Cooking
from the Heart

The HMONG KITCHEN *in* AMERICA

SAMI SCRIPTER *and* SHENG YANG

UNIVERSITY OF MINNESOTA PRESS

Minneapolis | London

Additional information is available on the book's companion Web site at www.hmongcooking.com.

"Slices with a Hmong Knife" by Kou Lor previously appeared in *Bamboo among the Oaks: Contemporary Writing by Hmong Americans*, ed. Mai Neng Moua (St. Paul: Minnesota Historical Society Press, 2002). Reprinted with permission by Kou Lor.

"The Year My Family Decided Not to Have Papaya Salad and Egg Rolls for Thanksgiving" by May Lee-Yang previously appeared in *Paj Ntaub Voice*, "War," 9, no. 2 (2004). Reprinted with permission by May Lee-Yang.

"Eating Habits" copyright 2009 by May Lee-Yang.

"Rice Rain" copyright 2009 by Song Yang.

Color photographs courtesy of Cenveo: Robin Lietz, photographer; Lara Miklasevics, food stylist; Rhonda Watkins, prop stylist.

Black-and-white photographs on pages ii, xvi, and 232 by Cheryl Walsh Bellville. Other black-and-white photographs courtesy of Sami Scripter.

Published by the University of Minnesota Press
111 Third Avenue South, Suite 290
Minneapolis, MN 55401-2520
http://www.upress.umn.edu

LIBRARY OF CONGRESS CATALOGING-IN-PUBLICATION DATA
Scripter, Sami.
   Cooking from the heart : the Hmong kitchen in America / Sami Scripter and Sheng Yang.
      p. cm.
   Includes index.
   ISBN 978-0-8166-5326-3 (hc : alk. paper)
   1. Cookery, Asian. 2. Hmong Americans—Food. 3. Hmong Americans—Manners and customs. I. Yang, Sheng. II. Title.
TX724.5.A1S34 2009
641.595—dc22   2009007778

Printed in the United States of America on acid-free paper

The University of Minnesota is an equal-opportunity educator and employer.

16 15 14 13 12 11 10 09   10 9 8 7 6 5 4 3 2 1

FOR CENTURIES the Hmong have been a people without a country, always making the best of each new situation and remaining true to their culture. This book is dedicated to the indomitable spirit of the Hmong people.

Contents ⁓ Rooj Ntawd Ntawm Nqe Lus

Color plate section follows page 174

Sheng, at age thirteen, wearing traditional Hmong clothing and jewelry.
This snapshot was taken when she was living with the Scripters.

Preface ⮑ Ncauj Lus

PEOPLE FROM TWO VERY DIFFERENT CULTURES can learn a lot about one another by cooking together and sharing their native food. That has certainly been true for us. Cooking together was one of the ways we got to know each other almost thirty years ago, when Sami was a young mother and Sheng was a young teen. Even before we had much language in common, our experiences in the kitchen and in the garden helped acquaint us with each other's cuisine as well as our cultures. Eventually, our friendship and these shared experiences led us to collaborate on this first-ever mainstream Hmong cookbook. This book evolved over time, but it would never have come to be if it had not been for a chance meeting and the eventual friendship between our two families. Sheng's family's roots are deep in Laos and China; they are Hmong. Sami's ancestors have been American for generations.

Sheng was born in 1970, in Luang Prabang, the old colonial capital of Laos, in Southeast Asia. Only a few memories from her early childhood remain: playing dolls with her friends; sitting outside on warm summer evenings enjoying movies projected onto the side of a building; and watching her mother cut up cassava roots and plantains for Sheng's favorite childhood food, a gooey, coconut-rich sweet treat. Sheng's life was that of a typical young Hmong girl. She learned how to embroider (*paj ntaub*, pronounced "pa dow") and helped take care of her younger siblings. Her father, Gnia Kao (pronounced "ne-ya cow") Yang, had been a soldier for six years fighting alongside the Americans against the Communist forces in Laos. Later, he worked for his Catholic church, serving the Hmong community as a deacon. When the United States abandoned the war in Vietnam and the Communists took control of their country, Sheng's family, along with thousands of other Laotians who had sided with the Americans, fled. Sheng's family first moved to a refugee camp in Thailand, where Sheng attended school, learning math and how to read and write using the Thai alphabet.

In 1979 Sheng and her family immigrated to the United States. In the course of a year, the family moved three times to different church assignments, living first in Kentucky, next in Oklahoma, and finally in Portland, Oregon. By then, there were seven people in Sheng's immediate family: her father, her mother, Mai (pronounced "my"), Sheng, two brothers, Ying and Meng, and two sisters, Blia and Der. In 1980 the Yangs became neighbors of the Scripters, and Sheng became a fifth grader in the school where Sami worked coordinating enrichment classes for gifted children. The Scripter family included Sami, her husband, Don, their daughter, Emily, who was a little younger than Sheng, and their son, Carl, who was the same age as Sheng's brother Meng.

Today, we cannot recall exactly what drew us together so quickly and strongly. In American terms Sheng was just a child, but in her own culture she was nearing young adulthood. At school, Sheng often came to Sami's office, sometimes to show her drawings she had made and sometimes to ask about the unfamiliar details of American life. Sheng was full of questions. How could she learn to play a guitar? Where did the water in the toilet go? Would Sami help her improve her penmanship? Soon the two families began to visit back and forth. They gardened together in the Scripters' big backyard, planting seeds that Sheng's mother had carried from Laos and Thailand. When the first of the long, dark green Hmong-style cucumbers ripened, Sheng sliced them and dressed them with tangy fish sauce and lime juice. When the raspberries turned dark red, Sami showed Sheng and her mother how to make and preserve jam. The Yangs graciously shared their culture with the Scripters, including them in many family functions, and the Scripters reciprocated. In this way, the families grew close and learned about one another's culture. When a sixth child was born to Mai and Gnia Kao, they named the baby girl Sami. When Sheng was in sixth grade, to help her become more proficient in English, she lived with the Scripters. Don built bunk beds so Emily and Sheng could share a room.

Eager to help around the house, Sheng assisted in preparing family dinners. However, Sami's Western-style kitchen often lacked the ingredients and equipment Sheng needed to make Hmong food. One time, after cleaning carrots, garlic cloves, and cherry tomatoes, Sheng searched through all of the cupboards for the tool she needed; in Hmong it is called a *tais tshuaj khib*. A trip to Sheng's house revealed what she was after—a stone mortar and pestle. Back at the Scripters', Sheng pounded the carrots together with the garlic. She then added fish sauce, lime juice, tomatoes, and MSG to make her favorite salad. The flavors were definitely a new experience for the Scripters. As time went by, the Scripters' pantry held jars of fish sauce, bags of rice, and cans of bamboo and coconut milk—all common ingredients in Hmong cooking. Sami learned to cook rice the Hmong way using an hourglass-shaped pot and woven basket steamer, and Sheng learned how to make Don's favorite dinner: meat loaf, baked potatoes, and peach pie.

Sheng followed her cultural tradition and married young. She and her husband had six children. While raising her large family, she attended college classes and pursued a career as a medical assistant. The Scripters moved from Oregon to the East Coast, returning to Portland nine years later. Sheng and all of her family eventually moved to the Sacramento area.

Through the years, in spite of the distances, we have remained friends. Whenever we see each other, food and cooking are always central features of our visits. From the very beginning, we jotted down lists of ingredients, measurements, and notes about Hmong food. Writing things down felt important, because no comprehensive written record of Hmong cooking seemed to exist. We talked many times about writing a Hmong cookbook to remedy that situation. As we began to collect recipes and information, we realized what a challenge we faced compiling such a cookbook. Hmong people learn to cook by following their mothers' and grandmothers' examples. They measure ingredients by the length of their fingers and by scoops. They decide by taste and by experimentation what ingredients and how much of each to include. Vegetables are chosen by what is in season and what is available. That means that for every Hmong dish, there are as many variations as there are Hmong cooks. Despite the challenges, we persevered, gathering recipes and putting them in order. Eventually we designed a Web site summarizing our vision. We were thrilled when Pieter Martin, an editor at the University of Minnesota Press, expressed interest in our project.

As the cookbook took shape, we agreed on several things. We determined that our readers would likely be young Hmong men and women who yearn for the tastes and fragrances they remember from their childhood. We also hoped to share the Hmong culture with non-Hmong people through the cooking and the traditions associated with food, just as we had learned about one another's culture by sharing food when we first met. Finally, we wanted our book to be a celebration of the Hmong culture as it is lived in the United States. We hope it can be a tangible way for Hmong people to experience their heritage with pride.

All of the recipes in this book originated in Hmong kitchens and have not been modified to conform to non-Hmong palates. We want our readers to experience the real flavors of Hmong cuisine—earthy, fiery, and wholesome. Although the flavors and textures may be unfamiliar, and may require some getting used to, we hope that everyone who uses this book will cook with an adventurous and creative spirit, as Hmong cooks do. They do not hesitate to try something new or add a twist of their own. After all, that is what is meant by "cooking from the heart."

Acknowledgments ⭣ Nco Txiaj Ntsim

FIRST, AN ENORMOUS THANK-YOU (*ua tsaug*) must go to our husbands, who were our steadfast partners in this endeavor. Sami's husband, Don, patiently proofread the text over and over. He is our "Comma King." In addition, he took over many of the housecleaning and dishwashing chores in the Scripter home while Sami wrote and cooked; plus, he taste-tested every single dish. Sheng's husband, Leo, generously shared his life experiences and expertise about Hmong cooking, language, culture, and history.

Next, we acknowledge Sheng's parents, Mai Her and Gnia Kao Yang. Without their love and guidance, this book would not exist. We also thank Sheng's sisters, Blia, Der, and "Little" Sami; her brothers, Ying and Meng; and Meng's wife, Koue, who all shared recipes and cooking know-how. Koue's mother, Nan See Lor, candidly shared her experiences as a young woman in Laos. Their contributions are woven into the text throughout this book. We thank Leo's mother, Saly Yang, who passed down her cooking expertise to Sheng. All of our children gave us encouragement and served as food tasters and photo models. They include Eddie and his wife, MaiKia, Susan, Sunny, Angie, Francis, and Paris (Sheng's children), and Emily and her husband, Paul, and Carl and his wife, Angie (Sami's children).

As novice writers, we are grateful to the people who gave us advice and support, especially our editor at the University of Minnesota Press, Pieter Martin, who found us on the Internet, pursued our project, and gave us wise counsel and encouragement. We are also grateful to Paula Tran, whose book *Living and Cooking Vietnamese* (San Antonio: Corona Publishing Company, 1990) inspired us to write our book. From the beginning, her suggestions and kind words spurred us on. We thank as well Beth Dooley and Chia Youyee Vang, who reviewed our book proposal; Beth Dooley also reviewed the final manuscript. Their insights helped us define our project. Pat Gerrard, Jennifer Fox, and Melody Lacina read various drafts of our book and gave helpful feedback. Marjory Reynolds and the Oregon Writers Colony writing group helped Sami gain confidence as a writer. We thank each of these people.

Many people contributed cooking and cultural information to this book. We hope we have not missed anyone. In the Portland, Oregon, area the following people shared their hospitality, recipes, and knowledge: Dr. Bruce T. Bliatout, Weena Chang, Molly Chong, True Her, Rev. Yee Khang, Joseph Kue and his wife, Zer, David Lee and his wife, Ma Her, Mai Yang Lee, Paj Lee, Mrs. Na Vang Lue, Ge Ly and his wife, Chou, Dr. Yer Thao (who allowed us to use part of Phoua Her's oral history from his book *The Mong Oral Tradition: Cultural Memory in the Absence of Written Language*), Kathy (Ka) Vang, Lee Vang and his mother, Chong Cha, Tia Vang, Mai Xee Vang, Sing Vang, Song Vang, Mao Xiong, GaoNa Yang, and May Tong (Cha) Yang, her mother, May Yer, and her sister May Chue Lawson, and the people in the congregation of the Hmong Missionary Alliance Church, who welcomed Sami into their community. In the Seattle area our gratitude goes to Bee Cha, John Hang, Julie Lor, and Ka Vue. In the Sacramento, California, area Chue Yang shared her great cracked crab recipe as well as personal insights. Mai Cha, Yer Xiong, and many other members of Sheng's extended family helped us whenever they were asked. We wish to thank these people in Minnesota for their contributions: Dr. Dia Cha, Charles Johnson, Xai Lor, Sharon Sawyer, Chang Thao, Steven Thao, Vallay Varro, Boua Xiong, Kao Yee Xiong, Blia Yang, Chia Yang, Fhoua Chee Yang, and Tino Yang and his wife, Ia Vang. The owners of the ABC Bookstore in St. Paul, Yuepheng L. Xiong and his wife, Shoua V. Xiong, loaned us Hmong stitchery for the photography and answered our many questions. We are very grateful to the creative crew at Cenveo in Minneapolis, who made the beautiful color photographs in this book, including Terry Holman (creative workflow coordinator), Robin Lietz (photographer), Chad Linderman (chef), Lara Miklasevics (food stylist), and Rhonda Watkins (prop stylist). In the Denver area we are thankful for the help of Chee Vang, Cindy Vue, Lee Moua Vue, Somxai Vue and Souzana (Vang) Vue, PaKou Xiong, and Txue Pa Yang. In Wisconsin Chuedang Vue and his wife, Gao Youa, graciously allowed Sami to shadow them while they worked in their restaurant, answering all her questions and also contributing recipes; Song Moua contributed a recipe as well. We thank food writer Terese Allen for sharing the recipe for chicken with cucumber and bitter melon. In North Carolina, Say Lee and her daughter, Becky Lee, shared food, hospitality, and their personal stories. We appreciate Manivan Larprom (of Toronto) and True Ly (of Paris), who provided recipes and cooking information.

We thank Lynne Rossetto Kasper, host of the American Public Media radio program *The Splendid Table*; Mee Moua, Minnesota state senator; and Kao Kalia Yang, author of *The Latehomecomer: A Hmong Family Memoir*, for writing such kind words to promote the book.

Finally, we extend a big thank-you to the writers who allowed us to reprint their poems and stories in this book: May Lee-Yang contributed the culturally insightful story "The Year My Family Decided Not to Have Papaya Salad and Egg Rolls for Thanksgiving" and the flavorsome poem "Eating Habits." Kou Lor graciously shared his evocative poem "Slices with a Hmong Knife." Song Yang let us include her lovely remembrance poem "Rice Rain."

COOKING *from the* HEART

Ger Xiong, of Sacramento, California, slices, chops, and minces mounds of herbs and vegetables in preparation for the many dishes she will serve at a family gathering.

Welcome to Our Dinner Gathering ❧
Zoo Siab Tuaj Koom Peb Rooj Mov

PEOPLE UNFAMILIAR WITH HMONG COOKING AND CUSTOMS might be overwhelmed when they experience a modern Hmong dinner gathering for the first time. Welcome to a Hmong home! Step inside the front door. Slip off your shoes and add them to the pile of oxfords, flip-flops, tennis shoes, and pumps. Accept a warm, respectful greeting and shake hands with your host.

A cloth-covered table stretches the length of the living room, its top barely visible under the profusion of serving dishes. Some bowls are heaped with steaming, jasmine-scented white rice. Others hold Ziploc packets of sweet, sticky purple rice. Platters spill over with garlicky long green beans glossy with bits of beef and dark brown sauce. Bowls full of warm, lemon-scented broth swimming with chunks of fat pork and bright green cooked vegetables are scattered along the table. Additional bowls hold fresh-cooked chicken paired with sour bamboo and topped with tangy cilantro. Wedged between the platters are tiny dishes filled with a fiery-hot chili sauce. Dishes of sliced mangos sit next to mounds of creamy, coconut-rich rice. Big bowls of glossy romaine lettuce, dotted with slices of hard-boiled eggs, tomatoes, and cucumbers, are arranged down the center of the table. Other plates hold stew, rich with meat and eggplants. Wedged between the plates and bowls are cans of coconut juice and Mountain Dew, and glasses filled with warm, pale-orange pumpkin juice. An assortment of chairs surrounds the table. Each place is set with a plate, a napkin, an Asian spoon, a fork, and a pair of chopsticks.

In the steamy kitchen, chatting, busy women chop up lemongrass and garlic. They pull apart sprigs of fresh mint, basil, and cilantro, shred green onions, and slice up juicy limes. The women fill still more serving bowls with food and somehow fit them on the table as well. They share gossip and eat tart ripe persimmons. Two women taste the creamy liquid from a huge tub of icy, brightly colored tapioca and coconut-milk dessert, checking its sweetness. A crew of young women washes, dries, and puts away pots and pans as fast as they accumulate. Little children race in and out, laughing, playing, and snacking on crunchy pink rice cakes. A muscular young man, dressed in sweats and a baseball cap with the bill pushed up, stands to one side, engrossed in a cell phone conversation. A heavy and wrinkled grandmother sits quietly on a folding chair, holding a sleepy child in her lap, seemingly oblivious to the loud babble of Hmong and English. Her steel-gray hair is covered with a knit cap, and her cloudy, gray-blue eyes seem focused on a far-off memory. In the family room, the women fill an equally lavish table for themselves.

To an outsider, things seem both casual and chaotic, but much of the business at hand is prescribed by age-old tradition. Finally, when all of the preparations are complete, and both tables are heavy with food, the men bow their heads and a respected elder offers a blessing. The men repeatedly kneel and bow to the ground to honor their ancestors and the occasion. Then they sit down and begin to eat and drink, laughing and chatting and toasting one another's prosperity with shot glasses full of rice liquor or beer. In the family room, the women also take their seats. They serve themselves and give the children plates full of the tasty food. At both tables, a serving bowl of each dish is within easy reach of every diner. People sip warm broth from their spoons and dip choice bits of meat into the hot chili condiment. When the meal is over, the young women quickly wash the stacks of dirty dishes. Leftovers are packaged in Tupperware and Ziploc bags for visitors to take home. Nothing is wasted.

This kind of meal is shared by close family and friends on important occasions. Everyone has plenty to eat and drink, and everyone is encouraged to eat more. Traditional roles are played, and customs important to the solidarity of the community are followed. Often such meals accompany rituals that have a spiritual or healing significance. At such gatherings, diners fill their stomachs with familiar, flavorful food, and their hearts fill with the warmth of tradition and the fellowship of community, family, and clan. Age-old cooking and eating traditions help Hmong people maintain their identity. Such meals serve to remind them of their roots and make them feel at home. This is Hmong cooking in America.

History of a People and a Cuisine

The first written reference to people believed to be Hmong dates back more than four thousand years to when they were an ethnic minority, living and farming in the lowlands of central China. Proud and stubbornly independent, the Hmong refused to be subjugated by Chinese rulers, and they fought to maintain their autonomy. Chinese records depict the Hmong as barbaric and fierce warriors. In the sixth century A.D. the Hmong controlled parts of central China. They were loosely governed by village and regional leaders under a Hmong king. This Hmong kingdom came to an end when the emperors of the Tang and Sung dynasties waged war to dominate China's ethnic minorities. Over centuries, the Hmong moved farther and farther south to escape persecution and enslavement, often living in isolation high in the mountains. No written records describing their cooking and way of life exist from these years. By the 1950s over half of the Hmong in the world lived in what was then called Indochina, mostly in the mountains of Cambodia, Laos, Thailand, and Vietnam.

In the 1950s, '60s, and '70s the Hmong were caught up in the political struggles in Southeast Asia. The civil war in Laos, between the Royalists and the Communists, and the war in Vietnam disrupted the traditional Hmong way of life. Hmong men were recruited by all of the armies. Thousands were trained by the United States' Central Intelligence Agency (CIA) to sabotage war supplies moving along the Ho Chi Minh Trail, and to rescue American pilots shot down over Laos. The Hmong became the United States' secret army in Laos. Their bravery, tenacity, ingenuity, and resourcefulness were highly valued. However, the Hmong paid dearly for their involvement in the war. Hmong soldiers were given some of the most dangerous jobs, and they died in far greater percentages than did their American comrades. Their families had to move from their mountain villages and farms to be close to military camps and American assistance. Over time, the women outnumbered the men.

In the spring of 1975, when the United States abandoned the Vietnam War, the Hmong were left behind, contrary to agreements they had with the CIA. Surrounded by their enemies, they were the target of persecution and genocide by the Pathet Lao (the ruling Communist government in Laos, then and now). At that time, thousands of Hmong families fled their country and went to refugee camps in Thailand. They often had to wait in the camps for years before humanitarian agencies resettled them in other countries. Most Hmong refugees went to the United States and France, with smaller numbers immigrating to Australia, Canada, and French Guiana.

They brought to their new homes a simple, earthy cuisine and cooking

Traditional Hmong Gatherings

Weddings *Tshoob*

Hmong weddings consist of a series of events that take place over several days: negotiating the wedding contract, welcoming the bride into the husband's family, and celebrating the union. Each event includes a meal with traditional food and beverages.

"Calling in the Soul" of a New Baby *Hu Plig*

Three days after a baby is born, a qualified elder conducts a ritual to summon the soul of the child into his or her body. This rite can be compared to a christening, since the child's first name is given by the caller of the soul at this time. It is customary to kill a pig or a cow and prepare many dishes using the meat to serve the guests who attend.

Recognition of Achievements

To honor such achievements as college graduation (*kev zoo siab rau tus neeg uas kawm tiav qib siab*) or acceptance into the armed services (*txais mus ua ib tug tub thab ham*), a celebration, complete with food and drink, is given by the honoree's family.

Bestowing an Adult Name on a Man after His First Son Is Born *Npe Laus*

A man receives a "mature" name after becoming a father. Typically the man's mother- or father-in-law selects the new name. As always, a wonderful meal is served to everyone in attendance.

Funerals *Kev Ploj Tuag*

The most important and complex of Hmong rituals is the funeral. It lasts three or more days, and all of the dead person's extended family and friends are involved. The purpose of the funeral rites for a traditional Hmong is for the soul of the deceased to travel safely back to her or his birthplace, then to the otherworld, and finally to be reincarnated as a member of the same clan. (This belief does not hold true for Christian Hmongs.) Funerals are very costly, because everyone in attendance must be fed three times a day.

Welcoming Visitors *Tuaj Los*

Visitors are always welcomed, and are honored at gatherings of family and friends with the best food and drink a host has to offer.

Healing Rituals *Ua Neeb Ua Yaig*

Although almost all Hmong Americans avail themselves of Western medicine, many still also consult a shaman. Traditional Hmongs believe that physical and mental illness is a result of loss of soul. Depending upon the problem, healing rituals are conducted with the aim of returning the soul to the body of the sick person. These ceremonies are usually a family affair at which cows, pigs, and/or chickens are sacrificed. Some meat is given to the shaman as a thank-you for services rendered. The rest goes to feed all in attendance.

Honoring and Protecting the Family Spirit *Ua Neeb Kab Plig*

Once every second or third year in traditional (not Christian) homes, a ritual is conducted to honor a family's ancestors, rid the home of bad spirits, and bring prosperity in the future. Gathering extended family members is important for such an event. The day always culminates with a big meal.

New Year *Xyoo Tshiab*

Throughout the United States, each Hmong community sponsors a big public celebration, complete with Hmong music, dancing, food, a beauty pageant, cultural displays, and concession booths, where Hmong clothing, jewelry, videos, and other products are for sale.

Tying Strings on Wrists to Protect Loved Ones *Khi Tes*

Traditional food is always provided for family and friends when they gather to tie strings on the wrists of loved ones who are about to undergo surgery or embark on a trip. A single red string guards against loss of soul and is used for health concerns. White strings are tied on the wrists to bind the soul to the body and keep a person safe when he or she is about to travel. White strings also signify good wishes and blessings.

traditions that reflected a rural lifestyle and ancient culture. Hmong cuisine was influenced by other ethnic cooking styles as the war forced them to move down from the mountains into cities, refugee camps, and other countries. The Hmong came into contact with lowland Laotians, Thai people, and other Southeast Asian refugees. Always pragmatic and inventive, the Hmong modified what they ate and how they prepared food, creating new dishes along the way.

For hundreds of years prior to these conflicts, most Hmong people lived an isolated, peaceful existence in small villages in the mountainous regions of China and Southeast Asia. Typical Hmong communities numbered ten or more households, many of them related. An individual household usually included people from two or three generations, under the leadership of the oldest man. For the most part, households were self-sustaining. Entire families, except for the very old or ill, walked or went on horseback each day to and from the family garden that was often miles away. The men hunted, and the rest of the family tended the garden. In the evening, they carried the harvested grain and vegetables back to their home in baskets strapped to their backs. Because rice was the staple of their diet, it was their most important crop. They also cultivated corn, soybeans, and a variety of other vegetables. The only cash crop was opium poppies, which grew well in the lime-rich soil of the mountainsides. Opium was traded for silver, and during the time the French were a regional power, the Hmong, and all other mountain-dwelling minority groups, were taxed in raw opium or silver bars. The Hmong raised pigs, goats, chickens, and turkeys for food. Fish and wild game were also part of their menus. However, rice remained the centerpiece of every meal. In fact, the Hmong words for "let's eat," *peb noj mov*, actually mean "let's eat rice."

The Hmong utilized several varieties of rice, the most common of which were long-grain and short-grain, glutinous ("sticky") rice. Rice was most often steamed using a water vessel and a porous cone-shaped basket with a lid. It was also boiled to make a soft cereal for the old and very young. Sticky rice was pounded with a large mortar and pestle into a soft, gooey paste and simply eaten, or it was shaped into little cakes that were toasted or steamed. The various ways of preparing rice remain essentially the same today. Meat and vegetables were usually boiled and served in the cooking liquid.

Historically, the Hmong seldom fried their food because oil and fat, other than what was rendered at home from animals, were costly and often not available. Beef was not common, although occasionally water buffalo was consumed. Homemade tofu was another common food. Dairy products were not available, so they were not part of the Hmong diet. Babies were breast-fed until they were several years old. Traditional cooking was simple and rather bland. To liven it up, the Hmong used herbs such as basil, mint, cilantro, and lemongrass as well as chili peppers to flavor cooking broth. A sauce made from fermented fish gave food a pungent, salty taste, and both salt and MSG were purchased when possible. Tropical fruits and nuts served as their only sweets. Cassava plants were grown. Their roots were dug from the ground, and then peeled and cooked to thicken puddings of coconut milk and plantains. Items from the forest, such as bamboo shoots and banana blossoms, also made dishes more interesting. Roots, bark, and many kinds of plants were gathered from the forest to flavor food in other ways. Some were used to treat illness and as health-sustaining tonics. In the mountains of Laos, Hmong men brewed and drank strong beer and liquor that were made from rice and corn. Women drank liquor only as part of formal rituals. Adults drank herbal teas, and everyone drank water. A common practice was to sip the "pot liquor" from a communal serving dish, using a spoon.

Hmong Culture in America

Hmong cooking and eating practices are closely associated with traditional beliefs and the social structure. Historically, most Hmongs practiced a form of animism (similar to Native American beliefs) as well as ancestor worship. They believed that many natural things, such as trees, streams, hills, and rocks, had individual spirits. Evil spirits inhabited wild places. House spirits and ancestor spirits could cause bad things to happen, or they could bring harmony to individuals or a household. Each person was thought to have a number of souls (different groups believed in different numbers). Illness, both physical and mental, happened when a soul left the body. All Hmongs had responsibilities to their ancestors and to the children, yet unborn, of their own lineage group.

In the United States, many Hmongs continue to believe and practice as they did in Laos. Others have cast those beliefs aside in favor of some form of Christianity. Still others maintain a traditional, although modified, lifestyle. These different choices have caused conflict between the old and young Hmong, and between family members who go separate ways.

Traditional believers place great importance on the shaman (*txiv neeb*). When someone is sick, a shaman is called upon to locate and negotiate with the spirit, to return the lost soul, and hopefully to restore the person's health. To do this, the shaman leaves this world and goes into the spirit world while in a trance. Some rituals call for a chicken, pig, or cow to be killed. The shaman enlists the help of the animal's spirit in his or her journey into the otherworld. Depending on the event, these sacrificed animals become part of the meal served to the people in attendance. Traditional events, such as weddings and funerals, include rituals that honor family ancestors and deal with the spirit world. At Hmong Christian gatherings, a pastor, hymns, and prayers take center stage, but the menu is often the same as for traditional events.

After Hmongs resettled in Western countries and became aware of other belief systems and worldviews, they (especially the young people) began thinking about the differences and their own identity. Although today most Hmong Americans embrace a mixture of worldviews, individuals are adamant about their beliefs. When asked to explain why they believe as they do, a typical response is "What a person believes to be true—is true."

Family units are still the most important element of Hmong society. Families related through a common male lineage, called *ib yim neeg* (one-family people), have an incredibly strong bond. Traditionally, family members respected and deferred to the elderly. Large families were the norm, and each new baby was cherished and pampered. Natural leaders emerged in these groups, and it was common for such leaders to serve as advisors and counselors, and even provide loans and other financial assistance to the entire group.

Eighteen Hmong kinship groups or clans are commonly recognized, each identified by a clan name: Cha (*Tsab*), Cheng (*Tsheej*), Chue (*Tswb*), Fang (*Faaj*), Hang (*Haam*), Her (*Hawj*), Khang (*Khaab*), Kong/Song (*Koo*), Kue (*Kwm*), Lee/Ly (*Lis*), Lor (*Lauj*), Moua (*Muas*), Pha (*Phab*), Thao (*Thoj*), Vang (*Vaj*), Vue (*Vwj*), Xiong (*Xyooj*), and Yang (*Yaaj*). Spellings of names vary. Lineage is traced through male bloodlines. When a woman marries she becomes part of her husband's family, although she is formally known by her birth clan name. Sheng maintains this age-old custom and uses her birth-family clan name, Yang, although her husband's clan name is Lee.

Because the Hmong stepped into modern history without a written language, all of their history and knowledge has been passed down orally. In the 1950s, missionaries developed a written language for the Hmong, called Romanized Popular Alphabet (RPA), which uses the Roman alphabet. Nowadays, most Hmong people throughout the world use RPA to write the language. However, the Hmong have yet to agree fully on the use of this alphabet for denoting Hmong sounds. Different spellings for the same word can be found in personal communications, dictionaries, and books. Although RPA is widely accepted as standard, many elderly Hmongs cannot write well in either Hmong or English, and numerous young Hmongs are not fully literate in written or spoken Hmong. A new mix of spoken English and Hmong used by many young people is called "Hmonglish."

There are two major Hmong dialects, Green Hmong (*Moob Leeg*) and White Hmong (*Hmoob Dawb*). Sheng's mother is White Hmong and her father is Green Hmong, so Sheng grew up hearing both dialects. We have chosen to use the White Hmong dialect for this book, since it is more widely used and understood by the Hmong community. Also, the Hmong language has no uniform capitalization rules.

Hmong words are tonal, which means that two words that sound the same except for different inflections will have completely different meanings. There are eight different tones, denoted by the final consonants at the end of a written word. The language contains no plurals, no possessives, and no present, past, or future tenses. All meanings are derived by the context of the message. "I cooked chicken soup for my brother's family last Saturday" would, in Hmong, be "Saturday past I cook chicken boil for my brother family."

The Challenge of a Hmong Cookbook

An old Hmong legend tells of a book in which all of the important information about people's journeys through life, death, and rebirth was recorded. In the distant past, so the story goes, the book was eaten by hungry animals. From that time forward, essential knowledge was passed along only by the spoken word, from the old to the young. Spiritual wisdom was revealed to people by a higher power, because those so chosen had a gift for understanding and using such knowledge. Wise elders shared information with younger people only when it was needed, and when the younger people were capable of understanding and using the information.

In the isolated mountain villages of their Laotian homeland, cooking was also the stuff of tradition, not the written word. Good Hmong cooks learned from their elders which ingredients to use, and how much of each, by sight, feel, and taste. Recipes were never written down and followed "to the letter." Cooking, like other Hmong arts and crafts, came "from the heart." Great Hmong cooks were, and still are, those who cook from the soul of their being. Therefore, this cookbook describes what individual Hmong cooks do and suggests how much of each ingredient and what techniques to use.

Writing down Hmong recipes is definitely a challenge for other reasons. First, although many favorite dishes—such as Sweet Pork, Papaya Salad, *Larb*, and boiled chicken—are considered traditional, Hmong cooks make them in amazingly different ways. The differences are not surprising, because Hmong people prize individuality. This diversity sometimes means that a Hmong cook in Minnesota is completely unfamiliar with a dish that a cook in North Carolina or California considers a standard.

Second, as is true of all good cooks, Hmongs like to keep their "secret" ingredients just that: secret. Fortunately, many Hmong cooks now feel that documenting the culinary aspect of their culture is important. A number of them have generously given their time and effort to work out complete lists of ingredients, measurements, cooking utensils, and techniques for inclusion in this book.

The final challenge, which is the biggest, is defining what Hmong cooking *in America* is. One young Hmong woman said, "That is easy. For old people it's fat pork and green vegetable soup. For young people it's chocolate chip cookies and McDonald's!"

Her words illustrate a reality about Hmong culture in this country; it is changing, and so is what Hmongs eat. Young Hmong people have different priorities than their parents, and different demands on their time. They work hard to become educated, have meaningful relationships, and find rewarding careers. To them, the old ways do not always seem relevant. Still, even young Hmong people worry that their culture will be lost. One thing seems to remain constant for both the old and the young: the desire to gather and enjoy "real Hmong food."

How to Use This Cookbook

Cookbooks are often organized around types of dishes, such as appetizers, salads, and desserts, or around what is traditionally served at a given meal, such as breakfast or dinner. However, these systems do not work well for Hmong cooking, because the first questions a Hmong cook asks when planning any menu are "What is in season?" and "What is available?" That means if fresh pork is available, it will be the main ingredient for every dish on the menu. If Chinese mustard greens are fresh and plentiful, they will become the center of a meal, whether it is breakfast, lunch, or dinner. Even the seasonings used in a dish are determined by what herbs are fresh and plentiful. Since that is the way Hmong people cook, that is the way this book is organized—by main ingredient.

One frequent ingredient in Hmong cooking is MSG (monosodium glutamate). Because of the heightened awareness of the health concerns associated with MSG, some people have stopped using it. In this cookbook, MSG is listed in a recipe when a Hmong cook has included it, but it is always optional. Some recipes call for "Asian-style bouillon cubes." Be advised that they contain MSG. If you want to stay completely away from MSG, substitute regular bouillon cubes.

A number of dishes in this book can be called "traditional." They are marked with a design like those found in Hmong stitchery (*paj ntaub*), indicating that the recipe has deep roots in Hmong culture. But even the most traditional recipes cannot replicate what was cooked in Laos. There, most families ate homemade foods from ingredients they farmed or harvested from the wild. Many of those ingredients are not available here, at least not exactly as they were found in Laos. This cookbook documents the way traditional dishes are made in America, using available ingredients. It also includes newer dishes that have been embraced widely by Hmong people. Some of these have been borrowed from other Asian cuisines, and some are creations of modern Hmong cooks. However, none of the recipes have been "Americanized," and cooking them will require a trip to a Hmong farmers' market or an Asian grocery store.

Variations of several dishes are found in more than one place in this cookbook. One of these dishes is *larb*, a Laotian meat salad that can be made with chicken, pork, fish, beef, or game meats. It can be very old-fashioned, using bitter ingredients and internal organs, or very modern, containing only fresh herbs and lean meat. Each way of making *larb* requires slightly different techniques and ingredients, hence the repetition. Another dish with several variations scattered throughout this cookbook is Hmong hot chili condiment (*kua txob*). There are so many ways to make this dish that we included eleven variations, each one listed with the dish it best complements. Because home cooking for large groups is so important for the Hmong, the final chapter, "Cooking for a Crowd," contains several recipes from other chapters, with directions for a crew of cooks and large quantities of ingredients.

As we gathered recipes and information about cooking from Hmong people across the country, we discovered a lot of diversity in even the most traditional dishes. Hmong cooks bring their innate ingenuity, pragmatism, and creativity to every dish they make. So, to the Hmong readers of this book, we apologize if a dish does not taste exactly as you remember it. We hope that everyone who reads this book learns a little about Hmong cooking and culture and how they are evolving in America. We have no doubt that, in the years to come, Hmong cooking will continue to evolve, and Hmong cooks will bring touches of their unique cuisine to mainstream American cooking.

Eating Habits

By May Lee-Yang

I didn't see them right away,
little lumps of apples hidden in the foliage.
My tongue salivated
contemplating their green, tangy forms
dipped in hot pepper.
When I spied them,
my hand instinctively went to pluck one.
Then I stopped,
remembering this was a public place.

My mother once asked,
Why do you kids always have to eat everything in the kitchen?
Why can't you be more like American kids who only eat when they're hungry?
My brothers and I were silent.
Because someone else will eat it didn't sound like a good enough answer.

What did you eat back in Laos? I asked.
My mother answered, Rice. Boiled vegetables. Chili peppers.
Sometimes ginger root dipped in salt.
But what about the animals? Didn't you have water buffalos and chickens and cows?
We only ate them at New Year or when someone was sick.

She didn't have to tell me New Year only came around once.

My mother said, After a woman gives birth,
for thirty days, she must eat chicken boiled with lemongrass.
That's so backward. What will boiled chicken do?
It will heal your body, so when you grow old,
you won't shake like American women.
You old people are too superstitious.

Years later, a Hmong doctor told me chicken was a good source of protein.
In Laos, it was a privilege, not a punishment.

In the middle of the night,
I remember images almost forgotten.
A family driving along the highway,
the kids *oohing* and *aahing* at every cow, horse, and sheep they see.
The parents licking their lips
imagining how the cow would make good larb
or how the red sumac berries,
a staple of the highway sidelines,
would taste good mixed with hot pepper.

I remember the apples and think,
Mother, we are not so different.

In a Hmong Kitchen ⟶
Hmoob Kev Npaj Noj Haus

Hmong-crafted knives such as these are kept very sharp. The knife on the bottom is stout enough to cut through big bones. The other knives are used to chop meat.

In a Hmong Kitchen ➤
Hmoob Kev Npaj Noj Haus

Diet as a Way of Life

From a Hmong point of view, food should contribute to a healthy balance of body and spirit. Some foods make the body warm and some serve to cool the body. Eating all of an animal corresponds to maintaining the wholeness of body and spirit. The goal is to eat what helps a person maintain a balance with nature and spiritual powers. Lots of rice, a wide variety and generous quantity of fresh, organic herbs and vegetables, fish, and sparing amounts of meat and seasonings comprise a typical old-fashioned Hmong diet. When the Hmong lived in Laos, that kind of diet, combined with a physically active farming life, helped them maintain the desired balance. The stresses and changes in diet experienced in America have upset that balance. To help them be healthy, many Hmong people try hard to cook and eat the old-fashioned way.

Cooking Techniques *Kev Npaj Noj*

Hmong food relies on two or three main ingredients per dish, flavored with fresh herbs and a few spices. Simple cooking techniques are the norm. All kinds of meat and vegetables are boiled in water flavored with lemongrass and served as a soup. In Laos, this method was the easiest way to cook on the commonly used clay stoves. Thickening agents, such as cooked rice or eggplants, are sometimes added to make a stew. Rice is boiled or steamed, depending upon the variety of rice being cooked and the texture desired. Fish, and sometimes other kinds of meat, are steamed by suspending the meat above boiling water on a tray or in a basket. For added flavor, rice and fish are first wrapped in banana leaves or other large leaves and then steamed. In modern kitchens, aluminum foil or parchment paper is sometimes used instead of the leaves. Grilling is another traditional cooking method. Food is marinated or basted and then grilled directly over burning coals or wood. Sometimes food is first wrapped in banana leaves and then grilled.

Cooking techniques embraced more recently by Hmong cooks include stir-frying, deep-frying, and also broiling, using either a conventional or a toaster oven. Hmong food is rarely baked.

Some traditional dishes call for raw meat, although many Hmong Americans shun this custom.

Cooking Equipment *Twj Taig Ua Noj*

Hmong cooks don't use measuring cups or spoons when making old standards, so such implements are not often found in Hmong kitchens. However, we have done our best to determine and include measurements in this book, so a basic set of measuring tools will be needed. Most standard pots and pans and other utensils can be utilized. In addition, a few tools not often found in American kitchens are necessary to make authentic Hmong food.

HMONG KNIVES RIAM HMOOB

Large, sharp, excellent-quality knives are needed to butcher animals and to mince meat and vegetables for popular dishes such as *larb*. In Laos, many Hmong men worked metal. Some turned out such fine knives that lowland Laotians would trade only with Hmong smiths. In America, Hmong men continue to fashion wonderful knives by using new and recycled metal and reworking old knives purchased at secondhand stores.

MOCHI OR BREAD MACHINES

In Laos, sticky rice was turned into a New Year's treat called *ncuav* by pounding it with heavy mallets in a large trough—hard, muscle-building work. Modern Hmong cooks prefer to use an electric *mochi* machine (the Japanese word for *ncuav*) or a bread machine to pound rice. A *mochi* machine both cooks and pounds the rice. Only the knead cycle of a bread machine is used with freshly cooked rice. Both machines produce a hot, thick, soft, elastic food that can be eaten as is or made into toasted rice cakes.

MORTAR AND PESTLES TSHUAJ KHIB THIAB QWS TXOB

Only by pounding (grinding and mashing) together ingredients such as garlic, chilies, and cilantro can cooks create a true Hmong taste. To pound ingredients, use a mortar and pestle, a wide variety of which is available at Asian stores. They are made of earthenware, wood, or stone. Inexpensive ones work just as well as more costly models. They come in many sizes, but Hmong cooking requires one with a several-cup capacity. The small mortar and pestles used to grind spices will not work to make dishes such as the popular papaya salad.

OUTDOOR PROPANE BURNERS AND LARGE POTS

Large, elaborate meals for many guests are a Hmong custom. They are often prepared in home kitchens. One way to do this is to set up portable propane burners on stands in the backyard. Look in the Yellow Pages under "gas—propane" to find stores that sell and rent propane burners in several different sizes. Be sure to follow all safety instructions and use propane burners only outside in well-ventilated areas. Large, round-bottomed aluminum or stainless-steel cooking pots are also needed to make meals for traditional gatherings. They can be purchased in larger Asian grocery stores.

STEAMERS

In Laos, few homes had ovens. Food was usually boiled or steamed over wood fires on small clay stoves. Hmong people used Thai rice steamers to cook their ever-present staple food. A Thai rice steamer is made up of a cone-shaped woven basket and an aluminum hourglass-shaped pot and a lid.

Other foods were steamed by wrapping them in banana leaves and simply elevating them an inch or two above simmering water on a metal rack in a pot with a lid. Some Hmong people now use Chinese-style stacked bamboo or stainless-steel steamers. Many varieties of steamers can be purchased in Asian supermarkets.

WOKS

Most modern Hmong cooks own one or two large woks. They are ideal for stir-frying and deep-frying. Flat-bottomed woks work best on electric stoves; round-bottomed woks work best on gas stoves and propane burner stands.

Slices with a Hmong Knife

By Kou Lor

I want to write an image poem and give you slices of who I am.
But first, I must board a plane to Laos
and I must buy a Hmong knife, forged by Hmong hands
from iron out of the belly of a sacred mountain
beside fires that consume lush green to feed Hmong mouths.

Then I must visit the village of my birth.
Perhaps the streets of earth and dust (and mud when it rains),
the single-room houses with their bamboo walls and bamboo-leaf roofs,
the plates of rice and meat left for spirits of ancestors,
the single spoon shared by a household during meager meals
(the spirits ate better than the living)—
perhaps all these things will help me remember those lost nights when
      magical words from distant tongues cured all fears.

Then I must board a plane to the U.S. and
I must return to Omaha, Nebraska,
where my family first landed after our long exodus from Laos,
where our sponsors taught us how to use sinks, toilets, and the TV,
where I almost drowned in our sponsor's pool
and got lost from my parents in a hospital elevator.
Perhaps all these things will help me remember
my parents' half-smiles and empty faces as they were forced to become
      children again.

Then I must drive to Appleton, Wisconsin,
(as my father did only six months after arriving)
where I learned how to speak English and how to forget my native tongue,
where I met my first American friend and my first American bigot,
where I played with friends in secret places in trees
that seemed to reach their roots to Laos.
Perhaps all these things will help me remember
the grizzled face of a boy innocently torn by two cultures.

And upon arriving back in Oshkosh,
I will find that the knife is dull and I don't have a sharpening stone
and the traveling has left my face white like my ancestors;
so the poem just waits silently kicking in its womb
beside its growing twin, who hums quietly in Hmong.

Packaged Ingredients *Npaj Li Cas*

Many ingredients common to Hmong cooking are not found in mainstream grocery stores. Therefore, a trip to a well-stocked Asian grocery store is necessary before cooking authentic Hmong food.

AGAR-AGAR POWDER

Agar-agar powder is the Asian Jell-O. Sold in 25-gram (about 5⅓ teaspoons) packets, the powder is a natural unflavored product made from red algae. The basic agar-agar recipe is 2 teaspoons of powder to 2 cups of boiling liquid. The gelatin becomes the consistency of very firm Jell-O in a couple of hours, sitting at room temperature. As with Jell-O, its ability to gel is affected by high-acid foods such as pineapple, kiwi, papaya, and mango. After it has been cooked and set, agar-agar gelatin should be refrigerated for storage.

BANANA LEAVES NPLOOJ TSAWB

These large, flexible leaves are found in the frozen section of most Asian grocery stores. They are used to wrap ingredients prior to steaming, baking, or grilling. Parchment paper can be substituted, but the dish will then lack the marvelous woodsy flavor the banana leaves add.

BLACK PEPPER FWJ TXOB LOS YOG HWJ TXOB

Although black pepper is a common American seasoning, it is included here because it is so important in Hmong food, especially the coarse-ground variety.

BOUILLON CUBES (ASIAN-STYLE)

Several name brands produce "Asian-style" bouillon cubes in beef, chicken, pork, vegetable, and fish flavors. They are similar to regular bouillon cubes, but they contain MSG. Regular bouillon cubes can be substituted.

CANNED BAMBOO SHOOTS KOOS POOM NTSUAG XYOOB

Many varieties of bamboo shoots are found in Asian grocery stores, including fresh, canned, and dried. Two Hmong favorites that come in cans and jars are sour bamboo (*ntsuag xyoob qaub*) and bitter bamboo (*ntsuag xyoob iab*), also called wild bamboo. Several Hmong families in North and South Carolina harvest, can, and sell a cold-hardy variety of bamboo that grows there.

CANNED TROPICAL FRUIT, NUTS, AND JELLIES
KOOS POOM TXIV HMAB TXIV NTOO

Any well-stocked Asian grocery store will have one entire aisle filled with high-quality cans of tropical fruits, nuts, and jellies, including, among others, logans, lychees, new coconut meat, jackfruit, and passion fruit, as well as products labeled "grass jelly" and "almond jelly." These sweet treats are eaten right out of the can for a snack, and are ingredients in the wildly popular Three-Color Dessert.

CHILI PASTES HMOOV KUA TXOB POOM

There are many choices of chili pastes in cans and jars. Look for ones that say "ground chili with fried garlic." Bottled paste tastes good, but good cooks make their own.

COCONUT MILK AND COCONUT CREAM KUA MAV PHAUB

Coconut milk is not the liquid found in the middle of a fresh coconut. It is a creamy extraction from shredded dried or fresh coconut. Although it can be made at home, virtually everyone buys it canned. Coconut cream is the first very thick, rich extraction from shredded coconut, and coconut milk is the second "squeezing" that is not as rich. However, be aware that both are very high in saturated fat. Coconut milk also can be purchased in powdered form in boxes and packets. Most Hmong cooks use canned and powdered coconut milk.

CURRY PASTES, CANNED (NAMYA) KOOS POOM KAS LIS

Hmong people use a red curry paste made in Thailand to flavor Chicken Curry Noodle Soup (*Khaub Poob*) and other curry dishes. Look for the word *namya* or a picture of curry noodle soup on the can's or jar's label.

DRIED FUNGI NCEB MOM LWM QHUAV

These dried edible fungi, also known as wood ears or cloud ears, can be black, brown, or white. They are soaked before using and are valued not only for the interesting texture they add to food, but also for their supposed medicinal value. They are often an ingredient in stuffed chicken wings and egg rolls.

DRIED SPICES

Most of the common Hmong seasonings, such as chilies, galanga, and lemongrass, can be purchased dried as well as fresh. The dried and fresh products are used interchangeably in recipes.

FISH SAUCE NAB PAM

Hmong people seldom use soy sauce, but fish sauce is an ingredient in many dishes. This clear, brownish, salty liquid is made from salted and fermented fish. Three Crabs is a favorite Hmong brand. Some cooks also like to use Squid brand fish sauce, which is made from anchovies.

FLOURS

Sweet rice flour, regular rice flour, sweet potato starch, and tapioca starch are just a few of the many varieties of flour-like products used in Hmong kitchens. Individual recipes in this book describe their specific uses.

MONOSODIUM GLUTAMATE (MSG) PEEB NUAS

The Food and Drug Administration (FDA) describes MSG as a safe food additive that "stimulates our taste buds and makes a variety of foods taste better." However, the FDA cites studies that show that eating large quantities of MSG (3 or more grams in a meal) is linked to a variety of symptoms, including numbness and headaches. There is also some indication that MSG stimulates people to eat more and can contribute to obesity. Some Hmong people accordingly never use it, but other cooks continue to include it in their recipes. We have noted MSG as optional whenever a cook has listed it as an ingredient.

NOODLES FAWM

In Laos, most manufactured noodles were unavailable to people living in remote mountain villages and typically were not part of Hmong cuisine. However, in America, Hmong people enjoy cooking with the amazing variety of noodles found in Asian supermarkets.

Noodles come in many shapes and sizes, both dried and fresh. Fresh ones need to be refrigerated and used within a day or two after purchase. Dried noodles should be stored in a dry place and will keep indefinitely. The following are some of the most common noodles used in Hmong cooking.

Rice Noodles

The primary ingredients in rice noodles are rice flour and water. Sometimes they also contain wheat or corn starch. They can be round or flat, thin or thick. Rice noodles have little flavor of their own, so they acquire the flavor of the foods with which they are cooked. You need to soak rice noodles in warm water for about 20 minutes, or until soft, before cooking them. When cooked, they have a terrific smooth and chewy texture. A medium-sized round or flat noodle is used to make Chicken Curry Noodle Soup (*Khaub Poob*). Each cook has his or her own favorite noodle. *Phở* is made with small (1/16-inch-wide) linguine-shaped rice noodles labeled "*bánh phở*." Very thin rice noodles are often called rice vermicelli, and the broader sizes are sometimes labeled "rice sticks."

Fresh Rice-and-Tapioca-Starch Flour Noodles

These delightfully chewy, fresh noodles can be found in the refrigerated section of Asian grocery stores. The Hmong name for them is *khaub-piaj*; the Vietnamese name is *banh canh*. They are thick, white noodles made with water, jasmine-rice flour, and tapioca-starch flour. Do not soak them before cooking, or rinse them afterward.

Rice Paper

Rice paper is made from a mixture of rice flour, water, and salt. It is rolled out by machine to paper thinness and then dried on bamboo mats. This process imprints a lovely cross-hatch pattern on the surface and gives the rice paper a slight fragrance and flavor of bamboo. Rice paper is sold in 8- and 10-inch round and wedge shapes, in packages of fifty and one hundred sheets. The sheets are fragile, so store them flat and handle them with care. Do not buy rice paper that is yellowed or broken, because it may be old or the package may have a hole in it. Rice paper is used to make Vietnamese-inspired spring rolls and salad rolls, and must be soaked briefly to make it pliable before using.

Another kind of rice paper is made at home using packaged flour for "wet rice paper." This rice-and-tapioca-starch flour is mixed with water and cooked to make glistening noodle-like pancakes that are filled with pork to make Rice Rolls (*Hmoov Ua Fawm Kauv*).

Wheat Noodles and Egg Noodles

Wheat noodles are made from wheat flour, water, and salt. They are white, while egg noodles are yellowish due to the egg added to the mixture. Plain and egg wheat noodles are sold fresh and dried, and they come in many shapes and sizes. They are only occasionally used by Hmong cooks.

Bean Thread Noodles

Sometimes called cellophane, vermicelli, or glass noodles, bean thread noodles are made of mung bean starch. Only available dried, they are often sold in packages of pink plastic netting composed of eight individually wrapped 1.3- or 2-ounce coils. Before they are cooked, bean threads are soaked in hot water for about 20 minutes until they are soft and pliable. Bean thread noodles are used in the stuffing for egg rolls and stuffed chicken wings.

OYSTER SAUCE KUA QWJ

Used extensively in Hmong households on stir-fried green vegetables, this Chinese product adds a savory, salty taste. A higher-priced brand is generally higher in quality.

PACKAGED SEASONING MIXES

Busy Hmong cooks use packaged seasoning mixes as a shortcut when making *larb*, sour fish soups, and Vietnamese Beef Noodle Soup (*Phở*). A stroll through the aisles of an Asian grocery store will reveal many brands and varieties.

SICHUAN PEPPER XYAB TXOB

These small, reddish-brown, flower-bud-shaped dried berries have a marvelous sharp, lemony, woody fragrance and taste. Not related to black pepper or chili peppers, they are the flower pods of a prickly ash tree. For a while, the FDA was unable to test and verify whether imported Sichuan pepper was contaminated with a citrus canker (dangerous to citrus crops, but not to people). During that time its import to the United States was banned. A simple way to ensure purity is now in place; however, finding Sichuan pepper in stores is still difficult. That is a shame, because Sichuan pepper is a favorite spice used in Hmong cooking and is worth tracking down. Sometimes the ancient spice can be found under the names "prickly ash," "red pepper powder," "wild pepper," or "Chinese pepper." For additional information and to purchase it, go to The Spice House Web site, http://www.thespicehouse.com/spices. Or visit one of their stores in Chicago, Milwaukee, and Evanston, Illinois. There is no good substitute for Sichuan pepper.

STAR ANISE TXIV PUAJ KAUM

Not used in traditional Hmong cooking, star anise has been borrowed from other Asian cuisines and is used to make *Phở* (Vietnamese Beef Noodle Soup).

TAMARIND TXIV QUAV MIV

This acidic fruit looks like a large, dark brown bean. Inside the brittle pod, a sticky brown flesh surrounds hard, shiny seeds. The pulp is both eaten as a fresh snack and dried and sold in packaged bricks. Tamarind is used to give soups and papaya salad a sour flavor.

Vegetables Used in Hmong Cooking, A to Z

LEAFY GREEN VEGETABLES ZAUB NTSUAB

Amaranth *Zaub Qiag*

This vegetable, sometimes called Chinese spinach, tastes a little like spinach and is full of vitamins. The Hmong customarily stir-fry or steam these delicate, oval, slightly rough-textured leaves and stems alone (with no meat). Red amaranth is purple-red in the center of its leaves and bright green on the edges. The water it is cooked in turns a lovely shade of pink. Green amaranth is entirely green. Young, small amaranth leaves are good in green salads.

Bok Choy *Zaub Kav Dawb*

Bok choy has tender, thick stems that can be ivory white or light green. Both types have deep green, broad, heavy leaves. Standard-sized bok choy plants are as large as, or larger than, a head of Chinese cabbage. When harvested small (between 3 and 5 inches tall), both white-stemmed and green-stemmed varieties are called baby bok choy. Bok choy is often available in mainstream grocery stores. It is almost always served stir-fried.

Cabbage *Zaub Qhwv*

Hmong people cook with several vegetables commonly called "cabbage." American cabbage is shredded and used in curry soups, and can be used as a substitute for bean sprouts in many recipes. Chinese cabbage, sometimes called napa cabbage, is tasty stir-fried and cooked in soups, and is also used as a wrap for savory fillings and then steamed. Chinese flowering cabbage looks a little like bok choy, with thick stems that are almost white and bright green oval leaves. It is recognizable by its yellow flowers and delicate cabbage flavor. It is delicious stir-fried. Hmong people also enjoy flat cabbage, which is related to bok choy, and which tastes more like bok choy than like cabbage. The plants grow close to the ground and have white stems and flat, oval-shaped dark green leaves 5 to 14 inches in diameter.

Chinese Broccoli *Zaub Ntsuag*

Delicious when stir-fried with garlic and oyster sauce, Chinese broccoli has a mild, slightly sweet taste and is often used in soups. It has smooth stems (¼- to ¾-inch thick), large, bright green leaves, and small white buds and flowers. In Chinese, it is called *gai lan*.

Garland Chrysanthemum Greens

This Japanese favorite (which has no Hmong name) often finds its way into Hmong soups. Sweet when young, the greens grow bitter with age. The light green, many-lobed leaves look a little like those of a common garden chrysanthemum.

Lettuce *Zaub Xav Lav*

Fresh lettuce leaves are used in green salads and soups and as an accompaniment for *larb*. Romaine lettuce is a favorite in salads. Boston lettuce and loose-leaf varieties are good to use as wraps for *larb*. Only iceberg lettuce leaves stand up to being blanched, stuffed, and steamed.

Mizuna *Yub Zaub Ntsuab*

Mizuna is sometimes called Chinese mustard. It has white stems and feathery, jagged, light green leaves. In America it is often harvested small and sold as part of a "mesclun" or "baby greens" salad mix. It has a slightly bitter taste like arugula, although it is not as pronounced. Mizuna pairs well with pork.

Mustard Greens *Zaub Ntsuag*

Hmong people are especially fond of an Asian variety of mustard that is sometimes called bamboo mustard cabbage and sometimes called swollen stem mustard. The Chinese call it *zuk gai choy*, and the Vietnamese label it *Sher-L-Hon* in their markets. These greens are boiled by themselves, or with a little chicken or pork. Bamboo mustard cabbage is often used to make sour pickled greens.

Oilseed Rape *Zaub Paj*

Every part of this leafy green vegetable is eaten—the crunchy stems, the glossy leaves, and the bright yellow flowers. The seeds of this plant are used to make canola oil.

Stem Lettuce *Zaub Nplaig Nab*

Its nickname is "snake-tongue lettuce," or *wo sun*. Stem lettuce has one very thick stem and long, light green, pointed leaves. The stem must be peeled before cooking and/or eating. This vegetable is not available everywhere.

Watercress *Zaub Dej*

Loved for its zesty bite, watercress is sold in bulk at Asian grocery stores when it is in season. Hmong people sometimes dress a watercress salad with stir-fried ground pork, herbs, oil, and vinegar.

Water Spinach *Phav Npoob*

Not really spinach, water spinach instead is related to the morning glory. It has long stems, long, thin, arrow-shaped leaves, and a very delicate flavor. It is stir-fried, and sometimes added to papaya salad. Its name in Hmong, *phav npoob* (pronounced "pa-nong"), is a phonetic Hmong spelling of the Lao words for the plant.

Bitter Melon *Dib Iab*

This melon illustrates perfectly the Hmongs' love for bitter flavors. Buy these cucumber-sized and -shaped wrinkly vegetables when they are light green and blemish-free. Dark green ones are immature and orange ones are overripe. Bitter melons are a very healthy food, although not everyone likes their bitter flavor. There is no good substitute for bitter melon.

Bottle Gourd *Taub Nyuv Nees Dawb*

These gourds can be shaped like a short baseball bat or a bottle. The bottle-shaped ones develop a hard shell when mature. In Laos they were hollowed out and used as scoops. Both varieties have smooth, light green skin and are sweet and tender when young. They are cubed and used in pork or chicken soup, and in stir-fries. They can be interchanged with fuzzy melons.

Chayote *Taub Maum los yog Taub Yaj los yog Taub Thaib* (known by three names)

This pear-shaped vegetable is a variety of squash. It has a mild, sweet flavor and can be used in stir-fries and soups.

Cucumber *Dib*

Cucumbers are very important in Hmong culture. Some groups celebrate a special ritual when the first cucumbers become ripe. Cucumbers can be stir-fried or sprinkled with fish sauce and eaten raw, and their pulp is mashed and mixed with sugar and eaten as a refreshing snack. Cucumbers are eaten at all stages of maturity.

Eggplant, Chinese *Lws Ntev*

Long purple eggplants are often pounded together with chilies and used as a condiment. Occasionally they are included in stir-fries.

Eggplant, Thai *Lws Pob Taub*

Hmong people use many varieties of round Thai eggplants. Although they also come in white, yellow, and purple, the most familiar ones are green; they are a little smaller than a golf ball and taste a little bit sweet. They are eaten raw as well as used in stir-fries and to thicken stews ("oh-la"). Other varieties taste bitter, especially the very small ones, and are used to impart a bitter flavor to food.

Fuzzy Melon *Taub Twg Nyuv Nees*

These melons are covered with soft fuzz when young. Shaped like very large cucumbers, they have smooth, splotchy-green skin and taste like a summer squash. They are cooked in the same way as bottle gourds.

Luffa Squash *Xwb Kuab Leej*

There are two varieties of luffas, angled and smooth. These gourds get tough as they mature, so they are used when young. Angled luffa is dark green and about 12 to 18 inches long with ridges that run down its length. Smooth luffa, which is less common, has a bat-like shape. Both varieties are ingredients in soups and stir-fries. No other squash has as firm a flesh as luffas, although other summer squashes can be substituted if luffas are not available.

Okra *Txiv Plaum*

Hmong people enjoy the combination of textures present in cooked okra: crunchy, spongy, and slippery. Okra is sometimes used as a thickening agent in stews, and it is also stir-fried.

Peppers, Sweet and Hot *Kua Txob Qab Zib thiab Ntsim*

All kinds of sweet peppers are good grilled or sautéed in oil. The ever-present hot chili condiment is made with Thai chilies or bird's-eye chilies. Jalapeños are sliced to accompany beef noodle soup.

Tomatoes *Txiv Lws Suav*

Tomatoes were seldom grown in Laos, so they do not often appear in traditional food. However, they play an important role in the food American Hmongs cook and eat. Cherry tomatoes are preferred in papaya salad, and larger tomatoes find their way into many fish dishes and salads.

Winter Melon Taub Twg

Hmong people cultivate a large, greenish-gray variety of winter melon that is often called Hmong pumpkin. For special occasions it is made into "pumpkin juice." It is also made into baked sweet desserts. Orange jack-o'-lantern-type pumpkins, simply called *taub*, are used in the same way.

ROOT-LIKE VEGETABLES

Carrots Zaub Ntug Hauv Paus

Carrots are often used as green papayas are in salads, and as an ingredient in egg rolls.

Cassava Root Qos Ntoo Ntug

Always peel and cook cassavas before eating them, to remove the peel's naturally occurring cyanide toxin. Cassavas are cooked and eaten the same as potatoes, but Hmong people more often use them in desserts, such as Cassava Root and Plantain Tapioca Dessert. There are no good substitutes for cassava roots, although taro roots are similar and can be used in a pinch.

Daikon Zaub Ntug Dawb

This long white or green turnip can be eaten raw or used in stir-fries and soups.

Jicama Qos Looj Pwm

This sweet-tasting, crunchy tuber is peeled and eaten fresh—sometimes sprinkled with salt, hot chilies, and lime juice—and occasionally stir-fried with beef. Most grocery stores stock jicama.

Kohlrabi Zaub Ntug Qe

This round, light green root is peeled, sliced, and served with *larb*.

Sweet Potatoes and Yams Qos Daj (Orange Ones),
Qos Liab (Dark Red Ones)

Hmong people like sweet potatoes and yams in soups, stir-fried, and made into tempura.

Taro Roots Qos Tsw Ha

Taro roots (actually rhizomes) come in a variety of shapes and sizes similar to potatoes. They all have a hairy brown skin and starchy mauve-colored flesh. They should be peeled and cut up before cooking, and are usually steamed or boiled. In Laos, the smaller varieties were sometimes roasted in their skin in hot ashes. There are no good substitutes for taro roots, although cassava roots are similar.

Water Chestnuts *Qos Dej*

These little corms, which grow wild in muddy areas in Laos, are peeled and eaten as a crunchy snack. When in season, fresh water chestnuts are sold in Asian markets. They taste very different from—and much better than—the canned variety. They are occasionally used to provide an interesting texture in Three-Color Dessert. Water chestnut leaves can be added to squirrel stew and are sometimes part of healthful tonics.

SHOOTS, SPROUTS, PEAS, BEANS, AND MUSHROOMS
NTSUAG, KAUS TAUM, TAUM QAB ZIB, TAUM, THIAB NCEB

Bamboo Shoots *Ntsuag*

Hmong people love to cook with bamboo shoots. There are dozens of varieties but just two basic categories—winter and spring. Winter bamboo shoots, smaller and more tender than spring ones, are considered more tasty. Bamboo shoots are available in Asian groceries two ways, fresh and cooked. Fresh ones look like green tusks, 5 to 10 inches long with a 2-inch-diameter base, that taper to a point. The coarse outer leaves tightly wrap around the shoot. Fresh shoots must be boiled about 30 minutes before being eaten or used in cooking. Fresh bamboo is sweeter and crunchier than the canned varieties. Cooked bamboo shoots come in an array of shapes and sizes in cans and plastic bags in Asian markets. The shoots in bags originally arrived in huge cans, so the two are interchangeable. Any of them will work in most Hmong dishes. In Laos, bamboo shoots were gathered in the wild, and Hmong people still love the flavor of wild bamboo. Labeled "bitter" bamboo (*ntsuag xyoob iab*), it is only available in cans.

Bean Curd (Tofu) *Taum Paj*

Bean curd, often paired with chicken in soup, is a special-occasion food. In America, Hmongs buy tofu ready-made, but for old times' sake some people still make it at home.

Bean Sprouts *Kaus Taum*

Fresh soybean sprouts are used as an accompaniment to *larb*. If they are not available, shredded cabbage is a good substitute.

Beans and Yard-Long Green Beans *Taum Hlab Tshos thiab Taum Ntev*

The short variety, a common American vegetable, is stir-fried, boiled, and added to stews. The long variety looks more exotic but tastes almost the same.

Mung Beans *Taum Pauv*

Mung beans are purchased dry. They are soaked, steamed, and mashed to be added to sticky rice packets, providing an interesting contrasting flavor.

Mushrooms *Nceb*

Oyster mushrooms come the closest to tasting like the wild mushrooms collected in Laos. In Hmong cooking, fresh mushrooms are cooked in a broth containing no other ingredients, so their flavor can be appreciated. Dried mushrooms and fungi are also used.

Rattan *Plawv Kav Theej*

Rattan's unique, woody taste is definitely worth trying. In the mountains of Laos, rattan shoots were harvested from the wild. More recently, a Laotian industry of farming and drying the shoots for commercial sale has developed. Hmong villagers dried rattan in the sun with no additives. Commercially farmed rattan is treated with citric acid and sodium metabisulfite, a preservative that may cause allergic reactions (although such allergies are rare).

Sweet Peas *Taum Mog*

Hmong people enjoy young sweet pea pods steamed and stir-fried.

Tendrils (Pea and Squash Vine Tips) *Ntsi Taum Mog*

Hmong people love the delicate tender tips and leaves from the ends of pea, melon, and squash vines. They are usually sautéed alone or with chunks of meat. The pruned vine will quickly grow a new end. Fresh tendrils are available in Asian grocery stores in season.

Mai Her, of Sacramento, California, explains a plant's healing qualities to co-author Sami Scripter. Very little information exists in English about the dozens of plants that Hmong people grow in their gardens and use in tonics and herbal remedies. The power of the plants often lies in the skill of the herbalist.

Herbs to Season and Medicate, A to Z

Hmong people use a variety of herbs. Some are available in grocery stores and others are grown in home gardens. These plants fall into three categories: seasoning herbs, herbs for health that are ingredients in soup, and bitter herbs used only as medicine. Some herbs fit in more than one category. A number of plants that flavor food also have health-giving properties, although there is no complete agreement about what medicinal properties each herb contains.

Herbs are listed here by their English common name (if one exists), their Hmong name, and other foreign names and nicknames that are used in the United States. Names and spellings of herbs vary widely. This list does not include all of the herbs utilized by Hmongs.

This category includes all of the plants used frequently to season food. Many have medicinal properties, but they are added to dishes primarily for their flavor.

Basil *Zaub Txwg Liab*

Thai basil and a home-grown, strong-flavored, forest-green "Hmong basil" (*zaub txwg theem Hmoob*) are ingredients in Lao meat salad (*larb*) and old-fashioned stews ("oh-la"); they also accompany soups.

Cilantro (Coriander) *Zaub Txhwb*

In their recipes, Hmong people like to include some of the root as well as the leaves and stems because the roots have a stronger flavor and more medicinal value.

Culantro *Txuj Lom Muas Loob los yog Nplooj Hniav Kaw* (known by two names)

Culantro is sometimes called duck-tongue herb or saw-leaf herb. Its grass-green individual leaves are 3 to 6 inches long and have a fine-tooth edge and a stiff spine. Although similar to cilantro in aroma and flavor, culantro is more pungent. Cilantro can be substituted in a recipe, although the flavor will not be as bold and sharp.

Dill *Zaub Txhwb Nyug*

Dill is tasty and good for digestion. Hmong people use dill when it is immature, without seeds—"baby dill."

Garlic Chives *Dos Ntaj*

Sometimes called Chinese chives, these long, flat, garlic-flavored chives are used in stir-fries. They lose their flavor if overcooked.

Green Onions *Dos Ntsuab*

Both the white and green parts are used raw and stir-fried.

Kaffir Lime Leaves *Nplooi Txiv Lws*

Although the fruit of a kaffir lime tree is too bitter to eat, the leaves are used to flavor soups. Lemongrass can substitute for kaffir lime leaves, but the flavor will not be as sharp.

Lemongrass Tauj Qaib los yog Tauj Dub (known by two names)

California Hmong often bring fresh lemongrass from their garden as a gift when visiting families in Minnesota and Wisconsin, where it does not grow well. Almost all Hmong soups are flavored with a stalk or two of this lemon-flavored herb. Lemongrass is very fibrous and is edible only when finely minced.

Mint Pum Hub

The Hmong grow and enjoy several varieties of mint. Spearmint, a favorite, is always included in Lao meat salad (*larb*).

Rice Paddy Herb

Rice paddy herb (which has no Hmong name) grows easily in wet places. It is used in soups and fish dishes for its flavor as well as in dishes and tonics for its medicinal properties. There is no good substitute for rice paddy herb. The Vietnamese name for it is *rau om*, which is how it is often labeled in Asian groceries.

Vietnamese Coriander Luam Laws

Sometimes called Asian mint or fragrant knotweed, this sprawling perennial with jointed stems can be recognized by the dark maroon, heart-shaped patches near the center of each leaf. Some Hmong people say that *larb* is not tasty without this strong, cilantro-flavored herb. There is no good substitute for Vietnamese coriander.

HERBS FOR HEALTH USED IN CHICKEN SOUP TSHUAJ RAU QAIB

This category includes all of the plants used in traditional chicken soup. These herbs, which Hmong people call "mints," are prized for their health-giving properties. Some of these plants have no common English names, and spellings of their Hmong names vary. They are listed here by their English common name (if one exists) and by their Hmong name.

Studies confirm that most of the plants Hmong people use for health have medicinal value, although the information here should not be used as treatment advice.

Angelica Koj Liab (Duck-Feet Herb)

This aromatic perennial with upright stems and divided, purple-flushed leaves looks like its name, "duck feet." It is an important postpartum tonic.

Hmong Herbal Medicine

WHILE MOST HMONG PEOPLE know something about culinary herbs (*txuj lom*) and those used in "good-for-you" chicken soup (*tshuaj rau qaib*), only a few are knowledgeable about strictly medicinal herbs (*tshuaj ntsuab*). The Hmong have practiced the art of using plants to treat illness and injury for centuries. In remote mountain villages in China, Thailand, and Laos, herbal remedies were often the only medicine available. Only a Hmong elder with experience and skill can utilize these herbs effectively. Some of the plants commonly used by Hmong herbalists, listed by their Hmong name, include *kaus luag, kuab dev, paj co ntiv, paj kaub tub sab, nrhab koob, paj tab, plauj tsuas, nplooj tsaj, qos tsov, raws liab, suv ntsim, txiv iab ntoo, uab noog ntxuam*, and *zej ntswg npua*. Any additional information must come from an experienced Hmong herbalist.

Women are herbalists (*kws tshuaj ntsuab*) more often than men. A good herbalist knows the medicinal capabilities of dozens of plants that she grows or gathers from the wild. Some are used fresh-picked and some are dried before they are used. Depending upon the nature of the plant and the nature of the illness, leaves, stems, fruit, blossoms, bark, and roots can be turned into healing tonics, poultices, washes, and wraps. Fresh herbs are usually supplemented by a variety of imported natural Chinese medicines that can be purchased on-line, at specialty stores, and from booths at New Year's celebrations and farmers' markets.

Traditionally, a person skilled in the use of healing herbs would pass down information to a younger interested person who showed an aptitude for learning and using the information. Sometimes a woman would pass down the knowledge to her daughter, granddaughter, or niece. Occasionally people would pay an herbalist to teach them "green medicine." It is widely understood that the effectiveness of any herbal medicine depends largely on the attention given to its preparation, and while one herb can be used to cure more than one illness, generally at least two or three herbs are combined to cure most complaints. An herbal remedy is also thought to be more effective if it is not explained or discussed. "Here, drink this and don't ask questions" is a common remark made when administering a medication.

The Hmong herbalist is a highly respected member of the community, and the same person sometimes, although not always, has command of several other traditional healing methods, including massage, dermal abrasion, and pressure-point techniques. Those who are highly skilled at these traditional healing arts are said to have "power hands" (*tes muaj tshuaj*).

In America, many Hmong fear the art of herbal medicine is dying off with the older generation. Few young Hmong Americans have the time or inclination to study traditional herbal healing methods, and some health-care providers forbid their Hmong patients to use medicinal herbs. As a result, herbal medicine know-how is declining. However, scientific research indicates that most Hmong herbs do have medicinal properties and that they are used wisely.

Skyler Vu's grandmother snipped healing herbs from the garden and plunged them into a cup of water. The "green medicine" is sipped through a straw.

Beefsteak Plant Nkaj Liab
This plant has big, bright red-purple leaves. The pungent, warming herb is used in soups, both for its flavor and for its health-giving properties.

Betel Zaub Kab Raus los yog Si Toj
Sometimes called pepper leaf or wild betel, this shrubby vine has heart-shaped leaves that smell spicy but taste medicinal. It is found in Asian markets labeled with its Vietnamese name, *lá lốt*. *Si toj* is a larger variety of piper betel that the Vietnamese chew like tobacco; they call it *lá trầu*. Hmong people use it in their cooking.

Cardamom Qhaus
Hmong cooks slice up the base of the stem and top of the root of this large-leafed perennial and include it in healthy soups.

Chinese Boxthorn Txiv Siav
The leaves of this shrub have a lemony, slightly bitter taste and are considered energizing, but the stems have thorns, so be careful when gathering them. The leaves are often added to soups. Parts of the plant are used as medicine.

Common Dayflower Tseej Ntug
The long, narrow leaves and stems of this weedy herb are always used in healthy chicken soup.

Elephant Ears Kav Ywm
The large, fleshy leaves of this plant are eaten with chicken. The root, called taro or malanga, is used like a cassava root.

Fish Mint Kab Si los yog Kab Raus (Smelly-Insect Vegetable)
This easy-to-grow herb has two Hmong names and a nickname derived from its unpleasant smell. Its flavor is slightly fishy.

Koj Ntsuab
This herb is always an ingredient of chicken soup for new mothers.

Lauj Vag
This herb is used for *larb*.

Mugwort Nrhab Koob
The lacy leaves of this plant go into healthy soups.

Ncaug Txhav
This green trailing plant grows close to the ground. It is always included in post-partum chicken soup.

Pennywort or Moneywort Lauj Vag
This creeping evergreen perennial that roots at the nodes is included in healthy soups.

Perilla Hnav Tsuj
Sometimes known by its Japanese name, *shiso*, perilla comes in purple varieties that are sold in Asian groceries. It has a strong mint-fennel flavor and many medicinal uses.

Sedum Sam Mos Kab los yog Sam Moj Kab
(Frighten Away Bad Spirits)
Several varieties of these succulents are used as food and as medicine.

Slippery Vegetable Hmab Ntsha Ntsuab
Sometimes called green vine or mederia vine, slippery vegetable is sold in season at Asian markets. When available, it is included in soup for new mothers.

Sweet Fern Ntiv
This pretty plant is another herb commonly grown and used in healthy chicken soup.

Sweet Flag Pawj Ia (large size), Pawj Qaib (small size)
These grass-like plants, also called Japanese rush, grow from rhizomes and smell strongly of licorice. Used since ancient times to promote appetite and digestion, and to invigorate health, they are always included in chicken soup for new mothers.

Tseej Ntug
Postpartum soup always contains this ingredient.

Tshuaj Rog (Fat Medicine)

There are several varieties of this herb, named after the color of the underside of its leaf. The herb is called "fat medicine" because it was an element in a weight-gain diet and was highly valued when being fat was a sign of wealth. Don't let the name fool you; it is actually a healthy food.

Zaub Iab

Only the elderly love this herb. Good when cooked with green beans, it is a little bitter.

Setting a Hmong Table and Eating Etiquette *Lub Tsum Mov*

Everyday family meals are simple. The menu always includes a big bowl of rice and two or three other dishes. Any food can be served at any meal. Hmong people eat with their fingers, forks, spoons, and sometimes chopsticks. Because ingredients are usually cut into bite-sized pieces before cooking, knives are seldom needed. At a family meal, the serving dishes are set in the middle of the table and everyone serves themselves. Dishes with a lot of broth double as beverages. "Hmong" or "Asian" spoons have a flat bottom and deep, sloping sides that make it easy to dip up broth from a bowl and bring it to your mouth without spilling a drop. At most meals, a small dish filled with minced hot chilies, cilantro, and fish sauce is also set on the table. Using their fingers, diners dip bits of meat and vegetables into the fiery condiment. Children are allowed to eat whatever they want. It is understood that children develop sophisticated tastes and eating habits as they grow older. Food is often cooked to order for children and the elderly.

Guests entering a Hmong home are always offered something to eat and drink. Turning down this hospitality is impolite. Guests receive the best food in the house and are encouraged to eat as much as they want. Hmong people will go without food to make sure that guests and loved ones have enough.

At formal traditional meals, each place is set with a plate, napkin, Hmong spoon, and chopsticks. A serving dish with each menu item is always within reach of each diner so that no one has to ask someone else to pass food. Traditional gatherings require that the men, seated together at one long table, eat separately from the women. In Laos, at such meals, the women sat down only after the men finished eating. Few modern families observe this custom. In America, it is more customary for the men to eat in one room and the women to eat in another room. Hmong Christians usually present food as a buffet, and men and women serve themselves and eat together. At gatherings of all kinds, it is still customary for the senior man to say a blessing before everyone begins to eat.

LET'S EAT ~ PEB NOJ MOV

Rice ～ Mov

Everyday Rice 51
Noj Mov Txhua Hnub

Sticky Rice 53
Txhuv Nplaum

Purple Rice 53
Txhuv Ntsav

Rice with Coconut Cream 54
Mov Xyaw Kua Mav Phaub

Sticky Rice in Banana Leaves—Two Filling Variations 54
Txhuv Nplaum Qhwv Nplooj Tsawb

Pounded Rice 57
Ncuav

Pounded Rice Cakes 58
Ncuav Ci

Sweet Steamed Rice Cakes 59
Ncuav Qab Zib Xyaw Taum

Saly's Rice and Corn Pancakes 60
Ncuav Pob Kws Kib

Toasted Sticky Rice Flour 61
Hmoov Nplej Kib

Plain Rice Porridge 61
Mov Kua Dis Tsuag

Rice Porridge with Meat 62
Kua Dis Nqaij

Rice Rolls 63
Hmoov Ua Fawm Kauv

Rice ⌇ Mov

Steam surrounds Chou Ly, of Hillsboro, Oregon, as she cooks rice the Hmong way, using a conical woven basket over a Thai hourglass-shaped steaming pot.

RICE IS SO IMPORTANT TO Hmong identity that they say, "To be Hmong is to eat rice." A large bowl of steaming rice is the centerpiece of every Hmong meal. Many varieties of rice are available in Asian grocery stores, and Hmong cooks enjoy using several kinds. Each variety has a different flavor and different cooking characteristics.

Jasmine rice is a fragrant, medium- to long-grain rice that cooks into tender, relatively dry, easily separated grains. Although it is grown in the United States, most of what is sold in Asian grocery stores is imported from Thailand. Jasmine rice is translucent prior to cooking.

Calrose rice is a high-quality medium-grain rice grown in California's Sacramento Valley. It has a rich, nutty flavor. Hmong people often cook a fifty-fifty mix of jasmine and Calrose rice to get just the right consistency and flavor. Jasmine or Calrose rice, or a mixture of the two, is "everyday rice."

Glutinous rice is called sticky rice, or sometimes sweet rice. Sticky rice has a high concentration of amylopectin, one of two types of starch found in rice (the other is amylase). When cooked, sticky rice becomes soft and the grains stick together. Sticky rice can be either long- or short-grain. It converts quickly to glucose in your mouth, making it taste a bit sweet. Sticky rice is opaque prior to being cooked. It is a special-occasion rice, used for desserts and to make pounded rice, a New Year's treat.

What is commonly called purple rice is a mixture of white sticky rice and unmilled rice that have been cooked together. The unmilled rice still has its dark husk, which infuses the cooked product with a deep purple color and gives it a somewhat nutty taste. Bags of unmilled rice labeled "black rice," "red rice," and "purple rice" are available at Asian supermarkets. All of them can be used to make purple rice.

Everyday Rice

◎◎ *Noj Mov Txhua Hnub*

Makes 8 cups cooked rice

Good Hmong cooks must master the art of preparing fluffy, delicious rice. Many people save time by using an automatic electric rice cooker. However, everyone loves the intense fragrance and flavor of rice cooked the old-fashioned way using an aluminum, hourglass-shaped Thai cooker and conical bamboo or plastic steaming basket. These inexpensive items can be purchased at Hmong, Thai, or Laotian grocery stores and supermarkets.

Cooking rice the old-fashioned way is a five-step process: washing, soaking, steaming, soaking a second time, and steaming the rice again to finish the cooking process. If you want to make authentic Hmong rice, here is how to do it.

INGREDIENTS

2 cups high-quality long-grain jasmine rice
2 cups high-quality Calrose rice
Water, for each step of the process

PREPARATION

Measure both kinds of rice into a large bowl. Cover the rice with cool tap water and rinse by swirling it around with your hand. Pour off the filmy water. Rinse the rice a second time, and again pour off the water. Cover the rice with cool water, and allow it to soak for several hours.

Fill a Thai cooking pot about two-thirds full with water, and set it on the stove over high heat to bring the water to a rapid boil. Set the steaming basket on top of the pot so the boiling water level is lower than the tip of the basket's cone. Completely drain the soaked rice and put it into the basket. Cover the rice; any lid that fits will work (neither the pot nor the basket is sold with a lid). Steam the rice for 15 to 20 minutes. The rice is ready for the next step when you pinch a grain and it is soft on the outside but still feels hard in the middle. After preparing this dish several times, you will be able to tell if the rice is ready simply by looking. The outer part of a grain of rice is translucent and the inner part is opaque.

Transfer the partly cooked rice into a large, clean bowl. Pour boiling water over the rice until it is just submerged. Stir with a plastic or wooden rice paddle and then allow it to sit in the water for 5 to 10 minutes. This process makes the rice fluffy and keeps it from sticking together. The water that is used to soak the rice the second time is called *kua ntxhai*. It is very nutritious, so do not discard it. Drain it from the rice and pour into a cup or bowl to use as a beverage or to make sour green vegetable pickles. Return the drained rice to the basket on top of the steamer.

Again, make sure that the boiling water does not touch the bottom of the steaming basket. Cover the rice again and finish steaming the rice, about 15 to 20 more minutes.

Now the rice is ready to eat. If you are not ready to serve the rice, store it in an electric rice cooker set to "warm," for serving later, or in a bowl to cool. Rice is eaten warm or cool, unaccompanied by any condiment or sauce. It is delicious just the way it is. Eat rice with a spoon, or with your fingers.

When a young child calls out "*Mov, mov!*" he or she is saying, "I am hungry." Grandmas can be counted on to lovingly pop a small ball of rice into the child's mouth.

"New grain" (*mov nplej tshiab*) is the first rice from a harvest season. It is cooked exactly the same way as Everyday Rice, but it is not mixed with any other kind of rice. It is picked a bit before it reaches maturity. It is a nostalgic treat for older Hmong people, who can remember when they grew and harvested rice by hand on their family farms in the mountains of Laos. After rice was harvested, it was roasted in the hulls and then winnowed to separate the hulls from the grains. The roasting process gave the rice a toasted flavor. It tastes different from rice grown, harvested, and processed commercially. Just after the first harvest, small packages of new rice are sold in Hmong grocery stores. Old people say that this dish is "pure Hmong."

Sticky Rice
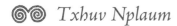 *Txhuv Nplaum*

Makes 8 cups cooked rice

Hmong cooks serve sticky rice simply steamed or made into a variety of special-occasion dishes. Sticky rice is often rolled into little balls and eaten with the fingers as part of a meal, or as a snack. Because sticky rice is softer than jasmine and Calrose rice, it requires less cooking time.

INGREDIENTS

> 4 cups sticky rice
> Water

PREPARATION

Soak and cook the rice the same as Everyday Rice, but steam it only once, for about 40 minutes. It is done when the grains are soft all of the way through.

Purple Rice
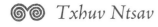 *Txhuv Ntsav*

Makes 8 cups cooked rice

Purple rice is always served at celebrations, especially New Year's. The vivid, dark purple is very pretty!

INGREDIENTS

> 1 cup purple rice
> 3 cups sticky rice
> Water

PREPARATION

In a food processor, grind the uncooked purple rice until it is about the size of sesame seeds. Mix it with the uncooked sticky rice, then soak, and steam the mixture as you would for sticky rice.

Rice with Coconut Cream

Mov Xyaw Kua Mav Phaub

Makes 16 servings (½ cup each)

The rich flavor and creamy texture of rice with coconut cream is a special treat. It is so sweet that it can be served as a dessert.

INGREDIENTS

8 cups cooked sticky rice
1 can (14 ounces) coconut cream

PREPARATION

Place the freshly steamed, hot sticky rice in a large bowl. Pour the coconut cream over the rice. Stir with a rice paddle to mix and fluff the rice. Return the mixture to the basket on top of the steamer, then cover and steam for 10 to 15 more minutes. Serve hot or at room temperature.

Sticky Rice in Banana Leaves— Two Filling Variations

Txhuv Nplaum Qhwv Nplooj Tsawb

Makes 16 packets

In Laos, Hmong men and boys hunted and fished to feed their families. In America, hunting and fishing are no longer necessary, but they are still favorite leisure-time activities. Many women make packets of sweet sticky rice in banana leaves for their husbands and sons to take with them on hunting or fishing trips. Plantains can be added to these little "to-go" snacks for extra flavor and texture. Another variation is to stuff the rice packets with a section of preserved sausage, creating a savory, salty snack.

INGREDIENTS

2 cups raw sticky (sweet) rice
1 cup canned coconut milk
4 tablespoons sugar

20 to 25 banana leaves (1 package)

Banana leaves can be found in packages in the frozen food section at larger Asian grocery stores. Thaw the package by allowing it to sit at room temperature for 1 hour.

PREPARE THE RICE FILLING

Soak the sticky rice overnight, or for at least 4 hours. Then steam it in a Thai steamer as in Everyday Rice, but for only 10 minutes. Transfer the partly cooked rice to a large bowl. In a small saucepan, mix the coconut milk with the sugar and bring to a simmer. Cook until the sugar is dissolved, about 3 minutes. Remove from heat and pour the coconut mixture over the sticky rice. Using a rice paddle, stir until the ingredients are thoroughly combined. Allow the mixture to cool.

PREPARE THE BANANA LEAVES

While the rice is cooling, prepare the thawed banana leaves. This is a delicate operation, because the leaves tear easily. To clean the leaves, lay them, one at a time, flat in the sink. Rinse each leaf under a trickle of water from the tap. Using your hands and a clean cloth or paper towel, following the grain of the leaf, wipe the leaf on both sides to clear away any residue. Turn the water off and dry the leaf on both sides. Stack the clean leaves on a flat work surface. Using a clean pair of scissors, cut the rib and all brown edges away from each leaf and discard. Cut each leaf into a 12-by-12-inch square. No matter how careful you are, some of the leaves will tear, and some may not be big enough. If necessary, overlap two leaves to get the correct dimensions.

STUFF AND STEAM THE PACKETS

Use about ¼ cup of rice for each packet. Place the rice on a banana leaf about 2 inches in from the edge. Pat the rice into a rectangular shape and then fold the banana leaf over the rice. Continue to wrap the banana leaf around the rice, and then fold the ends under as though you are gift-wrapping a package. Continue making packets until the rice is all used up. In the bottom of a steamer, bring 4 inches of water to a boil. Transfer the rice packets to the top of the steamer and steam for 40 minutes, or until the rice is very soft.

Plantain Filling

This version requires 2 ripe plantains, plus 1 lime.

Prepare the rice and coconut milk as in the preceding recipe. Just before you stuff the banana leaves, peel and cut 1 plantain in half the long way and then cut each half into five sections, making ten equal-sized pieces. Do the same with the second plantain. Put the plantain pieces in a small bowl of water together with the juice of the lime to keep them from turning brown. To make the banana-leaf packets, put 2 tablespoons of rice on a leaf and then 1 piece of plantain. Cover the plantain with 2 more tablespoons of rice. Then roll up the banana leaf and tuck in the ends, as described above. Steam the banana-leaf packets for 40 minutes, or until the rice is very soft.

Salty Sausage Filling

This version requires 4 preserved Chinese sausages.

Usually labeled "Kam Yen Jan," these hard, sweet, fatty pork and chicken sausages are found in 1-pound vacuum-packed packages at most Asian markets. They are the size and shape of slender hot dogs. The packaged sausages can be stored unrefrigerated, but they must be refrigerated after opening. Always cook them well before serving.

To make this filling, soak and cook the sticky rice as above, but do not add the sugar or coconut milk. Cut each sausage in half through the middle and then cut each piece in half the long way; each piece should be about 3 inches long. When stuffing the banana leaves, put 2 tablespoons of the sticky rice on the leaf, and then add a piece of Chinese sausage. Top that with 2 more tablespoons of rice and wrap up the packet as above. Steam the banana-leaf packets for 40 minutes, or until the rice is very soft.

Another version, with pork, preserved sausage, and mung beans, can be found on page 250.

Recipe shared by Lee Moua of Denver, Colorado

Pounded Rice

 *Ncuav*

Ncuav, or pounded sticky rice—sometimes referred to by its Japanese name, *mochi*—is a hot, thick, elastic food. In Laos, *ncuav* was made by pounding cooked sticky rice in a large wooden bowl or trough with heavy wooden mallets. In America, Hmong cooks buy premade *mochi* from an Asian store,

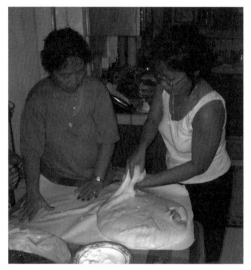

Sheng and her sister-in-law work with pounded rice (ncuav) to make New Year's rice cakes. They use no utensils to prepare the little toasted patties.

or they use an electric *mochi* machine or the knead cycle of an electric bread machine to pound rice. Although expensive, electric automatic *mochi* machines are superior. They are available occasionally from Web sites (use the search term "mochi machine"). In the Pacific Northwest (Seattle and Bellevue, Washington, and Beaverton, Oregon), Tiger-brand *mochi* machines are available at Uwajimaya Asian superstores. If you use a *mochi* machine, follow the manufacturer's directions to cook and pound the rice.

If you use a bread machine, begin with 4 cups of uncooked sticky rice. Soak the rice in warm water overnight. Drain and steam it as in the Sticky Rice recipe, which results in 8 cups of cooked rice. Spread the rice out on a clean surface to allow as much moisture as possible to evaporate, then put the rice into a large-capacity bread machine. Run the rice through the machine's knead cycle with the lid open (kneading time differs from machine to machine), which allows more moisture to escape. The drier the product, the easier it is to shape. After the rice is pounded, remove it from the machine with your hands. It will be very hot and sticky, so first rub your hands with hard-cooked egg yolk to keep the *ncuav* from sticking to your skin. Place the hot blob of *ncuav* on a large piece of freezer paper. *Ncuav* can be eaten as is, or it can be made into toasted rice cakes (see recipe below).

During New Year's celebrations in traditional Hmong homes, the first serving of pounded sticky rice is placed on the home altar as a divine offering: to honor and feed the spirits of the family's ancestors, to give thanks for prosperity, and to ensure good luck in the coming year.

Another way to enjoy *ncuav* is to deep-fry it around balls of sweetened, cooked mung beans; this dish is called *qe ncuav kib*. Make the mung bean filling by soaking 6 ounces of split mung beans in 5 cups of water for several hours. Drain, and put the beans in the top of a steamer and steam for 15 minutes. Next, put them in a blender along with ½ cup sugar. Blend until they look like small grains. Shape the mung beans into balls about the size of the tip of your thumb. Surround each mung bean ball with a golf ball–sized piece of the *ncuav*. In a deep wok, heat 4 or 5 inches of vegetable oil to medium heat. Slip several balls into the oil at a time and fry until golden brown, turning occasionally. Remove from the oil and drain briefly on paper towels, then roll in sesame seeds.

Pounded Rice Cakes
 *Ncuav Ci*

8 cups of ncuav *make about 20 cakes*

There are several ways to make rice cakes out of *ncuav*. To make a sweet fried cake, take a 2½-inch ball of pounded sticky rice and put it in the middle of one half of a 5-by-10-inch square of freezer paper. Fold the paper over the rice and press together so the rice blob becomes a flat, 4-to-5-inch-diameter pancake. Heat a dry (no oil) skillet over medium heat. Remove the patty from the paper and toast it in the pan, first on one side and then on the other, until it is puffy, golden brown, and a little bit crisp on the surface. To eat, dip the toasted rice cake into some palm or maple syrup. If you prefer a salty treat, form the pancake as above, and then brush the skillet with a thin layer of vegetable oil and fry the pancake on both sides (it will not puff up as the cake does when cooked in a dry pan). Sprinkle the rice cake with a little salt.

Rice cakes can also be broiled in the oven. Make several cakes and place them on a broiler pan covered with aluminum foil. Set the broiler pan about 4 inches from the oven's top elements. Broil the cakes at 300 degrees for 4 to 5 minutes on each side, or until they puff up and begin to turn golden brown.

Any way you cook these traditional little cakes, they are warm, delicious, and chewy!

Sweet Steamed Rice Cakes

Ncuav Qab Zib Xyaw Taum

Makes 3 dozen cakes

After these sweetened rice and mung bean cakes are steamed, toast them in a toaster oven and enjoy a Hmong-style "pop tart"!

INGREDIENTS

5 cups uncooked jasmine or Calrose rice
13 cups water (to soak rice and mung beans)
6 ounces whole mung beans
1 cup sugar

PREPARATION

Put the rice in a large bowl and rinse several times with cool water. Drain off the water and then add 8 cups of water to the rice. In another bowl, place the mung beans in 5 cups of water. Soak both the rice and the mung beans overnight. Remove and discard the papery skins that have separated from the mung beans. Drain the beans and add them to the bowl of soaking rice. Put about 1 cup of the mixture into a blender and blend on high until blended but still grainy—about the texture of commercial cornmeal. Transfer the blended mixture to a saucepan. Continue until all of the rice and bean mixture is blended. Add the sugar and stir. Place the pan over medium heat and stir constantly for 10 minutes. Turn the heat to low and keep cooking and stirring until the mixture is very thick. Remove the pan from the heat, cover, and allow to sit for 2 to 3 hours. The rice and bean grains will continue to absorb the water and puff up. Transfer the dough to a large, flat surface to cool completely.

To form each cake, take about ⅔ cup of the rice and bean dough and place it on a 12-by-12-inch piece of aluminum foil. Shape the dough into a 4-by-6-inch rectangle. First fold the foil over the two long sides of the dough and then the two short sides, overlapping the edges. Set the packets into a flat-bottomed metal steamer (they can be stacked) and steam the cakes over boiling water for about 30 minutes. These rice cakes can be eaten warm or cool. They are sweet, chewy, and a little bit gooey. Or, to make them crispy on the outside, open the packets and let the cakes cool. Then put them on another piece of foil in a toaster oven and toast on one side and then the other, until they begin to turn brown and slightly crispy.

Saly's Rice and Corn Pancakes

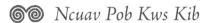 *Ncuav Pob Kws Kib*

Makes about 2 dozen pancakes

Saly Yang, Sheng's mother-in-law, was about eighty-four years old when this recipe was written down. She was born in a small mountain village in Laos. Her birth date was never recorded and has long since been forgotten. As a child, Saly walked each day with her family through the forest for four miles to their garden farm where she helped to tend the family's plots of rice, corn, and vegetables. Rice was the favored grain and corn was primarily used to feed the livestock. But if the rice harvest was inadequate, corn augmented the family's diet. Compared with the corn grown in America, Laotian corn was big, deep yellow, and dry. In Hmong gardens it was allowed to ripen and then dry on the stalks in the hot sunshine. For human consumption, the kernels were scraped off the cobs and ground into flour, using a hand- or foot-powered stone grinding mill.

In Laos, these pancakes were made with only corn, but because American corn is so full of moisture, Saly mixes the corn with rice flour to make the batter stiffer. These pancakes give elderly Hmong a taste of the old life. They are called "nostalgia food."

INGREDIENTS

> 5 cups yellow corn kernels (fresh or frozen)
> ½ cup sugar (more or less, to taste)
> 1 to 2 cups water
> 1 bag (16 ounces) glutinous rice flour
> Butter

PREPARATION

If using fresh corn, strip the husk and silk from 7 medium-sized ears. Remove any damaged kernels, rinse under running water, and dry with a paper towel. With a sharp knife, scrape the corn kernels off of the cobs into a big bowl. If using frozen corn, thaw first. Put the kernels in a blender and blend on medium until the corn is grainy (bits should be about the size of sesame seeds and a little larger). Pour back into the bowl and add the sugar, 1 cup of water, and the rice flour. Stir well, combining all ingredients. Continue to stir while adding water until the mixture is the consistency of thick, grainy pancake batter.

Coat a skillet with 1 teaspoon butter. Turn the heat to medium-low. When the skillet is hot, pour in ¼ cup of the batter. Fry the pancake on one side until it is golden. Turn it over and cook the other side. Continue cooking pancakes one at a time. These sweet pancakes are served warm from the skillet or at room temperature, with no accompaniment.

Toasted Sticky Rice Flour
Hmoov Nplej Kib

Makes ⅞ cup flour

Rice flour is an ingredient of *larb*, a traditional Laotian dish. You can buy packages of toasted rice flour in Asian supermarkets, or you can make it at home.

Put 1 cup of uncooked sticky rice in a nonstick skillet over medium heat. Stir constantly until the rice is uniformly browned (about 10 to 15 minutes). If the rice smokes as it is toasted, turn the heat down a little. Remove from the heat and let the rice cool. Grind the browned rice in a clean coffee grinder, or do it by hand using a mortar and pestle. Use the coffee grinder for only a few seconds; do not let the flour become too fine. The finished product should be a slightly grainy powder. Rice flour can be stored in an airtight container for several months.

Plain Rice Porridge
 ## *Mov Kua Dis Tsuag*

Makes 4 servings

A warm bowl of rice porridge is good for babies, the elderly, and anyone suffering from the flu. It is not just a breakfast food; serve it morning, noon, or evening.

INGREDIENTS

1 *quart water*
1 *cup hard-grained rice, such as jasmine rice*

Put the water into a pot and add the rice. Turn the heat to high. Bring to a boil and cook about 7 minutes, stirring constantly to keep the rice from sticking. Reduce the heat to medium-low so the porridge barely simmers. Cook the rice until it is very soft, even mushy. Add more liquid for a thin, soupy porridge.

Rice Porridge with Meat

Kua Dis Nqaij

Makes 4 servings

To make rice porridge more flavorful and hearty, add ground meat and seasonings.

INGREDIENTS

1 quart water
1 cup hard-grained rice, such as jasmine rice
½ stalk lemongrass (the tender part)
1 cup ground pork, beef, or chicken
A pinch salt
A pinch black pepper

PREPARATION

Put the water into a pot and add the rice and lemongrass. Turn the heat to high. Bring to a boil and cook about 7 minutes, stirring constantly to keep the rice from sticking. Reduce heat to medium-low so the porridge barely simmers. Cook the rice until it is soft.

Put the ground pork, beef, or chicken in a bowl and add a little water to break the meat apart. (The meat should not stick together like a meatball.) Pour the meat into the pot and stir. Add a pinch of salt and black pepper, or to taste. Cook for about 10 more minutes, until the meat is no longer pink. Remove the lemongrass. Serve the warm porridge in individual bowls.

Another way of adding flavor to the porridge is to cook the rice in chicken, beef, or vegetable stock instead of in water.

Rice Rolls

Hmoov Ua Fawm Kauv

Makes about 20 crepes

These rice noodle crepes glisten on the plate, making everyone's mouths water. Their mild flavor perfectly contrasts with the crunchy peanuts and the spicy sauce that accompany them. Asian grocery stores carry many kinds of flour made from different rice varieties and starches. Look for a bag with a picture of rice rolls on it, labeled "Flour for Wet Rice Paper" or "Flour for Steamed Rice Rolls"—*Fawm Kauv* in Hmong and *Bánh Cuốn* in Vietnamese. The flour is measured by weight; use an entire bag. Don't try to measure the flour with a cup because it is very, very fine and the result will be a big mess. The water measure listed below works for either a 12- or a 14-ounce bag of flour.

INGREDIENTS

8 green onions, white and green parts, chopped
Dried black fungus, soaked, drained, and chopped to equal ¼ cup
1 pound lean ground pork or beef (pork is traditional)
1 teaspoon salt
½ teaspoon coarse-ground black pepper
1 12- or 14-ounce bag rice flour for wet rice paper
3¼ cups water
Vegetable oil
Ground toasted peanuts and spicy chili sauce (see below)

PREPARATION

Clean and chop the green onions. Soak the black fungus (sometimes called black wood mushrooms) for 20 minutes to soften, and then drain and chop. Put the onions and fungus in a bowl and set aside. Fry the ground pork or beef in a hot skillet, stirring and breaking the meat into small pieces as it fries. Add the salt and pepper. Drain extra fat off of the meat and allow the meat to cool. Put it into a food processor and chop until fine. Mix the meat together with the green onions and fungus.

In another bowl, mix together the flour and water. Brush the bottom of a 10-inch flat-bottomed sauté pan with a very light coating of oil and heat the pan over medium-high. Pour ¼ cup of the watery batter into the pan. Shake and turn the pan so that its bottom is coated evenly. Cover and cook for about 1 minute, or until the crepe is cooked through. Flip the finished crepe onto a plate. Put a large spoonful of the filling onto the crepe and spread it into a line that does not reach the edge of the crepe. Roll the crepe up around the filling as you would an egg roll, tucking in the sides as you roll. If any of the crepe sticks on the pan, wipe it clean with a paper towel. Brush more oil on the pan and continue to cook and fill one crepe at a time until all of the batter is used. Top with toasted ground peanuts and serve with hot chili dipping sauce.

Ground Toasted Peanuts

Toast 1 cup raw peanuts in a dry skillet over medium heat, shaking the skillet constantly and being careful not to let them burn. After the peanuts cool, rub off the papery skins and discard. Grind the nuts using a mortar and pestle, a nut grinder, or a food processor. Sprinkle over the rice rolls.

Hot Chili Dipping Sauce

1 tablespoon bottled garlic chili sauce
3 tablespoons chopped cilantro
Juice of 1 large lime
2 tablespoons fish sauce
1 tablespoon soy sauce
½ teaspoon sugar

Mix together all ingredients. Pour into a small bowl and serve with the rice rolls.

Rice Rain

By Song Yang

Rice bags fall from the sky,
splitting open upon contact with the ground.
Specks of white spill out and
scatter throughout the landscape
like bomb craters.

Above, the sound of Air America planes
fades into the distant mountains.
Below, children run outside to watch.
Mothers scold at them
to stay out of the way.

Grandmother, with her purple hair wrap
and red sash around her waist,
waits in line for her meager ration.
Sweat on her brow from the blistering sun,
she remembers a mountainous field of rice.

How Father poked holes in the soil
with a wooden stick, followed by Mother
who filled in the seeds. A field where red
and orange poppies drowned out the sunset
and rice once came from the ground.

Vegetables and Herbs ~
Zaub thiab Tshuaj Ntsuab

Steamed Vegetables 71
Zaub Cub

Boiled Vegetables 71
Zaub Hau

Stuffed Bitter Melon 72
Dib Iab Ntim Nqaij Hau Ua Kua

Steamed Stuffed Cabbage Leaves 73
Nplooj Zaub Pob Qhwv Cub

Tofu 75
Taum Paj

Stir-Fried Pumpkin Vines 76
Ntsis Kaub Kib

Stir-Fried Water Spinach 76
Phav Npoob Kib

Cabbage and Tomato Stir-Fry 77
Zaub Pob Kib Xyaw Txiv Lws Suav

Garlicky Chinese Green Flower (Oilseed Rape) 78
Zaub Ntsuab Paj Kib

Stir-Fried Baby Bok Choy with Pork Belly 79
Zaub Ntsuag Dawb Kib Xyaw Nqaij Npuas

Wild Bamboo Stir-Fried with Chicken 80
Ntsuag Iab Kib Xyaw Nqaij Qaib

Sheng's Green Papaya Salad 81
See Taub Ntoos Qaub

Spicy Bamboo Salad 82
Ntsuag Tuav Kua Txob

Watercress Salad Dressed with Pork 83
Zaub Dej Xav Lav Xyaw Nqaij Npuas

Pickles, Condiments, and Sauces
Zaub Qaub, Kua Txob Ntsw, thiab Kua Txob Tuav

Sour Green-Vegetable Pickles—Two Variations 84
Zaub Qaub

Fried Green-Vegetable Pickles 86
Zaub Qaub Kib

Hot Chili Condiment 87
Kua Txob Ntsw

Hot Chili and Eggplant Sauce 88
Lws Tuav Kua Txob

Chili Garlic Paste 89
Kua Txob Qej Kib Xyaw Roj

Vegetables and Herbs ～
Zaub thiab Tshuaj Ntsuab

Chong Cha, of Portland, Oregon, uses herbs and vegetables fresh from her backyard garden to give her food a distinctly Hmong flavor.

VEGETABLES ARE THE SOUL OF Hmong cuisine. Hmong cooks use a fabulous variety: leafy greens of all kinds, squashes, melons, pods, shoots, tendrils, tubers, mushrooms, roots, and seeds. Only fresh, good-looking vegetables appear in Hmong dishes. Menus are often decided upon by which vegetables are available and in their prime. In Laos, Hmong families raised all of their own vegetables. In America, many Hmong families make a living by growing, harvesting, and selling vegetables at farmers' markets. So strong is the desire to be connected to the land and growing things that even Hmong professionals make space for a backyard garden.

At first glance, to a non-Hmong, a Hmong garden may appear haphazard, with cucumbers and beans vining up mismatched branches stuck into the ground and unidentified weeds growing among more cultivated crops. But on closer inspection everything makes sense. The rough bark of the branches is a perfect surface for vines to take hold and climb, and what others may consider a weed is given space in a Hmong garden because of its medicinal properties. Hmong gardeners have a deep understanding of plants, and they work with nature to obtain bountiful, organic harvests.

Just as fat pork on the table is a symbol of wealth and prosperity, vegetables—even though they are much-loved—are a symbol of being poor. Marriage feasts do not include vegetables, because their presence would be an omen of a poor life for the married couple. Vegetables are not served at funerals, either, because the Hmong desire a rich afterlife for the deceased. At all other meals, vegetables and herbs play a major role.

"In a Hmong Kitchen" (page 15) contains lists and descriptions of the vegetables and herbs most closely associated with Hmong cooking, including those used differently than in other cuisines and those not often found in mainstream supermarkets. Each one is listed by its commonly used American name (if there is one) and its Hmong name (if there is one), as well as other names by which it is identified in American stores.

Steamed Vegetables
Zaub Cub

The simplest method for cooking vegetables is to steam them. Steaming emphasizes their fresh flavor, and vegetables are very healthful when steamed. Hmong cooks steam every kind of vegetable and present them plain without seasoning or accompaniment. Steam vegetables in a double boiler or in a Chinese bamboo steamer inside a wok, or simply place them on a heat-proof plate elevated 1 inch above boiling water on a rack inside a pot. Steaming vegetables takes twice as long as boiling them, but be careful not to overcook them. They should retain their shape and some crunch.

Boiled Vegetables
Zaub Hau

Makes 6 servings

The Hmong like to eat vegetables cooked in a light broth. Such a dish graces the table at most Hmong meals. Follow this recipe to cook leafy greens, oyster mushrooms, or any kind of young squash.

INGREDIENTS

1 pound vegetable of choice (such as bitter melon vines,
    bamboo mustard cabbage, garland chrysanthemum greens,
    or cubed chayote squash)
8 cups water
1 stalk lemongrass, tough outer leaves and root removed,
    bulb smashed with the flat edge of a knife, and cut into
    3-inch pieces
1 teaspoon salt
2 hot Thai chili peppers, sliced thinly on the diagonal (optional)
Dash coarse-ground black pepper
Several sprigs cilantro and 2 green onions, white and green parts,
    cut into 2-inch lengths, for garnish

Wash and prepare your choice of vegetable. Coarsely chop leafy greens, cut mushrooms into bite-sized pieces, or peel and cut young squash into 1-inch cubes. Bring the water to boil in a pot. Add the vegetable, lemongrass, and salt. Add the hot pepper, if desired. Cook until the vegetable is done. Add the black pepper, and garnish with cilantro and green onions. Pour into individual serving bowls. Diners can sip the broth as a beverage.

Stuffed Bitter Melon

Dib Iab Ntim Nqaij Hau Ua Kua

Makes 8 servings

Many Western people are unfamiliar with bitter melon. It is found only at Hmong farmers' markets and in Asian grocery stores. While some may find it an acquired taste, bitter melon is good for you and is low in fat; it is considered a good vegetable for diabetics. In this recipe, the bitter melon adds a zing to the rather bland pork filling.

INGREDIENTS

6 medium-sized ripe bitter melons (the seeds will be red)
1 pound lean ground pork or chicken
½ bunch cilantro, stems and leaves, chopped fine
  (to equal about ½ cup)
4 green onions, white and green parts, chopped fine
½ teaspoon salt
Dash black pepper
½ teaspoon MSG (optional)
1½ quarts water (or enough to cover bitter melon as it cooks)
1 stalk lemongrass, cleaned and chopped into 3-inch pieces

PREPARATION

Clean and then cut each bitter melon crosswise into two pieces. With a small spoon (a long-handled iced-tea spoon works well), scoop out the seeds and surrounding pith, leaving the melon's thick shell intact. Set aside.

If you prefer to cut your own meat rather than buy ground pork or chicken, chop it very finely with a cleaver. Mix the meat with the chopped cilantro and green onions. Add the salt, pepper, and MSG (if desired). Mix well. Fill the hollowed-out bitter melons with the meat mixture. If any filling is left over, form it into 1-inch meatballs to cook along with the stuffed bitter melons.

Bring the water to boil. Add the stuffed bitter melons and the lemongrass. Lower the heat to keep the water gently simmering. Cook for about 20 minutes, or until the filling is cooked and the bitter melon is just getting soft. After it is done, snip the stuffed bitter melons into 2-inch lengths with kitchen shears. Serve the melon pieces floating in the broth in a large, shallow bowl. Diners dish the stuffed bitter melon pieces onto their plates and with a spoon sip the flavorful broth directly from the serving bowl.

Recipe shared by Sami Yang (Sheng's youngest sister and Sami Scripter's namesake) of Sacramento, California

Steamed Stuffed Cabbage Leaves
Nplooj Zaub Pob Qhwv Cub

Makes 10 stuffed leaves

The mixture used to fill these glistening, fat cabbage bundles is similar to egg roll filling, and, like egg roll filling, every Hmong cook makes it a little bit differently.

INGREDIENTS

> 10 outer leaves from 2 large heads of American or napa cabbage
>   (or substitute iceberg lettuce leaves)
> 3 packages (2 ounces each) vermicelli noodles
> 1 pound ground pork, chicken, or turkey
> 4 green onions, white and green parts, chopped fine
> ¼ cup cilantro, finely chopped
> 1 small can water chestnuts, drained and chopped
> 3 medium-sized carrots, finely shredded
> 6 pieces black fungus, soaked until soft and then chopped fine
> 6 medium-sized white mushrooms, chopped fine
> 1 teaspoon salt

1 teaspoon MSG (optional)
½ teaspoon coarse-ground black pepper
2 tablespoons oyster sauce
A few drops sesame oil
2 eggs, stirred

PREPARATION

Remove and wash the large outer leaves of the cabbage (or lettuce), being careful not to tear them. With a paring knife, cut any tough root-end away from each leaf. In a large pan, bring 3 quarts of water to boil. Once the water is boiling, submerge 1 cabbage or lettuce leaf at a time in the water for a second or two. The leaves should become pliable but not limp. Drain and lay the leaves on a plate and set aside.

While preparing the leaves, soak the vermicelli noodles in a bowl of warm water for 30 minutes, or until soft. Using a fine-mesh colander, completely drain the noodles. With kitchen shears, snip the noodles into approximately 1-inch lengths. In a large bowl, use your hands to mix the ground meat with the noodles, green onions, cilantro, water chestnuts, carrots, black fungus, and mushrooms. Add the salt, MSG (if desired), black pepper, oyster sauce, and sesame oil. Add the eggs and mix thoroughly.

Using a plate as a working surface, place 1 cabbage leaf on the plate and about ⅓ cup of the filling on the leaf. Roll up the leaf as you would an egg roll, tucking in the sides as you roll. Discard any leaves that have large tears, since the filling would leak out. Small tears do not matter. To steam the stuffed leaves, fill a large, flat-bottomed bamboo or metal steamer half full of water and set it on the stove over high heat to boil. Gently place each stuffed leaf in the top part of the steaming pan. The stuffed leaves can be stacked on top of each other. Cover the pan and steam the stuffed leaves for about 30 minutes. Remove the steamer from the stove, take the lid off of the steamer, and allow the steam to escape. Then carefully lift each stuffed leaf onto a serving platter. Serve hot.

Tofu

Taum Paj

Makes 1 brick tofu

In Laos, the Hmong made soybean curd (*taum paj*) at any time of the year, from soybeans grown in their fields and stored dry in the attic. The beans were first soaked in water and then ground in the stone mill, yielding a wet mush, which was boiled in a cast-iron pan (*lub yias*) and drained through a cloth. The liquid was saved and the solids were discarded (though some would fry the solid part in grease and eat it). Then the liquid was heated to boiling and some kind of acid (lemon juice or the juice of certain leaves or vines) added, causing the liquid to thicken. The resulting tofu could be eaten hot or left to cool. The following recipe is a modern version.

Tofu is highly esteemed by the Hmong. Older Hmong especially like to eat a good tofu soup. Sometimes chunks of tofu are added to boiled chicken or capon, particularly at the first meal of newly harvested rice. Tofu is served on other special occasions, such as visits between in-laws.

INGREDIENTS

1 pound soybeans
½ cup lemon juice
½ cup warm water, plus enough to soak and cover beans

PREPARATION

Edible soybeans are available at Asian grocery stores. Buy 1 pound, put the beans in a bowl, and cover them with cool water. Allow to soak for 8 hours. Then drain, and remove the skins that have separated from the beans.

Put ¼ cup of the beans in a blender. Add enough water to cover the beans. Blend until the beans are mashed. Repeat until all of the beans are processed.

Put the mashed beans in a clean cloth rice bag or in several layers of cheesecloth, tied to enclose the beans. Hang the bag over a large bowl. Let the liquid drain into the bowl. Twist the bag, squeezing it tighter and tighter to force the liquid out. Keep the drained liquid. Throw away the solids with the bag.

Pour the liquid in a saucepan. Over a low heat, carefully bring it to a "little boil" (don't stop watching). Add the lemon juice to the warm water. Add the lemon mixture to the liquid until it changes from white to clear and solids separate from the liquid. When the top part is solid and the bottom part is liquid, it is done.

With a slotted spoon, remove the solid part and put it in a clean rice bag or cheesecloth. Hang the bag over a bowl for 2 hours. The tofu is in the bag. The liquid can be drunk or used as a soup base. Remaining liquid can be refrigerated and used during the next two days. This homemade tofu is not as solid as store-bought tofu bricks.

Recipe adapted from the Hmong Recipe Cook Book, *edited by Sharon Sawyer (First Presbyterian Church, South St. Paul, Minnesota, 1986)*

Stir-Fried Pumpkin Vines
Ntsis Kaub Kib

5 cups of vines make 2 or 3 servings

Pumpkin vines, or vines from luffa squash, bitter melon, and sweet peas, can be stir-fried. Buy them at an Asian grocery store, or snip off the last 6 to 7 inches of vines growing in your garden. Wash them and drain in a colander. If thick vines have a tough outer fiber, peel it off. Cut the vines into approximately 3-inch lengths, or leave intact. For every 5 cups of vines, use 1 tablespoon of vegetable oil. Add the oil to a large wok and heat it to medium. Toss the vines into the wok and stir-fry for a few minutes, until the leaves begin to wilt, though the vines should remain crunchy. Add a little water, rice juice, or broth. Cover and steam for a few minutes. The vines are ready when they are bright green and still a bit crunchy. Sprinkle with a little salt and serve hot.

Stir-Fried Water Spinach
Phav Npoob Kib

Makes 4 servings

This vegetable is available only in the spring and early summer. Because of its hollow stems, its Chinese nickname means "empty heart vegetable." It tastes delicate and sweet, and the hollow stems soak up the flavor of accompanying ingredients. This recipe is fresh and flavorful, with just a touch of heat. The trick is to cook the spinach so that the leaves are wilted but the stems remain crunchy. For a Western twist, mash 2 anchovies with the garlic, and omit the oyster sauce.

INGREDIENTS

1 large bunch fresh water spinach
2 tablespoons vegetable oil
2 large cloves garlic, minced
2 jalapeño peppers, sliced thin on the diagonal (discard the seeds
  for less heat)
½ teaspoon salt
½ teaspoon MSG (optional)
3 tablespoons oyster sauce

PREPARATION

Wash the water spinach in lots of cold water. Pick off any tough stems and discolored leaves and discard. Drain thoroughly in a large colander. Heat the oil in a large wok or frying pan over medium-high heat. Add the garlic and peppers. Stir-fry until the garlic just begins to turn brown. Add the water spinach, salt, MSG (if desired), and oyster sauce, and stir-fry for about 2 minutes. Cover and cook for 1 or 2 more minutes, until the leaves are wilted, the stems are still crunchy, and the flavors are combined. Serve hot.

Cabbage and Tomato Stir-Fry
Zaub Pob Kib Xyaw Txiv Lws Suav

Makes 4 to 6 servings

This healthy veggie dish has a wonderful flavor and can be served for any occasion.

INGREDIENTS

¼ cup vegetable oil
2 cloves garlic, smashed and then chopped

½ head cabbage, cut into 2-inch cubes

2 medium-sized tomatoes, cut into 1-inch cubes

3 green onions, white and green parts, cut into 2-inch pieces

1 bunch cilantro, cut into 2-inch pieces

2 teaspoons salt

2 tablespoons oyster sauce

Dash MSG (optional)

1 teaspoon black pepper

PREPARATION

Heat the oil in a large wok to medium-hot. Fry the garlic until fragrant and golden brown. Add the cabbage and tomatoes, and stir-fry for a few minutes. Then add the rest of the ingredients. Stir-fry for about 5 to 7 minutes, until the cabbage is tender but still a bit crunchy. Serve hot.

Garlicky Chinese Green Flower (Oilseed Rape)
Zaub Ntsuab Paj Kib

Makes 6 servings

Co-author Sami loves this vegetable more than any other Asian leafy green. It is delightfully sweet and crispy and has a beautiful, glossy, deep green color. Because oilseed rape is not imported, it is available only in season, during the summer. Chinese broccoli, bamboo mustard cabbage, or bok choy can be substituted.

INGREDIENTS

1½ pounds oilseed rape, cut into 5-inch pieces

5 green onions, white and green parts, cut into 3-inch pieces

½ bunch cilantro, cut into 3-inch pieces (about 2 cups)

1 bunch baby dill, cut into 3-inch pieces (about 2 cups)

¼ cup chopped garlic (about 6 cloves)

¼ cup vegetable oil

2 teaspoons salt

1 tablespoon soy sauce

You need a wide-bottomed, non-stick pan with a lid for this dish. Be sure to have all of the ingredients ready before you begin cooking.

Clean and cut up the oilseed rape. Cut up the green onions, cilantro, and baby dill and toss them together in a bowl. Chop the garlic. Heat the oil in the pan until it is quite hot, but not hot enough to smoke. Stir-fry the garlic until it is fragrant and golden brown. Add the oilseed rape, salt, and soy sauce. Stir-fry quickly for a few minutes, making sure the mixture does not stick to the bottom of the pan. Add a little water and cover the pan for 3 to 4 minutes. Remove the lid, add the green onions, cilantro, and dill, and then stir again. Do not overcook. The leaves should be limp, but the stems should still be a little crunchy.

Stir-Fried Baby Bok Choy with Pork Belly
Zaub Ntsuag Dawb Kib Xyaw Nqaij Npuas

Makes 6 servings

Any leafy green vegetable can be substituted for the bok choy. Hmong people are especially fond of pork belly because it has wonderful textures and flavors. When cooked, the skin is chewy, the fat is soft, and the lean meat is very tasty. Pork belly, usually sold in a slab, is available at some mainstream supermarkets and most Asian grocery stores.

INGREDIENTS

½ pound pork belly (for a more Western flavor, use loin roast
    with some fat on it)
1 bunch baby bok choy (about 10 small heads)
2 tablespoons vegetable oil
1 teaspoon salt
1 chicken bouillon cube (Asian-style or regular)

PREPARATION

Cut the pork belly slab or loin roast into pieces about 1 inch long and ⅛ inch thick, and set aside. Carefully wash the bok choy, pulling each leaf off of the head. Cut each leaf in half from tip to stem. Drain on paper towels. Heat the oil in a wok over high heat. Add the pork, salt, and bouillon cube. Stir-fry about 10 minutes. Add the bok choy and stir-fry about 5 more minutes. The dish is done when the meat is cooked, the bok choy leaves are limp, the stems are still a bit crispy, and a glossy glaze covers all. Serve hot, accompanied by Everyday Rice (page 51).

Recipe shared by Sami Yang (Sheng's youngest sister and Sami Scripter's namesake) of Sacramento, California

Wild Bamboo Stir-Fried with Chicken
Ntsuag Iab Kib Xyaw Nqaij Qaib

Makes 4 servings

Wild bamboo is usually labeled "bitter" bamboo, and it sometimes has a photograph of a woman in a Hmong headdress on the can or jar.

INGREDIENTS

2 cups wild bamboo strips (16-ounce can)
1 teaspoon vegetable oil
1 cup ground chicken breast
1 stalk lemongrass, tough outer leaves and root removed, bulb
   smashed with the flat edge of a knife, and cut into 3-inch pieces
4 hot Thai chili peppers, sliced thinly on the diagonal
1 teaspoon salt
¼ teaspoon black pepper
¼ teaspoon MSG (optional, but using MSG reduces
   the bitterness)
2 teaspoons water

PREPARATION

Open the can of bamboo and drain it in a colander. Rinse well with cool water. Heat the oil to medium-hot in a frying pan or wok. Add the chicken, lemongrass, and chilies. Cook about 7 minutes, stirring continuously to break up the chicken. Add the bamboo, salt, pepper, MSG (if desired), and water. Stir the mixture and then cover the pan. Allow to cook a few more minutes. Remove the lemongrass before serving.

Sheng's Green Papaya Salad

See Taub Ntoos Qaub

Makes about 6 servings

This salad, a Hmong favorite, can be made with green papaya or shredded carrots. Sheng prepared it with carrots the day she came to live with the Scripters in 1980. For non-Hmong people, the combination of flavors is definitely an acquired taste. Sheng always includes MSG in papaya salad, although it can be omitted. Shrimp and crab paste have strong fishy flavors, and although they are essential to Hmong papaya salad, a non-Hmong may want to taste some before including the full amount called for in this recipe.

A recipe for papaya salad to serve at a large gathering appears on page 239.

INGREDIENTS

> *4 cups shredded green papaya or 4 medium-sized carrots*
> *2 to 4 cloves garlic (depending upon your taste—some people like it very garlicky)*
> *1 to 3 hot Thai chili peppers (depending upon desired heat)*
> *1 to 2 tablespoons fish sauce*
> *½ tablespoon shrimp paste (optional)*
> *½ tablespoon crab paste (optional)*
> *1 tablespoon sugar*
> *1 teaspoon MSG (optional)*
> *Juice and some of the pulp of 1 lime*
> *6 cherry tomatoes*
> *3 cups shredded cabbage (optional)*

PREPARATION

Some Asian markets sell shredded green papaya, or you can shred it yourself after peeling, using a special tool (pictured on page 239; also available in Asian markets). If preparing this dish with carrots, scrub them well and cut off the top ends. Peel them into long, thin strips with a vegetable peeler and set them aside. Remove the papery skin from the garlic cloves and put the cloves into a large mortar. Remove the stem ends of the chilies and add the chilies to the garlic. With a pestle, pound the garlic and chilies until they are mushy. Next, add the green papaya or carrot strips, fish sauce, shrimp and crab paste (if desired), sugar, and MSG (if desired). Squeeze the lime juice into the mixture, discarding the seeds. Use a spoon to scrape some of the lime pulp into the salad. Pound together a minute or two, turning the mixture over with a spoon. Continue until the flavors are extracted and mixed, but the papaya strips or carrots still retain their shape.

Cut the cherry tomatoes in quarters, and mix them into the salad. Put ½ cup of the cabbage on each of 6 individual salad plates and top with the salad mixture.

Spicy Bamboo Salad
Ntsuag Tuav Kua Txob

Makes 5 servings

Everyone has a favorite dish. Co-author Sheng makes this salad whenever her husband's uncle visits, because it is his favorite. No wonder—it is full of bright and hot flavors. This dish is prepared in the same way as papaya salad.

INGREDIENTS

6 hot Thai chili peppers (more or less, depending upon desired heat), grilled

1 30-ounce can of bamboo, shredded into ¼-inch strips

2 cups Vietnamese coriander, chopped into 1-inch pieces (for a more Western flavor, substitute cilantro)

1 clove garlic

2 teaspoons shrimp paste (for a more Western flavor, substitute anchovy paste)

1 teaspoon fish sauce

1 teaspoon salt

1 teaspoon MSG (optional)

Grill the peppers over an electric or gas burner, using a stove-top dry-roasting grill. Or you can hold the peppers over the burner with a long-handled fork. Turn the peppers as they cook until about half of the skin has brown patches. Open the can of bamboo and drain the liquid. Using your fingers, shred the bamboo into thin strips. (To save time, use already-shredded fresh bamboo; some Asian grocery stores sell it.) Chop the Vietnamese coriander. Put the chilies, bamboo, and coriander into a large wooden mortar. Add the peeled garlic, shrimp paste, fish sauce, salt, and MSG (if desired). Pound all of the ingredients together until everything is well mixed, but the bamboo maintains its shape.

Watercress Salad Dressed with Pork

Zaub Dej Xav Lav Xyaw Nqaij Npuas

Makes 4 servings

INGREDIENTS

2 large bunches fresh watercress
3 tablespoons vegetable oil
¼ pound very lean ground pork
1 tablespoon fish sauce
Salt and coarsely ground black pepper, to taste

PREPARATION

Wash the watercress and pick off and discard any damaged leaves and stems. Dry in a salad spinner or on paper towels. Heat the oil in a skillet over medium heat. Sauté the pork until it is fully cooked, stirring to break the meat apart. Season with the fish sauce, salt, and pepper. Right before serving, pour the meat and oil over the watercress and toss to coat the salad. Serve immediately.

Pickles, Condiments, and Sauces
Zaub Qaub, Kua Txob Ntsw, thiab Kua Txob Tuav

Sour Green-Vegetable Pickles—Two Variations
◎◎ *Zaub Qaub*

Bamboo mustard cabbage, found at Asian groceries, is the best vegetable choice for zesty Sour Green-Vegetable Pickles. Other leafy greens can be substituted.

An old Hmong tale says that if you use the bathroom while making these pickles, they will not turn sour. Perhaps that is true; although the process is simple, sometimes they just don't turn sour. However, these pickles are worth the effort because their piquant, slightly hot, fresh-vegetable taste is so good.

Most Hmong cooks make a big batch of Sour Green-Vegetable Pickles and then store the pickled greens in the refrigerator or freezer to be eaten a little at a time over weeks or months. As with most Hmong dishes, each cook does things a little differently. Here are two versions of Sour Green-Vegetable Pickles.

Zaub Qaub Version One

INGREDIENTS

2 large bundles bamboo mustard cabbage (about 3 pounds)
½ cup jasmine rice
4 cups water, plus enough to cover vegetables
Salt
Hot chili pepper, minced

PREPARATION

Be sure you select fresh, good-looking bamboo mustard cabbage. Pull each stem away from the bunch and wash carefully under running warm water. After all of the bamboo mustard cabbage is clean and drained, hold several stems in your hands and crush the stems and leaves by rubbing them back and forth against each other. This action is very much like trying to scrub out a tough spot from an item of laundry. Transfer the crushed vegetables to a large glass or earthenware container that has a lid. Boil the jasmine rice in 4 cups of water until the rice is soft, about 25 minutes. Drain the rice well, reserving the rice water. Pour the rice water over the bamboo mustard cabbage and add just enough warm water to cover the vegetables. Stir with your hand to combine the rice water and clear water. Put the lid on the container and allow it to set for seven or more days.

When you are ready to serve the pickles, put the desired amount into a serving bowl and drain away most of the water. Add about ¼ teaspoon salt and ¼ teaspoon minced fresh hot chili pepper per cup of mustard cabbage, or to taste. Eat immediately, or refrigerate. Once pickled, the greens keep in the refrigerator for as long as two months. Or freeze in serving-sized Ziploc bags for later use.

Recipe shared by Somxai Vue and Souzana Vang of Denver, Colorado

Zaub Qaub Version Two (Americanized)

INGREDIENTS

1 pound bamboo mustard cabbage or other leafy green vegetable
Warm water, enough to cover the greens
3 tablespoons salt
1 tablespoon sugar
2 tablespoons distilled white vinegar
Chili flakes (optional)

PREPARATION

Twist and crush the green vegetables, as in the preceding recipe, to equal 8 cups crushed greens. Place them in a lidded glass or earthenware container. Cover with a brine made of the water, salt, sugar, and vinegar. Put on the lid.

Set at room temperature for three days. Using a slotted spoon, remove the greens from the brine; retain the brine in the container. Wash the greens in clear water and then return them to the brine. Refrigerate or freeze until served. If desired, add chili flakes to the greens before serving.

Recipe from Hmong Recipe Cook Book, *edited by Sharon Sawyer*
(First Presbyterian Church, South St. Paul, 1986)

Fried Green-Vegetable Pickles

Zaub Qaub Kib

Makes 4 servings

This recipe, adapted from several dishes encountered in Hmong homes across America, is full of explosive flavors.

INGREDIENTS

> 3 cups pickled green vegetables (see previous recipes), with excess
>   water squeezed out
> 6 strips lean bacon, sliced width-wise, or ¼ pound pork belly,
>   thinly sliced
> 1 teaspoon vegetable oil
> 2 green onions, crushed
> ½ teaspoon salt, or to taste
> 1 teaspoon fish sauce, or to taste
> 1 tablespoon water
> 2 green onions, white and green parts, chopped
> ¼ cup loosely packed, chopped cilantro
> Red chili flakes (optional)

PREPARATION

Place the squeezed-dry pickles in a bowl. Slice the bacon or pork belly. Heat the oil in a wok over medium-high heat. Stir-fry the crushed green onions until they smell good. Add the bacon or pork belly and continue to stir-fry until the pork is golden brown. If a lot of fat has cooked out of the meat, spoon off all but 2 tablespoons. Add the green-vegetable pickles, salt, fish sauce, and water. Mix well. Taste for saltiness and add more salt or fish sauce if desired. Sprinkle with the chopped green onions and cilantro. Sprinkle with chili flakes if you want more heat. Stir-fry 1 more minute to combine all of the flavors. Serve hot.

Hot Chili Condiment

Kua Txob Ntsw

Makes 1 cup

Hmong people simply call this dish "pepper." It accompanies almost every meal, and it is never made exactly the same way twice. Several recipes for pepper are scattered throughout this book, each one a different cook's accompaniment for a particular dish. The basic recipe below can be served with any meal. Good chilies to use are the small red and green Thai ones. Hmong people like this condiment very hot, so the seeds are usually included.

Chop and combine the herbs and seasonings for a fine relish, or, to get the maximum flavor from the ingredients, use a mortar and pestle to pound everything together. If you are chopping a lot of chilies, or if your skin is sensitive, wear disposable gloves to keep the chilies from burning your skin.

INGREDIENTS

6 to 10 small hot chili peppers, chopped (more or less,
depending upon desired heat)
4 green onions, white and green parts, chopped
¼ cup chopped fresh cilantro
1 teaspoon salt and ½ teaspoon MSG (or 2 teaspoons salt)
3 tablespoons fish sauce
Juice of 1 large lime

OPTIONAL INGREDIENTS

1 to 2 teaspoons sugar
2 to 3 cloves garlic, chopped
2 to 3 Thai eggplants, chopped
2 tablespoons minced lemongrass (the tender part)

PREPARATION

Chop or pound the herbs and vegetables. Add the seasonings and stir well.

Hot Chili and Eggplant Sauce

Lws Tuav Kua Txob

Makes 3 cups

This sauce, which is more like a relish, is milder than other Hmong chili condiments. You will need a medium-sized mortar and pestle to make this dish.

INGREDIENTS

> *3 Chinese eggplants (the long, purple kind)*
> *2 to 3 hot Thai chili peppers*
> *1 teaspoon salt*
> *¼ teaspoon MSG (optional)*
> *¼ cup chopped green onion, white and green parts*
> *¼ cup chopped cilantro*

PREPARATION

Steam the eggplants about 20 minutes, or until they are soft. Remove from the steamer and allow them to cool. Remove the stems and peel off the skin and discard. Measure 1¾ cups of the eggplant pulp into a bowl and set aside.

Using a mortar and pestle, pound the chilies until they are soft. Add the salt and MSG (if desired), and continue to pound and mix for another minute. Add the eggplant, green onion, and cilantro and continue to pound until everything is well mixed.

Chili Garlic Paste
Kua Txob Qej Kib Xyaw Roj

Makes 1 cup paste

This paste is an ingredient of Chicken Curry Noodle Soup (*Khaub Poob*). The dried chilies are a Mexican product.

INGREDIENTS

> 2 packages (3 ounces each) dried mild chilies
> 5 cloves garlic, chopped
> ½ cup vegetable oil
> 1 tablespoon salt

PREPARATION

Cut the stems off of the chilies and then soak the chilies in a bowl of warm water for about ½ hour, until they are soft. Drain the chilies. Bring a pot of water to a boil and add the chilies. Boil them for 15 to 20 minutes. With a slotted spoon, lift the chilies out of the water and put them on a cutting board. Mince the chilies. Chop the garlic. Put the oil into a medium-sized skillet and heat it to medium-hot. Add the garlic and sauté for 1 to 2 minutes, until it is light brown and fragrant. Add the chilies and continue to sauté for 5 minutes. Remove from the heat and allow the mixture to cool. Stored in a closed jar in the refrigerator, the chili paste will be good for a month.

Recipe shared by Song Vang of Portland, Oregon

Chicken ~ Nqaij Qaib

Fresh Chicken with Hmong Herbs (Soup for New Mothers) 94
Nqaij Qaib Hau Xyaw Tshuaj

Old-Fashioned Chicken Soup—Four Variations 95

    Chicken and Bitter Melon Soup 98
    Nqaij Qaib Hau Xyaw Dib Iab

    Chicken and Oyster Mushroom Soup 98
    Nqaij Qaib Hau Xyaw Nceb

    Chicken Soup with Tofu 98
    Nqaij Qaib Hau Xyaw Taum Paj

    Chicken Rattan Soup 99
    Nqaij Qaib Hau Xyaw Kav Theej Iab

Coconut Lemon Chicken Soup 99
Nqaij Qaib Hau Xyaw Kua Mav Phaub Qaub

Chicken Noodle Soup 100
Nqaij Qaib Khaub Piaj

Stir-Fried Chicken with Luffa Squash 101
Nqaij Qaib Kib Xyaw Xwb Kuab Leej

Stir-Fried Chicken with Tomatoes 105
Nqaij Qaib Kib Xyaw Txiv Lws Suav

Stir-Fried Chicken with Cucumber and Bitter Melon 106
Nqaij Qaib Xyaw Dib thiab Dib Iab

Chicken *Larb* (Laotian Chicken and Herb Salad) 107
Laj Nqaij Qaib

Chicken and Bean Sprout Salad 110
Hauv Siab Qaib thiab Kaus Taum Xav-Lav

Stuffed Chicken Wings 111
Kooj Tis Qaib Ntim

Breaded Stuffed Chicken Wings 113
Mov Ci Ntim Kooj Tis Qaib

Chili-Peanut Dipping Sauce 114
Kua-Kua Txob Xyaw Txiv Laum Huab Xeeb

Whole Roasted Coconut Chicken 114
Qaib Ci Xyaw Kua Mav Phaub

Chicken Drumsticks with Hmong-Style Barbeque Sauce 116
Nqaij Qaib Pleev Kua Barbeque

Chicken ⤳ Nqaij Qaib

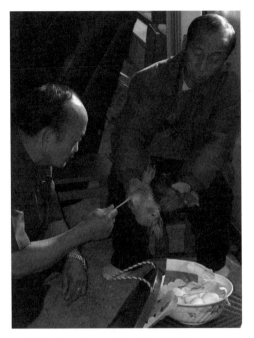

At the door of a traditional family's home, a shaman and his assistant burn joss sticks (xyab) and hold two chickens (a male chicken represents the female members of the household, and a female chicken represents the males) to call souls of family members. This is just one part of the ua neeb kab plig *ritual, which serves to protect and ensure the health of each living family member.*

CHICKENS FIGURE PROMINENTLY IN the Hmong way of life. According to the anthropologist Dr. Dia Cha, they are considered one of the "eight most important spirits in the Hmong cultural tradition" (*yim tus tswv dab nyob hauv Hmoob kev cai dab qhuas*). Chickens play a role in many traditional Hmong practices. They help heal the sick, divine providence, and guarantee good fortune. A Hmong shaman may employ a chicken's spirit to assist in dealings with the otherworld. Chickens have an important part in birth, soul-calling, naming, marriage, and death rituals. Ask any Hmong person, old or young, what their favorite Hmong food is and the answer often is "boiled chicken."

Hmong farmers take pride in raising vigorous, beautiful chickens for their own dinner tables. Hmong professionals who are busy with nine-to-five jobs often treat their families by cooking such a chicken that has been purchased at a Hmong grocery store. These chickens have been hand-raised and butchered quietly and quickly using an age-old technique. Although the meat is tender, it is very lean and flavorful. The difference between a Hmong-raised chicken and one purchased at a mainstream grocery store is tremendous.

Fresh Chicken with Hmong Herbs (Soup for New Mothers)
◉◉ Nqaij Qaib Hau Xyaw Tshuaj

Makes 1 pot of soup

If Hmong people have a signature dish, this is it. This very simple soup incorporates a fresh whole chicken cooked gently in a lemongrass-flavored broth. The addition of Hmong herbs—some of which do not have common English names—makes it unique. The herbs help new mothers stay warm and gain strength after the strain of giving birth. Women who eat this soup after bearing a child also maintain strong bones in old age. Hmong custom dictates that, for one month after a baby is born, a mother's diet consist of only this chicken soup, freshly cooked rice, and the warm water drained from the second soaking of rice (*kua ntxhai*), or clear, warm water. Hmong Americans often add vegetables to keep their diet well balanced. This soup also is eaten at regular meals by the entire family.

Which herbs are used in the soup depends upon a family's customs and what is available. Some of the herbs in the following recipe are not available in any store in America. They are lovingly grown in backyard plots and on the patios and windowsills of most Hmong homes. Many of these plants originated from seeds and starts carefully brought to the United States from Laos in the handbags and pockets of Hmong women striving to preserve their healthful cooking traditions. In Hmong booths at farmers' markets, bouquets of these herbs are sometimes available in season. The herb bundles are called *Tshuaj Rau Qaib* (pronounced "chua chao kai"). This soup will not taste the same if mass-produced and -processed chicken pieces are used.

INGREDIENTS

    1 whole fresh chicken (the kind purchased from a
      Hmong market or farm)
    10 cups water
    1 stalk lemongrass, tough outer leaves and root removed
    1 tablespoon salt, or to taste
    ½ teaspoon black pepper

Hmong herbs
Each cook cites favorite herbs, often including *hmab ntsha ntsuab* (slippery vegetable), *koj liab* (angelica, sometimes called duck-feet herb), *ntiv* (sweet fern), *pawj qaib* (sweet flag), *tseej ntug* (common dayflower), and *ncaug txhav* and *tshab xyoob* (for which no English translations are available).

PREPARATION

Clean and chop up the chicken into about 16 pieces. Refrigerate the giblets for other uses. Pick or buy the herbs shortly before using, and wash them carefully. Several sprigs of each herb is the customary amount. In a medium-sized pot, bring the water to a boil. Add the lemongrass, salt, and pepper. Bring the water back to a boil and add the chicken pieces. Boil 15 minutes (do not overcook the chicken). Add the herbs and cook a few more minutes. Remove the lemongrass and serve with rice.

Old-Fashioned Chicken Soup—Four Variations

Makes 10 servings

Chicken paired with a vegetable and simmered in a simple broth is a typical everyday Hmong meal. The following four recipes are variations on a theme using distinctly Hmong flavors. A mass-produced frying chicken will make a meaty, fatty soup. For a more traditional flavor, use a homegrown chicken, including the head and feet, or one purchased frozen in an Asian market.

INGREDIENTS FOR BASIC SOUP

1 whole chicken, 2 to 3 pounds
10 cups water
1 stalk lemongrass, tough outer leaves, root, and top 1 or 2 inches
   removed; cut into 3-inch lengths
1½ teaspoons salt
1 chicken-flavor bouillon cube (Asian or regular)
¼ teaspoon MSG (optional)
¼ teaspoon coarse-ground black pepper
About 16 sprigs cilantro, cut into 2-inch lengths, for garnish

Using Food to Heal

THE HMONG PREPARE another kind of soup, called medicinal chicken (*qaib tsaws tshuaj*), to help heal injuries. They make it with a very small breed of chicken cooked in water along with strictly medicinal herbs (*tshuaj ntsub*). Most elderly Hmong know which herbs treat what illness, and they grow many of them in their backyard gardens. Depending upon the ailment, additional herbs, pods, tree barks, and roots are purchased from Hmong herbalists. Only a few of these plants have common English names. Because healing herbs taste bitter, and because medicinal chicken contains no salt and pepper, this food definitely tastes like medicine!

Food remedies, such as medicinal chicken and medicinal eggs, are used to help heal wounds or to ease problems such as indigestion and coughs, but they are not utilized to treat diseases such as cancer or heart problems. Most modern Hmong people supplement Western medicine with herbal food remedies.

A personal experience of Sami and Sheng demonstrates this Hmong practice. When Little Sami (Sheng's youngest sister, named in honor of Sami Scripter) suffered at age twenty-four a broken leg and pelvis in a sledding accident, doctors used metal rods and pins to set the bones and hold her leg and pelvis together. Afterward, the medical staff were unsure how well—or even if—she would be able to walk again. When she was finally released from the hospital, Little Sami's family and friends provided the support she needed. "Big" Sami (this book's co-author) came to help around Little Sami's home and to care for her two young children during the day while Little Sami's husband was at work.

Each morning during the first week that Little Sami was home from the hospital, her father, Gnia Kao, delivered a pot of cooked medicinal chicken for her breakfast. He also applied a traditional herbal ointment to her many incisions. Gnia Kao instructed his daughter to eat every bit of the chicken, beginning with the chicken's left leg (corresponding to Little Sami's leg most damaged in the accident). The two Samis decided that this must have something to do with restoring the wholeness of her body. But, as is always the case with Hmong healing, the logic and healing properties behind the prescription were not explained.

Fresh Hmong chicken and medicinal herbs, ready to be made into the traditional soup that nourishes a new mother after giving birth. Clockwise from the left: tshab xyoob, pawj qaib, koj liab *(sometimes called duck-feet herb),* nplooj tsaj, luam laws *(Vietnamese coriander),* sam mos kab, ntiv, ncaug txhav, tseej ntug, *and* zej ntshua ntuag.

They also laughingly agreed it was a good thing that Little Sami did not have a broken skull!

Some people scoff at such remedies, but the home-health professionals who visited were astounded at Little Sami's rapid rate of healing and progress. By the end of the third week after her accident, Little Sami was hopping around, only partly supported by her crutches, fixing everyone's dinner and baking her famous chocolate chip cookies. She was even able to dance with her husband at a nephew's wedding reception.

Making medicinal food is a gift of love and skill. To prepare the dish, Little Sami's father had to drive for miles to a farm that raised the right kind of chickens. Her mother knew exactly how to cook the chicken and which herbs to include.

Clean and chop up the chicken into about 16 pieces. Chop right through the bones, so the marrow will cook out and flavor the soup. In a medium-sized pan, bring the water to a boil. Add the lemongrass, salt, bouillon cube, and MSG (if desired). Add the chicken and return to a boil. Reduce the heat so that the water boils gently. Cook for about 15 minutes. Proceed, using one of the variations below.

Chicken and Bitter Melon Soup

Nqaij Qaib Hau Xyaw Dib Iab

Cut a medium-sized bitter melon in half the long way and scoop out the seeds. Wash and chop the melon into bite-sized pieces. Add to the basic soup and continue to cook for about 15 more minutes or until the chicken meat is white and tender and the melon is soft but not mushy. Taste the broth and add more salt, if needed, and the black pepper. Serve in individual bowls garnished with the cilantro sprigs, with rice on the side.

Serve bitter melon during cold weather, because it brings warmth to the body.

Chicken and Oyster Mushroom Soup

Nqaij Qaib Hau Xyaw Nceb

Cook the basic soup until the chicken is just about done, about 20 minutes. Clean and slice 1 pound of oyster mushrooms. Add to the basic soup and cook for about 15 more minutes. Taste, adjust the seasonings, and serve as above.

Chicken Soup with Tofu

Nqaij Qaib Hau Xyaw Taum Paj

Cook the basic soup until the chicken meat is white and tender, about 25 minutes. Cut 2 bricks (12 ounces each) of firm tofu into bite-sized pieces. Add the tofu to the soup and cook for 5 more minutes. Taste, adjust the seasonings, and serve as above. Chicken Soup with Tofu is a nostalgic dish, because it was often served on special occasions in Laotian villages. This very nutritious soup is especially beloved by elderly Hmong.

Chicken Rattan Soup

Nqaij Qaib Hau Xyaw Kav Theej Iab

Add 3 cups of dry rattan to the basic soup. Cook an additional 15 minutes. Taste, adjust the seasonings, and serve as above.

Coconut Lemon Chicken Soup

Nqaij Qaib Hau Xyaw Kua Mav Phaub Qaub

Makes 4 small servings

This chicken soup is more modern than the previous four recipes. It is quick to make, and it has a tongue-pleasing combination of mildly sweet, salty, and tart flavors.

Coconut milk separates in the can, so be sure to stir it until the consistency is uniform before measuring.

INGREDIENTS

½ boneless, skinless chicken breast
2 cups cubed chayote squash
1 lemon
2½ cups low-sodium chicken broth
1 inch fresh ginger root, sliced
3 tablespoons fish sauce
3 tablespoons minced lemongrass, tough outer leaves
  and root removed before mincing
1 cup coconut milk
Fresh cilantro sprigs, for garnish

PREPARATION

Cut the chicken and the squash into ½-inch cubes and set aside. Wash the whole lemon and cut it in half. Cut one half into eight wedges. Shave thin strips of lemon peel from the other half and cut them into very thin matchsticks, for garnish. In a 3-quart saucepan, combine the chicken broth, lemon wedges, sliced ginger, and fish sauce. Turn the heat to medium-high and bring the mixture to a boil. Reduce the heat and simmer for 10 minutes. Strain the soup and return it to the pan, discarding the solids. Bring it back to a simmer, then add the chayote and lemongrass. Cook for 10 minutes, until the squash is soft but not mushy. Add the chicken and coconut milk. Cook for 2 to 3 more minutes, or until the chicken becomes opaque. Serve this soup in individual bowls, garnished with cilantro sprigs and the lemon peel shavings.

Chicken Noodle Soup
Nqaij Qaib Khaub Piaj

Makes about 10 servings

Everyone calls this soup "ko-pia," after the fresh rice and tapioca flour noodles with which it is made. Find these thick, white noodles in the refrigerated section of Asian grocery stores. They are usually produced in the store where they are sold, and they are seldom labeled by weight. The Hmong name for them is *khaub piaj*; the Vietnamese name is *bánh canh*. These delightfully chewy noodles thicken the soup a little and they soak up a lot of liquid when cooked, so make plenty of broth.

INGREDIENTS

> 1 frying chicken (4 to 5 pounds), chopped into about 16 pieces,
>   or 2 whole chicken breasts with bone and skin
> 1 tablespoon vegetable oil
> 6 cloves garlic, smashed and sliced
> 6 quarts water
> 1 stalk lemongrass, tough outer leaves and root removed, bulb
>   smashed with the flat edge of a knife, and cut into 3-inch pieces
> About 2 tablespoons salt (add half during cooking, then taste
>   before adding more)
> 3 chicken bouillon cubes
> 1 teaspoon MSG (optional)
> 3 pounds fresh rice and tapioca flour noodles (about 1½ packages)

4 cups finely shredded cabbage
1 bunch cilantro, cut into 2-inch lengths
1 bunch Vietnamese coriander, cut into 2-inch lengths
Hot chili garlic sauce (purchase at an Asian grocery store)
Coarse-ground black pepper

PREPARATION

If using a whole chicken, chop it into about 16 pieces and set aside. In a small skillet, stir-fry the garlic in the oil for 1 or 2 minutes, until it is golden and fragrant. In a large pot, bring the water to a rolling boil and add the chicken and garlic along with the lemongrass, 1 tablespoon salt, bouillon cubes, and MSG (if desired). Boil 15 to 20 minutes. While the chicken cooks, wash and prepare the cabbage, cilantro, and Vietnamese coriander, and arrange them on a large tray. When the chicken is done, turn the heat to low and transfer the chicken to a bowl to cool. After it cools, if using chicken breasts, remove the skin and bones, and shred the meat. Put the meat back into the broth and discard the skin and bones. If using a whole chopped-up chicken, leave the pieces intact. Taste the soup and add more salt if desired. Remove the lemongrass. Return the soup to a boil and then add the noodles a little at a time, so they do not stick together. The noodles are done when they rise to the surface. They cook very quickly. Ladle the soup into large individual bowls. Leave plenty of room in the bowls for the accompaniments.

Stir-Fried Chicken with Luffa Squash
Nqaij Qaib Kib Xyaw Xwb Kuab Leej

Makes 6 servings

Hmong people cook with all kinds of squash and gourds, taking advantage of whatever is in season. We favor luffa squash for this recipe. However, fuzzy melon, bottle gourd, or chayote can be substituted. Make sure the luffa is young and tender, and cook it within a day or two of purchase. Squash blossoms can be purchased in season in Asian groceries, or use zucchini or other squash blossoms from the garden. Yucca plant blossoms also can be substituted.

Hmong Weddings

IN ADDITION TO JOINING two people as husband and wife, a Hmong marriage is a negotiated contract and union between two families, made to strengthen the fabric of Hmong society. In Laos, parents often arranged unions, although it was hoped that the couple would find one another attractive and be happy together. In America, old-world marriage customs are not always strictly followed. However, most Hmong families still honor their culture by including what they can in the series of events that make up a traditional Hmong wedding. Having their union blessed by their church is important to Christian Hmongs, but even Christians observe many of the old customs that do not conflict with their beliefs.

A Hmong wedding begins with either an elopement or a formal request from the groom's family to the bride's parents for their daughter's hand in marriage. After that, the sequence of events is essentially the same. The bridal couple and family representatives travel between the two households several times to accomplish all of the rituals that comprise a Hmong wedding. For each trip a basket of food is packed, which includes boiled chickens, new spoons, and rice that is wrapped in a new white cloth. In Laos, these journeys often meant long hikes

MaiKia and Edward Lee, of Sacramento, California, wear silver necklaces and colorful Hmong clothing for their traditional wedding.

through the jungle, the travelers stopping along the way to eat. In America, the picnics serve a more symbolic purpose, since the bride's and groom's houses may be minutes apart by car, or clear across the country.

At the Bride's Home

Both of the bridal couple's families are represented by one or two negotiators, called *mej koob*, whose job is to iron out problems between the families and to work out details of the contract, especially the dowry, sometimes called the "bride price" or "bride wealth" (*nqe mis nqe no*). Negotiations may take a day or more. Two boiled chickens and shot glasses of liquor or soda are offered to and ritualistically consumed by the negotiators. Negotiations can be heated if the two families have disputes, or they can be cheerful and full of word games and songs if the families are harmonious.

A huge meal is then prepared and served to the bride's extended family and the groom's negotiators. This meal is for luck. All food, beverages, and eating utensils must be presented in pairs during this and all of the wedding meals. This pairing signifies that the bride and groom will walk together through life as a couple. The meal is simple, although plentiful. A whole roasted pig, boiled chickens, and lots of fresh-steamed rice are served. Since vegetables signify a poor person's diet, they are not on the menu; only food available to the wealthy is presented. This menu means the marriage will be a rich one. Wedding food is never seasoned with hot chilies, because they would make the marriage "hot": full of anger and disagreements. Fruit and other snacks are shared while preparing the meal, but they do not appear on the wedding table. Beverages include water, soft drinks, and liquor (for ritual use).

The bride and groom wear beautiful new traditional Hmong clothing. The groom is attended by a young kinsman who helps the groom fulfill all of the traditional obligations, such as bowing to the ground to honor each of the bride's ancestors and male elders. The bride is attended by a maid of honor, a young woman related to the groom, who chaperones the bride. A knowledgeable elder lectures the bridal couple about the keys to a successful marriage and about their obligations to their families as young married people. After the wedding ceremonies, the souls and good fortune of the young couple are symbolically wrapped up inside an umbrella that is tied with the sash that was part of the bride's turban.

At the Groom's Home

Next, the couple and the negotiators travel back to the groom's home. Traditionally the groom carries the bride price and another picnic packed by the bride's family, which includes a bottle of wine, three boiled chickens, two packages of freshly cooked rice tied in a white cloth, a packet of salt, a new blanket, a fine Hmong knife, and a side of pork in a woven basket. The new spoons and other incidentals are doubled for luck on this trip. The groom's kinsmen help carry the load. To honor their cultural traditions, the couple and their attendants always stop halfway between the houses to eat the chicken and rice. However, one of the chickens, the wine, and a small packet of cooked rice are saved to be presented to the head of the groom's household to feed his ancestors in thanks for their blessings.

When the bride comes to her husband's family's home, she becomes a part of their clan. At this time, traditional families do a series of formal rituals to welcome her soul into her new home and into her husband's family. The umbrella is hung on the wall by the front door. Another plentiful meal is cooked and served to welcome the bride and to thank the negotiators. The menu is the same as at the bride's house—a roasted pig, boiled chickens, and rice—this time to be shared by the groom's extended family.

In Hmong culture, all of these events comprise a "wedding," and some may take place weeks or months apart. If they can afford to do so, both Christian and non-Christian Hmong families often add an American-style wedding reception, complete with a catered banquet, white bridal gown, bouquets, and dancing. An elaborate wedding cake is always part of these less traditional meals. A "tying of strings," or *khi tes* ceremony, is sometimes included by non-Christian families, to honor ancestors and to offer best wishes and safety to the couple as they travel through life together. During this ceremony, the bride and groom stand or sit in front of the guests, and each holds a plate in one extended hand. Every guest in turn approaches and ties a length of white cotton string around the wrist of one of the bridal couple and then the other, wishes each one well, and puts money on the plates.

　2 teaspoons vegetable oil

　2 cups lean ground chicken

　5 cups sliced luffa squash (peel the tips of the ridges, but not the
　　skin, with a vegetable peeler before slicing) or other variety of
　　summer squash

　2 cups squash blossoms

　1½ teaspoons salt

　¼ teaspoon MSG (optional)

　¼ teaspoon black pepper

　2 cups lemon basil leaves

　1 cup water

PREPARATION

Heat the oil to medium-high in a wok. Add the chicken and stir-fry for about 4 minutes, breaking the meat apart as it cooks. Add the squash slices, squash blossoms, salt, MSG (if desired), black pepper, and basil leaves. Stir-fry for 1 minute. Pour the water over the ingredients and bring the water to a simmer. Stir, and put a lid on the wok. Cook for 5 minutes, remove the lid, and stir again. Cook until the squash is soft but not mushy. Serve hot.

Stir-Fried Chicken with Tomatoes

Nqaij Qaib Kib Xyaw Txiv Lws Suav

Makes 4 servings

Cindy Vue, who contributed this recipe, is a newly married, young professional who has adopted a progressive, healthy way to cook. This simple dish is typical of the food prepared by younger Hmong people for an everyday family meal. She uses a minimum of oil and no MSG. This dish nevertheless has a distinctly Hmong taste because of the garlic, cilantro, and oyster sauce.

 ½ boneless, skinless chicken breast
 1 tablespoon vegetable oil
 2 cloves garlic, chopped
 10 cherry tomatoes, each cut in half
 4 green onions, white and green parts, chopped
 Cilantro, chopped to equal ¼ cup, loosely packed
 ½ teaspoon salt
 ½ teaspoon coarse-ground black pepper
 1 tablespoon oyster sauce

PREPARATION

Wash the chicken breast and pat dry with a paper towel. Cut the chicken into ½-inch cubes and set aside. In a medium-sized skillet, heat the vegetable oil to medium-hot. Add the garlic, tomatoes, and green onions and stir-fry for 2 or 3 minutes, until they are aromatic but not brown. Add the chicken and continue to stir-fry until the meat is no longer pink, about 5 to 7 minutes. Add the cilantro, salt, pepper, and oyster sauce and stir-fry for 2 or 3 more minutes, until the flavors are combined. Serve hot with rice.

Recipe shared by Cindy Vue of Denver, Colorado

Stir-Fried Chicken with Cucumber and Bitter Melon
Nqaij Qaib Xyaw Dib thiab Dib Iab

Makes 2 to 3 servings

Asians relish the taste of bitter melon, but the flavor seems strange to others. In this recipe, the bitterness is lessened by treating the melon (actually a variety of squash) with salt, and by including sugar.

INGREDIENTS

 1 small bitter melon
 1 tablespoon salt
 2 tablespoons vegetable oil
 ½ pound skinless chicken breast meat, diced
 1 teaspoon minced garlic

2 green onions, white and green parts, chopped
1 large cucumber, peeled, seeded, and diced
1 tablespoon soy sauce
1 tablespoon sugar

Cut the bitter melon in half lengthwise, scoop out the seeds, and dice. Toss with the salt in a colander; let stand 20 minutes. Rinse well; then, with your hands, squeeze out the excess liquid.

In a large, heavy skillet, heat 1 tablespoon of the oil over high heat. Add the chicken, garlic, and green onions; stir-fry until barely tender, 3 to 4 minutes. Remove to a bowl. Wipe out the pan and heat again with the remaining oil. Add the bitter melon and cucumber; stir-fry until barely tender, 3 to 4 minutes. Stir in the soy sauce and sugar. Then stir in the chicken and heat through. Serve with white rice and hot pepper sauce.

This recipe, shared by food writer Terese Allen, was first published in Wisconsin Trails *magazine (copyright 1997).*

Chicken *Larb* (Laotian Chicken and Herb Salad)
Laj Nqaij Qaib

Makes 8 servings

Light, healthy, and full of flavor—nothing can beat chicken *larb* for a simple but elegant meal with friends on a warm summer evening. This version is easy to make and can handily be halved or doubled, and the ingredients can be found in almost any grocery store.

Use only fresh, blemish-free herbs. Chop and slice them by hand, because a food processor will bruise them. Loosely pack the herbs into the measuring cup. Although you can use ground chicken or turkey, chopping the meat yourself gives the dish a finer, more desirable texture.

2 whole boneless chicken breasts or 3 pounds ground chicken
* or turkey*
Juice of 2 large limes, plus 1 lime for garnish

About *Larb*

FRESH-FLAVORED *LARB* is often called "the national dish of Laos." This wonderful meat salad is made of finely chopped raw or cooked meat or fish, combined with mint and other herbs. *Larb* is also seasoned with lime juice, fish sauce, and minced chili peppers. Finely ground toasted sticky rice grains are included as well, giving *larb* a slightly dry, crumbly texture. It is often served in a hand-held lettuce wrap accompanied by other fresh vegetables and plenty of sticky rice. No one prepares *larb* better than Hmong cooks, and every cook has an opinion about what makes great *larb*. Hmong people often include a variety of "backyard" herbs and spices, such as rice paddy herb and culantro, that add distinctive tangy flavors. Another key ingredient in the *larb* made by Hmong people is Sichuan pepper, which can be difficult to find; it is sometimes labeled "red pepper powder" in Asian grocery stores. *Larb* is one dish that is frequently made by men, often as a group effort. After the meat is prepared, and all of the herbs and seasonings are chopped and ready, the men set about combining them. Often a lot of good-natured arguments ensue about how much of each ingredient to include. No festive occasion or holiday is complete without *larb*.

Good *larb* is virtually fat-free. It can be made with any extremely fresh, lean meat—venison, duck, and turkey, as well as chicken, pork, and beef. Fish is always used raw, although it is first minced and then marinated in lime juice. The acid from the lime changes the structure of the proteins in the fish, essentially "cooking" the fish without using heat. It is customary to cook minced pork and chicken to well-done and beef to medium-rare. After the meat is cooked, it is allowed to cool before being mixed with the other ingredients. *Larb* is always served at room temperature.

We have chosen the spelling *larb*, since Hmong people usually spell the word that way, although in other cookbooks it is sometimes spelled *laap, larp, laab,* or *lob*.

Because many wonderful *larb* recipes come from Hmong kitchens, five variations appear in this cookbook: in this chapter, and in the "Pork," "Beef and Water Buffalo," "Fish and Game," and "Cooking for a Crowd" chapters.

2 tablespoons rice wine

2 teaspoons minced fresh ginger (for a more traditional taste,
  substitute galanga)

1 stalk minced lemongrass, tough outer leaves, root,
  and top several inches removed before mincing

3 teaspoons grated lemon peel

2 small hot chili peppers, minced, or 1 teaspoon crushed
  chili flakes

1 clove garlic, minced

1 tablespoon fish sauce

1½ teaspoons salt

½ teaspoon white pepper

3 tablespoons Toasted Sticky Rice Flour (page 61)

1 chicken bouillon cube

1 heaping cup chopped fresh mint

1 heaping cup chopped cilantro

Several additional stems of mint and cilantro, for garnish

1 bunch green onions, green part chopped, white part
  sliced diagonally

½ cup chopped Thai basil

1 large head leaf lettuce (16 leaves, for wrappers)

PREPARATION

On a large, clean chopping board, chop the chicken with a heavy knife or cleaver. As you chop the chicken, fold it over on itself. Continue to fold and chop until the meat is very finely chopped. Put the meat in a large bowl and squeeze the lime juice over it. Add the rice wine. Cook the chicken mixture in a nonstick skillet (don't use any oil) over medium-high heat, tossing and stirring constantly just until the meat turns white. Return the mixture with any accumulated juice to the bowl and allow it to cool to room temperature. While the chicken cools, prepare the fresh herbs. Add the ginger (or galanga), lemongrass, lemon peel, chili peppers (or crushed chili flakes), garlic, fish sauce, salt, white pepper, and rice flour to the cooled mixture. Break apart the chicken bouillon cube and sprinkle it on top. Toss the ingredients together until they are well mixed. Then add the mint, cilantro, green onions, and Thai basil. Gently toss everything together. Break lettuce leaves away from the head, and wash and dry them.

Scoop ¼ cup of *larb* onto each lettuce leaf and arrange the leaves on a large platter. Garnish with mint and cilantro sprigs and wedges of lime. Diners pick up a lettuce leaf and roll it up to eat. Serve *larb* with cool sticky rice.

Chicken and Bean Sprout Salad

Hauv Siab Qaib thiab Kaus Taum Xav-Lav

Makes 6 servings

In this recipe, the lemongrass and basil impart a delicate flavor to the chicken. The bean sprouts add crunch, and—as usual—the cilantro provides the Hmong touch.

INGREDIENTS

*1 stalk lemongrass, tough outer leaves, root, and top several
    inches removed*
1 quart water
4 or 5 Thai basil leaves
1 teaspoon salt
1 teaspoon MSG (optional)
1 whole chicken breast, skin and fat removed
4 cups fresh bean sprouts
½ to ⅔ cup chopped cilantro, stems and leaves included
4 green onions, white and green parts, chopped
½ cup broth reserved from cooking the chicken
Juice of 1 lime

PREPARE THE CHICKEN

Cut the lemongrass into 3-inch pieces. Bring the water to a boil over high heat. Add the lemongrass, Thai basil, salt, and MSG (if desired). Add the chicken breast and allow it to simmer gently for about 15 minutes, until it is white all the way through and tender. Remove the chicken from the water and place it in a large mixing bowl. Strain the broth through a sieve and save ½ cup of the liquid to moisten the salad. When the chicken is completely cool, shred the meat with your fingers. Set aside.

Wash the bean sprouts and then drain. Mix the shredded chicken with the bean sprouts and the chopped cilantro and green onions. Squeeze the lime juice over the mixture and add the reserved broth. Taste the mixture and add more salt if desired. Mix gently with your hands. Serve immediately.

Stuffed Chicken Wings
Kooj Tis Qaib Ntim

Makes 20 wings

Chee Vang, of Denver, makes stuffed chicken wings in her home.

Stuffed chicken wings are a recent innovation of Hmong cooks. In Laos, the luxury of preparing just one part of many chickens was not possible. The finished wings are incredibly plump and golden brown. They are crispy on the outside and chock-full of vegetables, meat, and vermicelli noodles on the inside. Although removing the bones from the chicken wings can be tricky and time-consuming, it is worth the effort, because the finished product is so beautiful and tasty.

PREPARE THE CHICKEN WINGS

Buy 20 large, whole chicken wings—the larger, the better. Remove the bone and most of the meat from the first two joints of each wing, but not the wing tip. This process is like pulling your leg out of a pair of pants: after you remove your leg (the bones and meat), all you have left is the pant leg (skin).

Beginning at the large, "drumstick" end of 1 chicken wing, use a small, sharp knife to cut away the bone and as much of the meat as you can from the skin. Push the skin down as you empty the wing, and continue cutting away the meat and bone on the middle section. Separate the bones at the joint between the middle part of the wing and the wing tip and remove the bones and meat. Do not remove the bone in the tip of the wing.

If you are careful, this paring will leave the skin from the first two-thirds of the chicken wing in one piece, without any tears. Most, but not all, of the chicken meat will be removed along with the bones. Repeat this procedure on each chicken wing. Set the wings aside. Cut as much meat as you can from the bones. With a cleaver, mince the meat. Discard the leftover bones, or save them to use another time in a soup broth. Wash the empty chicken wings under cold running water and pat dry with paper towels. Sprinkle about 2 teaspoons of salt over the wings.

INGREDIENTS FOR FILLING

3 2-ounce packages vermicelli noodles
1 pound ground pork
Minced chicken from the wings
4 green onions, white and green parts, chopped
¼ head cabbage, finely shredded (about 4 cups loosely packed)
1 medium-sized carrot, finely shredded
1½ teaspoons salt
1 teaspoon MSG (optional)
½ teaspoon coarse-ground black pepper
2 tablespoons oyster sauce
2 eggs, stirred

PREPARE THE FILLING

Soak the vermicelli noodles in a bowl of warm water for 30 minutes. Bring 2 quarts of water to boil in a medium-sized pot. With a fine-mesh sieve, lift the noodles out of the bowl of warm water and submerge them in the boiling water for a second or two. Quickly lift the noodles from the boiling water and drain them completely. Using kitchen shears, snip the noodles into short lengths. In a large bowl, use your hands to mix the ground pork and minced chicken together with the noodles, green onions, cabbage, carrot, salt, MSG (if desired), black pepper, and oyster sauce. Add the eggs and mix thoroughly.

Using your fingers, stuff about ½ cup of the meat-noodle mixture into each chicken wing. If the skin has no tears, the chicken wing will look very fat. If the skin has a tear, sew it up with a sterilized needle and clean thread before stuffing. Pull the skin around the stuffing at the open end. If filling is left over, use it to stuff cabbage leaves (page 73).

COOK THE STUFFED WINGS

Broil about 6 inches beneath the upper element of an oven set at 400 degrees. Cook for about 25 minutes, or until golden brown on one side. Turn the wings over and broil on the other side until done, 15 to 20 more minutes. Or use a large toaster oven to cook the wings. Either way, make sure there is a place for the fat to drain while the wings cook. The thread used to sew up tears usually burns away during broiling. If any thread does remain, remove and discard it before serving. Serve hot.

Recipe shared by Chee Vang of Denver, Colorado

Breaded Stuffed Chicken Wings
Mov Ci Ntim Kooj Tis Qaib

Prepare the chicken wings as in the previous recipe, adding to the filling ½ cup loosely packed chopped cilantro and 4 pieces of dried black fungus that have been soaked for 30 minutes, drained, and chopped fine (about ¼ cup). Stuff the wings as in the previous recipe. Next, beat an egg in a bowl and coat each stuffed wing with the egg mixture. Roll each stuffed wing in purchased Italian bread crumbs (you will need about 3 cups of crumbs). Make sure each wing is well coated with crumbs. Lay the wings side by side on a broiler pan. Bake in a preheated 350-degree oven for 45 minutes. Serve hot with Chili-Peanut Dipping Sauce (page 114).

This variation of stuffed chicken wings shared by Der Yang of Sacramento, California

Chili-Peanut Dipping Sauce

Kua-Kua Txob Xyaw Txiv Laum Huab Xeeb

Makes ½ cup

INGREDIENTS

> 2 tablespoons fish sauce
> Juice of 1 lime
> 1 teaspoon salt
> 1 teaspoon sugar
> 1 teaspoon MSG (optional)
> 1 to 2 fresh red chili peppers, minced
> ¼ bunch cilantro, chopped fine
> 4 green onions, white and green parts, chopped fine
> 1 small tomato or 6 cherry tomatoes, chopped
> 2 tablespoons chopped raw peanuts
> 1 tablespoon peanut butter

PREPARATION

In a small bowl, mix the fish sauce, lime juice, salt, sugar, and MSG (if desired). Stir until the salt and sugar are dissolved. Next, add the chili peppers, cilantro, green onions, tomatoes, and peanuts. Add the peanut butter and stir until the sauce is of uniform consistency.

Whole Roasted Coconut Chicken

Qaib Ci Xyaw Kua Mav Phaub

Coconut milk is a natural tenderizing agent, making this roast chicken super-tender and very rich.

INGREDIENTS

> 1 young frying chicken, at least 5 pounds
> 3 teaspoons salt
> ½ pound lean ground pork

4 to 6 hot Thai chili peppers, minced (more or less, depending
   upon desired heat)

1 teaspoon coarse-ground black pepper

1 cup toasted peanuts, coarsely ground (page 64)

1 cup mint leaves, chopped

1 cup fresh cilantro sprigs, chopped

5 green onions, white and green parts, chopped

1 can coconut milk (14 ounces)

1 tablespoon fish sauce

PREPARATION

Preheat oven to 350 degrees. Wash the chicken well with cold water and pat dry with paper towels. Remove the giblets and refrigerate for use in another dish. Sprinkle the chicken inside and out with 2 teaspoons of the salt.

In a large bowl, mix the ground pork, chili peppers, pepper, and the remaining teaspoon of salt. Add the peanuts, mint, cilantro, green onions, and half of the can of coconut milk and mix well. Stuff the chicken with about two-thirds of the pork mixture. Put the chicken in a baking dish, breast side up. Tuck the wings underneath. Loosen the skin over the breast and push the rest of the stuffing under the skin, patting the surface to distribute the stuffing equally. Sprinkle the chicken with the fish sauce, and cover. Bake for 40 minutes. Remove the lid and pour the rest of the coconut milk over the chicken. Baste several times with the pan drippings while the chicken continues to cook. It is done when a meat thermometer inserted into the middle of the stuffing registers 170 degrees and the chicken is golden brown (about 30 more minutes).

Recipe adapted from the Hmong Recipe Cook Book, *edited by Sharon Sawyer*
(First Presbyterian Church, South St. Paul, 1986)

Chicken Drumsticks with Hmong-Style Barbeque Sauce

Nqaij Qaib Pleev Kua Barbeque

This basting sauce is delicious on chicken broiled in an oven or grilled over coals. In either case, the chicken is cooked until almost done and then brushed with the sauce for the final few minutes of cooking. This recipe calls for drumsticks, but any chicken pieces can be used.

INGREDIENTS

> ¼ cup finely minced fresh lemongrass, tough outer leaves, top,
>   and root removed first
> ½ cup finely chopped fresh cilantro
> ½ cup finely chopped green onion, white and green parts
> 2 tablespoons sugar
> ¼ cup oyster sauce
> 2 tablespoons dark soy sauce
> 4 pounds chicken drumsticks (about 15 drumsticks)
> 3 teaspoons salt
> 1 teaspoon black pepper

PREPARATION

Mince the lemongrass. Chop the cilantro and green onion. In a bowl, mix the lemongrass, green onion, and cilantro with the sugar, oyster sauce, and soy sauce.

If you are using an oven, remove the broiler pan and preheat the broiler to 400 degrees for 10 minutes before the chicken is ready to cook. For an outdoor grill, light the coals and allow them to become medium-hot.

Wash the drumsticks and dry them with paper towels. Mix the salt and pepper in a large bowl and then add the chicken. Toss the drumsticks until they are thoroughly coated. To broil in the oven, put the chicken on the broiler pan about 6 inches from the heat. On the grill or in the oven, cook the chicken about 20 to 25 minutes until the pieces have browned on one side. Then turn the chicken over and continue to cook until the meat is still juicy but no longer pink (20 to 25 minutes). Brush the chicken on all sides with the basting sauce and cook it a little longer, turning so that all sides are a rich, dark brown. Serve hot.

Eggs ～ Qe

Besides being a special treat for children, eggs have spiritual significance and figure in traditional Hmong healing practices.

Eggs ～ Qe

TO THE HMONG, a warm, smooth egg just plucked from a chicken's nest is much more than a cooking ingredient. Eggs have a special place in Hmong cultural traditions. They figure in marriage negotiations and ceremonies, naming ceremonies, and funeral rituals. Eggs signify good fortune, and they are used to symbolically feed ancestral spirits. Eggs also serve as a diagnostic tool when a person is ill. Hmong people eat freshly laid eggs and ones that have a partly formed "baby chicken" inside. Chicken soup sometimes includes the not-yet-laid eggs from inside the chicken. They bob around in the broth, adding an interesting visual element and taste. However, according to an old tale, if a girl eats them, her labor will be hard when she has children. Another superstition maintains that a young woman should never eat a double-yolked egg, because eating one—or a double banana or lychee nut—will give her twins. Nansee Lor, a grandmother from Sacramento, California, explains this traditional belief: "In Laos, life was very hard and poor. Carrying, giving birth, and trying to care for twins increased the health risks to the mother and the babies. That's where the old idea comes from. In America, twins are not so dangerous, but the old beliefs remain in our hearts."

"Baby Chicken Eggs" (Is It a Chicken or Is It an Egg?)

Qe Mi Nyuam

Makes 1 dozen balut *eggs*

Although some people wrinkle their noses at them, steamed eggs that contain partly formed baby chickens inside are a special treat for many Hmong Americans. Hmong people call them *qe mi nyuam* ("baby chicken eggs"). In Asian grocery stores these eggs, which are about fifteen days into gestation, are labeled "*balut*." *Balut* can refer to either chicken or duck eggs. Either can be used for this recipe. Steaming eggs takes at least twice as long as hard-cooking eggs. You don't want them to be only partly cooked, so err on the side of overcooking, not undercooking.

Almost all Asian cultures enjoy "baby chicken eggs." They are potent symbols of rebirth and springtime. Hmong people serve them paired with spicy sauce and fresh green herbs.

PREPARE THE SPICY SAUCE

2 hot chili peppers, seeded and finely chopped
3 tablespoons finely chopped cilantro
1 green onion, white and green parts, finely chopped
½-inch lemongrass bulb, very finely minced
3 tablespoons fish sauce
1 teaspoon sugar

Combine all of the ingredients and mix thoroughly, until the sugar is dissolved and all of the flavors are united.

PREPARE THE GREEN HERBS AND LETTUCE

1 bunch fresh mint
1 bunch Thai basil
½ bunch chives
1 head lettuce, separated into leaves

Wash, dry, and arrange the fresh herbs and lettuce on a plate with a small bowl of the spicy sauce.

COOK THE EGGS

Bring a dozen *balut* eggs to room temperature and then put them in the top of a steamer. Bamboo and metal stacking steamers that fit over a wok or saucepan are available in Asian markets, or you can use a vegetable steamer. Make sure the water in the pan or wok does not touch the eggs. Turn the heat on medium-high. When the water begins to boil, turn the heat down so the water remains at a simmer. Steam the eggs for about 40 minutes. Do not boil them, as boiling tends to crack them.

SERVE THE EGGS

Remove the eggs from the steamer and allow them to cool enough to handle. With a teaspoon, crack away the shell at the round end of the egg to make a fifty-cent-piece-sized hole. Then sip the liquid accumulated there. This liquid is very nutritious. Next, spoon some of the spicy sauce into the hole and then scoop the cooked egg out a little at a time with some of the sauce. Eat the egg and sauce with bits of the herbs and a leaf of lettuce. The entire "baby chicken," including the beak and bones, is soft enough to eat. Some people also like "baby duck eggs" cooked and served the same way.

Sami notes that she has eaten "baby chickens" and, except for the fact that, upon close inspection, the feathers and bones can be identified, she finds them enjoyable. The texture is that of a hard-cooked egg and the taste is unique— not quite "egg" and not quite "chicken." Sheng suggests that Westerners not look too closely when they eat balut; *simply enjoy the flavor.*

Der's Egg and Cucumber Salad
Dawb Nkaub Qe thiab Dib Xyaw Xav Lav

Makes 4 to 6 servings

The most important role for a traditional Hmong woman is motherhood, and one of the most important parts of mothering is feeding children well. Little children are allowed to eat whenever they are hungry. Although Hmong mothers try to provide healthy food, children are permitted to choose what they eat. This choice helps children learn about who they are. Hmong parents know that as children grow older they will develop tastes for all kinds of food. Sheng's sister Der speaks from experience. When her son, Aden, was three years old, he would pass up chicken, rice, and other dishes in favor of green salad with eggs and cucumbers. He did this whenever the salad was served. In fact, Der thinks he would have liked to eat it at every meal! Here is Der's recipe for green salad with eggs and cucumbers.

INGREDIENTS

8 large eggs
3 tablespoons lemon juice
3 tablespoons Italian salad dressing
½ teaspoon salt
½ teaspoon sugar
¼ teaspoon black pepper
1 tablespoon fish sauce (optional)

1 large head lettuce
Several sprigs fresh dill
¼ cup chopped cilantro
2 medium-sized firm cucumbers
10 cherry tomatoes (optional)

MAKE THE DRESSING

Hard-cook the eggs; cool and remove the shells. Separate the yolks from the whites. Chop the whites coarsely and put them into a salad bowl. In a small bowl, mash 4 of the yolks and mix them with the lemon juice and Italian salad dressing. Save the rest of the egg yolks for other uses. Add the salt, sugar, and black pepper. Add the fish sauce if desired. Blend thoroughly with a wire whisk.

MAKE THE SALAD

Tear up freshly washed and dried lettuce leaves, dill, cilantro, and any other salad greens you like. Cut the cucumbers down the middle lengthwise and scoop out the seeds. Slice the cucumbers. Der's son doesn't like tomatoes, so she doesn't use them, but if your family does, wash the cherry tomatoes and cut them in half. Toss the vegetables with the salad dressing and the chopped egg whites. Enjoy!

Egg Soup

Qe Hau Ua Kua

Makes 1 serving

Hmong comfort food includes this very simple egg soup.

INGREDIENTS

3 cups water
2 eggs
Salt and pepper, to taste

PREPARATION

In a saucepan, boil the water. Crack the eggs into a dish and whisk briefly.
Pour the eggs into the boiling water and stir briskly, so that the eggs become
wispy and do not stick to the bottom. When the eggs are cooked, remove
from heat and season the soup with salt and pepper. Serve hot. This dish
is often given to someone who is sick, and it also serves as an alternative to
the standard chicken-and-rice diet new mothers traditionally eat during
the month after giving birth.

College students like a similar recipe called Qe Hau Xyaw Mij *(Quick Egg
and Noodle Soup), incorporating beaten eggs into their Top Ramen.*

Scrambled Eggs with Pickled Greens

Qe Keb Xyaw Zaub Qaub

Makes 4 servings

INGREDIENTS

6 large eggs
2 cups Sour Green-Vegetable Pickles (page 84)
2 tablespoons vegetable oil
½ teaspoon salt

Break the eggs into a bowl and stir them well. Squeeze the excess liquid from the pickles. Heat the oil in a medium-sized skillet, add the pickles, and stir-fry for 3 minutes. Reduce the heat to medium. Add the eggs and salt. Stir until the eggs are thoroughly cooked. Serve hot.

Recipe shared by Somxai Vue of Denver, Colorado

Omelets, Hmong-Style

Hmoob Ncuav Qe Kib Xyaw Zaub Ntsuab

Makes 2 servings

In Laos, most rural Hmong people did not use oil, butter, or shortening. All frying was done with rendered fat from animals. However, in America even the most traditional cooks use vegetable oil. Sometimes, to approximate that old-world flavor, they substitute lard.

INGREDIENTS

Leafy green vegetables of your choice, about 3 or 4 cups
½ cup chopped fresh herbs of your choice (optional)
4 large eggs
2 tablespoons water
¼ teaspoon salt
Dash coarse-ground black pepper
1 teaspoon fish sauce

PREPARATION

Wash and dry your choice of leafy green vegetables, such as mustard greens, spinach, or sweet pea or melon tendrils. Steam them until they are bright green and limp. Remove the greens from the steamer and set them aside in a bowl. If you want the flavor of herbs, wash, dry, and chop one or two, such as cilantro, dill, Thai basil, or green onion. In a bowl, whisk the eggs with the water. Stir in the salt, pepper, and fish sauce. Pour the egg mixture into a well-oiled wide skillet. Cook over medium heat. As the eggs cook on the bottom, lift the edges of the omelet and allow the uncooked egg to flow underneath. When the egg mixture is just set, turn it over and cook the other side briefly. Remove from the heat and spoon the steamed vegetables down the middle of the omelet. Sprinkle the herbs on top of the greens. Fold one side over the filling. Serve with bacon or Hmong sausage.

Egg and Ginger Omelet

Qe Kib Xyaw Qhiav Tsoo

Makes 2 servings

Ginger is both refreshing and good for digestion. This omelet's flavor is very strong, so adjust the amount of ginger to suit your taste.

INGREDIENTS

Fresh ginger root, peeled and grated
4 eggs
1½ teaspoons salt
¼ teaspoon black pepper
1 tablespoon vegetable oil

PREPARATION

Peel and grate a fresh ginger root. Break the eggs into a bowl, add the grated ginger (about 1 teaspoon to 1 tablespoon per egg), salt, and pepper, then whisk until completely blended and frothy. Heat the oil to medium-hot in a small skillet. Pour in the egg mixture. Lift the edges of the omelet to allow the liquid egg to flow underneath, but do not scramble. When the underside is a little brown, turn the omelet over and continue to cook on the other side. When the omelet is puffy and slightly browned, remove to a plate, fold in half, and cut in half. Serve with warm rice and cooked Hmong sausage.

New Year's Eggs Tais Qe Hu Plig

EGGS ARE IMPORTANT good-luck symbols. In many Hmong homes, during the Hmong New Year's celebration, a two-part ceremony is conducted. First, raw eggs—one for each family member, plus a few extra eggs for visitors—are set in a bowl of uncooked rice, accompanied by burning joss sticks (*xyab*), a special kind of incense. Later, the eggs are hard-cooked and returned to the bowl, and a blessing is conducted by a shaman, another religious leader, or the head of the family. When everyone gathers for the traditional family New Year's feast, each child is given one of the eggs to eat.

In America, this tradition is not always strictly adhered to, especially in Christian families. However, this and many other traditional practices have taken on new and meaningful forms. Sheng's mother, who is Catholic, gives each of her children a devotional candle nestled in a bowl of rice grains surrounded by eggs, one for each family member.

Herbed Eggs
◎◎ *Tshuaj Cub Xyaw Qe*

Hmong groceries sometimes sell these savory hard-cooked eggs as "to-go" treats. Although making them at home requires patience, they are so tasty and unique it is worth the effort. Grocery store herbed eggs are often seasoned with only salt, pepper, and fish sauce. We like to add cilantro or baby dill, with a bit of green onion. Grated ginger, basil, or Vietnamese coriander are also good. Feel free to be creative.

INGREDIENTS

>   6 large fresh eggs
>   2 tablespoons finely chopped savory herbs (optional)
>   1 teaspoon salt
>   1½ teaspoons coarse-ground black pepper
>   1 tablespoon fish sauce

PREPARATION

Using a large darning needle, tap a chopstick-sized hole in the pointed end of 1 egg. Prick the yolk inside to break it. Carefully drain the liquid egg white and yolk from inside the shell into a bowl. You may need to guide the liquid out with the needle and pull the membrane out with your fingers. Discard the membrane. Repeat with each egg. After all the eggs have been emptied, whisk the eggs in the bowl. Chop the herbs very finely. Add to the eggs the herbs, salt, pepper, and fish sauce. Whisk again. After mixing in the seasonings, carefully pour the egg mixture back into the shells. Steam the eggs over boiling water in a steamer for about 25 minutes, making sure they are sitting upright so none of the liquid egg drains out. You may need to prop up the eggs with stones or steam other eggs with them to keep the herbed eggs from tipping over. Steaming eggs takes twice as long as hard-cooking them. When the eggs are cooked, run cold water over them so the shells will peel off easily.

To save time, you can steam the prepared eggs in custard cups. To do this, crack the eggs into a bowl and whisk with the herbs, salt, pepper, and fish sauce. Pour the prepared eggs into six custard cups. Steam the eggs in a covered pan partly filled with simmering water. The water should be only half the depth of the custard cups.

Herbed eggs are a variation of an old-fashioned remedy called qe tshuaj *(medicinal eggs). Sick people often receive specially prepared eggs that contain medicinal herbs for treating their illness. Medicinal eggs taste bitter, because some of the herbs are bitter and the eggs are never seasoned with salt, pepper, or fish sauce.*

Pork ~ Nqaij Npuas

Pork and Mustard Greens Soup 132
Nqaij Npuas Hau Xyaw Zaub Ntsuab

Sweet Pig's Feet 133
Nqaij Qabzib

Hmong Sausage 134
Nyhuv Ntxwm Hmoob

Cabbage with Pork Sausage 135
Zaub Pob Kib Xyaw Nyhuv

Pork-Stuffed Tofu 136
Feev Choj Ntim Taum Paj Hau

Quick and Easy Pork *Larb* 137
Laj Nqaij Npuas

Sour Liver/Bitter Liver (Traditional Pork Organs and Entrails) 138
Siab Qaub/Siab Iab

Pork with Squash Tendrils and Blossoms 142
Nqaij Npuas Hau Xyaw Xwb Kuab thiab Ntsis Xwb Kuab

Fried Pork Skin 144
Kiav Roj

Smoked Pork and Young Asian Pumpkins 144
Nqaij Npuas Sawb Hau Xyau Qe Taub thiab Ntsis Taub

Smoked Pork and Bitter Eggplant 145
Nqaij Npuas Sawb Kib Xyaw Txiv Pos Lws Iab

Pork Meatballs 146
Qe Nqaij Npuas

Hot Chili Garlic Sauce 147
Kua Txob Qej

Pig Brain Pâté 147
Hlwb Npua Tuav

Pork and Chicken Salad with Peanuts 148
Nqaij Npuas thiab Nqaij Qaib Xav Lav

Pork ~ Nqaij Npuas

PORK IS THE FOOD that the Hmong most closely associate with prosperity. Numerous dishes featuring pork are eaten during New Year's celebrations as a way to ensure success and wealth in the coming year. A whole roasted pig is served at marriage rites, to signify a rich life for the bridal couple. The menus for most traditional rituals and big celebrations include pork. Dishes featuring pork are favorites for many Hmong Americans.

In the mountains of Laos, a pig would be processed, cooked, and eaten right after butchering, because there was no refrigeration to keep the meat fresh. Many of the following recipes reflect that facet of Hmong history.

This pig has been prepared for a "jingle-bell party"—a ritual that can have a number of purposes, including treating an illness (hu plig) or ensuring prosperity in the new year (ua neeb kab plig).

Pork and Mustard Greens Soup

◎◎ *Nqaij Npuas Hau Xyaw Zaub Ntsuab*

Makes 6 servings

This old-fashioned, simple dish is everyone's favorite and is typical of everyday Hmong cooking. Serve it accompanied by a dish of Hot Chili Condiment (page 87) and plenty of fresh steamed rice. Any leafy dark green vegetable can be substituted for the mustard greens.

INGREDIENTS

> 7 cups water
> 1 pound pork meat with some fat and bones
>   (neck or ribs are good), cut into pieces
> 2 inches fresh ginger root, washed and sliced
> 1 tablespoon salt
> ¼ teaspoon MSG (optional)
> 1 big bunch tender Chinese mustard greens, washed

PREPARATION

Put the water in a pot. Add the pork with bones, ginger root, salt, and MSG (if desired). Bring to a simmer and cook until the pork is well done (no longer pink inside), about 15 to 20 minutes. Skim off any residue and foam from the soup as it cooks. Add the mustard greens and continue to simmer until the greens are bright green and tender. Taste and add more salt, if needed.

Diners ladle some of the soup into their own bowls. They sip the broth from their spoons and dip the meat and greens into a bit of the hot chili condiment before eating.

Sweet Pig's Feet
Nqaij Qabzib

Makes 8 servings

This recipe is a smaller, simpler version of Sweet Pork (page 244).

INGREDIENTS

3 pounds pig's feet (or any pork with fat and bones)
3 quarts water, to blanch the pig's feet
1 cup brown sugar
4 cloves garlic, smashed
4 inches fresh ginger root, peeled and sliced
1 bulb lemongrass (base of a stalk), smashed
2 cups water
1 teaspoon salt
1 tablespoon fish sauce
1 tablespoon dark soy sauce
1 dozen hard-cooked eggs, shells removed

PREPARATION

Ask your butcher to split the pig's feet in half lengthwise, then cut crosswise into 1-inch pieces. Blanch the pig's feet by submersing them in boiling water for 2 minutes. Remove to a plate. Heat a deep pan or large wok to medium-hot and add the sugar. Stir constantly until the sugar is melted and dark brown but not burned. Add the garlic, ginger, and lemongrass. Stir for 2 or 3 minutes. Add the water, pork, salt, fish sauce, and soy sauce. Bring the mixture to a "little boil" and cook for about 1 hour. Add the peeled, whole hard-cooked eggs, stir them into the sauce, and cover the dish. Cook over low heat for another hour, stirring occasionally, until the meat is very soft, but not falling apart, and the eggs are deep brown. Serve with warm fresh-made rice.

NQAIJ NPUAS — 133

Hmong Sausage

◎◎ *Nyhuv Ntxwm Hmoob*

Makes 8 servings

Long, fat tubes of hot-off-the-grill Hmong sausage are sold at Hmong New Year's celebrations around the world. For everyday eating, Hmong families usually buy sausage from delicatessens; however, some families like to make their own. Most Hmong cooks no longer chop the meat by hand or use intestine casings. To save time, they have adopted modern technology and utilize meat grinders, sausage stuffers, and synthetic casings.

Good cooks guard their sausage recipes, and everyone makes sausage a little differently. If you want to try your hand at making Hmong sausage the old-fashioned way, here is a step-by-step guide. Ingredient amounts are suggestions. Cooks must decide for themselves their preferred quantities of pork, fat, and seasonings.

INGREDIENTS

3 pounds pork meat with some fat (depending upon how fatty
  you want the sausage), finely minced or ground
1 cup finely chopped ginger
3 to 4 cloves garlic, minced (optional)
2 to 3 hot chili peppers (more or fewer, according to desired heat),
  minced
2 teaspoons salt
1 teaspoon black pepper (optional)
1 to 2 teaspoons MSG (optional)
2 pig's intestines turned inside out and washed and then turned
  right side out again (or use synthetic casings)

PREPARATION

Chop the ginger and garlic with a mini-chopper. Put all of the ingredients into a bowl. Using gloved hands, mix ingredients well. Take a small amount of the mixture and fry it in a nonstick skillet. Taste, and adjust the seasonings. With a sausage-stuffing machine, fill a section of the pig's intestine or synthetic casing with the pork mixture. To make links, stuff a portion and then make two knots between each link. To separate the links, cut between the knots. If you do not have a sausage-stuffing machine, remove the cap from an empty plastic ½-liter water bottle and cut off the top third. Insert

A vendor grills fat tubes of Hmong sausage at the Sacramento New Year's celebration.

the cap end into the intestine or sausage casing and, holding the casing onto the bottle, fill the sausage by pushing the meat mixture in with your fingers.

After assembly, Hmong sausage rests for a day or two to let the flavors blend and allow the sausage to become firm. Traditionally, sausages were hung in an airy place protected from flies. Health concerns now require that the sausages rest in a refrigerator. Cook the sausages within two days of making them. Grill the meat about 6 inches over hot coals, turning several times so all of the sides are brown. The sausages are done when a meat thermometer inserted into the interior registers 170 degrees. Cool and refrigerate if not eaten immediately. Freeze if not eaten within three days.

Cabbage with Pork Sausage
Zaub Pob Kib Xyaw Nyhuv

Makes 4 servings

Make this dish with the homemade Hmong sausage of the previous recipe, or purchase sausage ready-made from a Hmong meat market.

INGREDIENTS

½ head American cabbage, cut into 2-by-2-inch squares
2 teaspoons vegetable oil
2 cloves garlic, minced
½ Hmong sausage, sliced into ½-inch pieces
1 teaspoon salt
½ teaspoon Mrs. Dash
4 green onions, white and green parts, cut into 3-inch pieces
½ bunch cilantro, cut into 3-inch pieces

Blanch the cabbage in boiling water for ½ minute. Drain it in a colander, and then quickly plunge the cabbage in cold water and drain it again. The cabbage should remain crisp. In a medium-sized skillet, heat the oil to high and fry the garlic for 20 seconds. Add the sausage and stir 3 to 5 minutes. Quickly add the cabbage, salt, and Mrs. Dash. Stir just long enough to reheat the cabbage. Add the green onions and cilantro. Toss and serve on a platter accompanied by plenty of hot rice.

Pork-Stuffed Tofu

Feev Choj Ntim Taum Paj Hau

Makes 12 servings

For American New Year, Mai Xee Vang always serves roast turkey with savory bread stuffing and all the American-style fixings, but the place of honor on her table goes to a big dish of stuffed tofu. She makes this dish in remembrance of her mother, who always included it in her Thanksgiving menu. This is Mai Xee's dad's favorite dish.

Packaged squares of fried tofu are available in several sizes in most large Asian groceries.

INGREDIENTS

1 small bundle rice vermicelli noodles, about 1½ ounces (optional)
1½ pounds ground pork
½ cup chopped cilantro
4 green onions, white and green parts, chopped
1½ teaspoons salt
½ teaspoon black pepper
36 pieces fried tofu, in about 3-by-2-inch chunks (depending upon available size)
About 5 cups water
1 to 2 cans chicken broth (liquid measurements to vary, depending upon desired soupiness)
Ginger root, 1-inch piece, peeled, sliced, and smashed with the side of a cleaver

Low-carb dieters may prefer to omit the rice vermicelli. If you want to include the noodles, soak them in warm water for 30 minutes, until they are soft. Drain the noodles and cut them with kitchen shears to make ½-inch pieces. In a bowl, mix the pork, noodles (if used), cilantro, green onions, salt, and black pepper. Cut a broad, deep slit in one of the pieces of tofu, creating a pocket almost the size of the tofu piece. Fill the pocket with the meat mixture. The resulting stuffed tofu should be nice and plump. Continue until all of the tofu pieces are filled. If any filling is left over, make meatballs out of the remainder and boil them along with the stuffed tofu. In a large pot, bring the water and chicken broth to a gentle boil. Add the ginger. Slip each piece of tofu into the boiling water and broth. Bring the liquid back to a simmer and maintain the heat until the tofu filling is thoroughly cooked, about 20 minutes. Serve the stuffed tofu in a large bowl along with the ginger-flavored broth.

Recipe shared by Mai Xee Vang of Portland, Oregon

Quick and Easy Pork *Larb*
Laj Nqaij Npuas

Makes 4 servings

This simple recipe (which can easily be halved or doubled) can be made with very lean ground pork, beef, or chicken. The brand-name seasoning mix includes ground garlic, chili, lemongrass, galanga, toasted rice powder, and salt. The jar also contains a separate pouch with very hot chili powder in it, to add according to taste.

INGREDIENTS

1 pound lean ground pork (or chicken or beef)
1 kaffir lime leaf, minced
½ cup coarsely chopped fresh mint
¼ cup coarsely chopped cilantro
¼ cup coarsely chopped Vietnamese coriander
Juice of 1 large lime
1 tablespoon fish sauce

1 tablespoon OK brand Laab (larb) Powder Seasoning Mix
3 green onions, white and green parts, chopped
Fresh lettuce leaves, for wraps
1 cucumber, sliced (or other fresh vegetables, as accompaniment)

PREPARATION

Cook the pork in a nonstick skillet without oil over medium heat for about 7 minutes. Break the meat apart as it cooks. Do not overcook. Transfer to a bowl and allow to cool to room temperature.

While the meat cools, wash and mince the lime leaf, and coarsely chop the herbs. Squeeze the lime juice over the cooled meat. Add the fish sauce, seasoning mix, mint, cilantro, coriander, and green onions. Gently toss everything together and taste. Add the hot chili powder to taste (¼ teaspoon makes it mildly hot). Serve with lettuce leaves, sliced cucumber, and other vegetables as desired. *Larb* is always served with cool sticky rice. Add a bowl of fresh fruit and you have a meal!

Sour Liver/Bitter Liver (Traditional Pork Organs and Entrails)
 *Siab Qaub/Siab Iab*

This dish is key to Hmong identity and is relished by many people. Since it is very traditional, the recipe contains an old-fashioned set of directions. Some of the earthy ingredients and the lack of precise measurements may make it difficult for Westerners to enjoy or follow. But to omit the unusual ingredients or to quantify the measurements would remove the Hmongness. This dish is made when a pig is butchered. The ingredient amounts depend upon the size of the pig.

The old saying about butchering a pig, "Everything is eaten, except the squeal," is the philosophy behind Sour Liver/Bitter Liver. Like farmers everywhere, the Hmong waste nothing. They take pride in eating every edible part of an animal.

The dish usually includes the pig's liver, lungs, stomach, pancreas, and large intestine (but never the small intestine). Different Hmong clans have different beliefs regarding the consumption of organs. For instance, men of the Yang clan supposedly will become ill or die if they eat the heart. Therefore, the heart is included only when no men of the Yang clan are in attendance.

To give the dish a bitter flavor, the gallbladder is boiled separately from the other organs, and some of its cooking liquid is added to the mixture. However, some people prefer to make the dish sour, not bitter, by adding lime or lemon juice instead. The herbs are used only as seasoning; their flavor should not overwhelm the meat.

INGREDIENTS

Edible organs of 1 freshly butchered pig
Several cups salt (to clean the organs)
Lime juice (to clean the organs)
Water (to clean the organs, and for boiling)
2 stalks lemongrass, tough outer leaves and root removed
2 to 3 teaspoons salt, or to taste
2 to 4 cups chopped Hmong herbs, your choice (listed below)
2 to 3 tablespoons fish sauce, or to taste
Hot Thai chili peppers, chopped, to taste
Gallbladder "juice" (for a bitter flavor; optional)
Lime juice (for a sour flavor; optional)

PREPARATION

Wash the organs and entrails several times with liberal amounts of salt, lime juice, and water. Turn the stomach and intestines inside out and wash them several more times. With a sharp knife, cut or scrape off any impurities. Cut deep slashes in the large organs so that they will cook through completely. Put a large pot of water on to boil. Add the lemongrass and the teaspoons of salt. When the water boils, add the organs and entrails. Cook for 40 minutes. Using a slotted spoon, remove the pork pieces from the cooking water and put them in a large bowl. Discard the lemongrass but not the broth, because some of it is added to the dish later on. When the organs and entrails are cool enough to handle, thinly slice everything and return the sliced meat to the bowl. Chop and add traditional herbs, such as green onions, cilantro, culantro (saw-leaf herb), mint, and Vietnamese coriander. Add the fish sauce and hot chili peppers. To make the dish bitter, add some of the gallbladder juice, or to make it sour, add lime juice. Sometimes the sliced meat is mixed and then divided into two bowls: one made bitter for elderly people and the other made sour to suit younger people. Taste and adjust the seasonings. Add some of the pork broth and mix well.

Hosting a Shaman Ritual in America—A "Jingle-Bell Party"

THE HMONG PEOPLE who helped with this book estimate that about one-third to one-half of Hmong Americans have converted from their traditional animist and ancestor-worship belief systems to some form of Christianity. The rest of Hmong Americans continue to follow the old ways, which include seeking a shaman's assistance in spiritual matters. To fully understand Hmong cooking practices and menus, some insight into the family-affirming, age-old customs involved in hosting a shaman event is necessary. These rituals are the legacy of the Hmong, and even as their belief systems evolve, remnants of the old ways are revealed in the food Hmong people love and in the party etiquette they continue to follow.

In America, Hmong rituals that require a shaman are often called "jingle-bell parties," because one of the shaman's tools is a large metal ring equipped with metal disks that jingle when the shaman shakes it while performing the traditional rites. Co-author Sheng explains, "We use those words because they help to engage the children in the activity, and we want our children to learn about our traditions."

One ritual observed by families that continue to follow the traditional ways is the *Ua Neeb Kab Plig*. Such a ritual must be hosted about every other year. This shamanic rite is performed for the welfare of a single family. It is held in early spring to honor family ancestors, to rid the house of evil spirits, and to ensure health and prosperity in the coming year. Although the basic components of this ritual and other rituals conducted by a shaman are the same throughout Hmong culture, each family group's traditions vary, depending upon the customs of the family's original home region and village and the family's current circumstances.

A day or two before the party, the children begin to anticipate the day's special treats and the fun they will have with their visiting cousins. Meanwhile, the adults begin to carry out their traditional responsibilities. The male head of the household is in charge of selecting an auspicious day for the ceremony—a day that also accommodates everyone's schedules—engaging a shaman who can perform the rites in accordance with the family's needs, and inviting extended family and friends. The Herculean tasks of menu planning, shopping, recruiting cooks and cooks' helpers, preparing the house for dozens of guests, and cooking fall to his wife.

The day before the party, various components of Three-Color Dessert are prepared and refrigerated. Early the next morning, pots of sticky rice and jasmine rice are made and packaged in serving-sized plastic bags. A big kettle of Chicken Curry Noodle Soup is begun. The soup will serve as a hearty breakfast for guests as they observe the sacred events, and while they help prepare the big meal that is the culmination of the day.

Although they have no active role in the ritual, closely related family members from near and far come to provide support. Their presence is vital to the success of the day. Such rituals require the sacrifice of a pig and two chickens (one male, one female). On the morning of the event, the family leaders go to a farm and select a healthy, young, "pretty" pig. It is then quickly killed and cleaned. The pig's carcass is brought back home. The shaman uses the pig's released spirit to communicate with the spirit world, and an offering of paper spirit money is burned to thank the pig for its supreme sacrifice. A string then encircles the family and joins it to the spirit of the pig. The shaman uses all the ritualistic tools: a mask, the metal jingle rings, a set of split buffalo horns, a ritual sword, and a wooden platform (horse) that the shaman rides into the otherworld.

After the pig's role in the ritual is finished, the men efficiently turn the carcass into chops, steaks, and ground pork. The head and one upper quarter of the pig are given to the shaman. Then the women get busy and cook a variety of dishes, including Sweet Pig's Feet, Quick and Easy Pork *Larb*, Pork and Mustard Greens Soup, Sour Liver/Bitter Liver (all recipes in this chapter), and blood pudding.

It is considered poor manners for any guest to have to ask for a dish to be passed, so tables are crammed with duplicate dishes of food. The family would be shamed if any guest left hungry or empty-handed. Therefore, far more food than can be eaten in a day is made, and every guest is heaped with leftovers to take home.

Even with the continual rapid changes to Hmong culture in America, some of these customs and dishes grace the homes of even the most ardent Christian Hmong Americans.

Pork with Squash Tendrils and Blossoms

Nqaij Npuas Hau Xyaw Xwb Kuab thiab Ntsis Xwb Kuab

Makes 4 servings

Hmong gardeners know that if the end of a squash vine is pinched off, it will quickly grow again. Any kind of squash or pumpkin vines and blossoms can be used for this recipe. Tendrils are sold in Asian stores in season. The bright green of the tendrils together with the orange blossoms makes this a brightly colored dish.

INGREDIENTS

> *4 boneless pork chops, sliced into strips 3 to 4 inches long*
> *and about ½ inch thick*
> *2 tablespoons vegetable oil*
> *1 clove garlic, smashed*
> *2 inches ginger root, peeled and sliced*
> *1 teaspoon salt*
> *½ teaspoon coarse-ground pepper*
> *1 cup pork broth (reserved from cooking pork bones),*
> *or pork bouillon or water*
> *1 teaspoon soy sauce*
> *4 cups squash tendrils, about 4 to 6 inches long*
> *8 to 10 squash blossoms*

PREPARATION

Heat the oil to medium-hot in a wok or large skillet. Add the garlic, ginger, salt, and pepper, and stir-fry until aromatic but not brown. Add the pork and continue to stir-fry for 5 minutes or until the meat is almost cooked (it may still be a bit pink in the middle). Add the pork broth and soy sauce and stir to combine. Place the tendrils and blossoms on top and cover with a lid. Steam until the tendrils are bright green and the blossoms are wilted. Remove lid, stir once, and taste. Adjust seasonings as desired. Serve hot with rice.

Pork or Chicken Blood Pudding ("Live Blood")
Ntsha Npua los yog Ntsha Qaib Teev

MAKING "LIVE BLOOD" (*Ntsha Npua Teev*) with pork blood requires experience and skill. Traditionally, only men prepare this dish. The blood from a freshly killed pig is mixed with salt and stirred until it gels. Clean cooked and chopped internal organs, such as the liver, stomach, and large intestine, and some cooked sliced pork skin and pork meat are then added. Salt, Sichuan pepper, MSG, and all kinds of Hmong herbs are also mixed in, except for lemongrass, which prevents pig's blood from gelling. Heart meat is seldom included because of the taboo against Yang men eating it. Many young Hmong Americans are not interested in making this dish, but those born in Laos enjoy the camaraderie of preparing it as well as the old-world flavor.

Chicken Blood Pudding (*Ntsha Qaib Teev*) is made in a similar fashion. When a chicken is killed, its blood is drained into a clean bowl. The blood congeals easily when allowed to sit mixed with a little room-temperature water. The chicken is plucked, cleaned, and cooked in boiling water flavored with lemongrass and salt. After the blood has cooled enough to handle, it is mixed with cooked chopped chicken meat and giblets, plus chopped fresh mint, green onions, and Vietnamese coriander, and minced lemongrass. Usually, fish sauce, roasted and ground Sichuan pepper, and MSG are also added, to taste. These dishes should be eaten immediately or refrigerated.

The refrigerated section of many Asian groceries stocks pint tubs filled with cubes of congealed pork blood. This ingredient is used not in live blood pudding but in soup in much the same way as tofu cubes. The drained blood cubes are added for the last 5 or 10 minutes of cooking time. Do not overcook; the cubes will harden if they are cooked for a long time. The blood makes any soup richer and heartier.

Fried Pork Skin

Kiav Roj

Fried pork skin serves as a snack or as an ingredient in other recipes to add a chewy texture. Pork skin can be purchased at Asian grocery stores. Clean the pork skin well and cut it into 2-by-3-inch pieces, or whatever size suits the recipe. To minimize spattering, use corn oil to fry the pork skin. Pour about 4 inches of oil into a deep wok and heat until it is hot but not boiling. Slip several pieces of pork skin into the oil and fry, turning them over as they cook. They are done when they are yellowish-brown and fairly hard. Drain on paper towels and sprinkle liberally with salt. (Some people add the salt to the oil instead.)

Smoked Pork and Young Asian Pumpkins

Nqaij Npuas Sawb Hau Xyau Qe Taub thiab Ntsis Taub

Makes 4 servings

This recipe is pure Hmong—very simple and flavorful. Hmong smoked pork tastes a little like bacon. It is available at Hmong meat markets. If it is not available, substitute any Asian smoked pork, or for a more American flavor, use thick-sliced bacon. Asian pumpkins have gray-green skin and bright orange flesh. They are similar to pumpkins, which can serve as a substitute.

INGREDIENTS

> ½ bunch pumpkin vines, chopped
> 1 medium-sized young Asian pumpkin (or American pumpkin)
> 1 pound Hmong or Asian smoked pork, or bacon, cut into
>   bite-sized pieces
> 5 cups water
> 1 teaspoon salt
> ½ teaspoon MSG (optional)
> 1 stalk lemongrass, tough outer leaves and root removed, bulb
>   smashed with the flat edge of a knife and cut into 3-inch pieces

First, wash and peel the tough veins from the pumpkin vines and chop the vines into 6-inch lengths. Peel and remove the seeds and strings from the pumpkin. Then cut it into bite-sized pieces. Cut the pork into bite-sized pieces and set the vines, pumpkin cubes, and meat aside. Put the water, salt, MSG (if desired), and lemongrass in a soup pot and bring it to a boil. Add the pork and boil gently for about 10 to 15 minutes, until the meat is almost cooked (it should still be a bit pink in the middle). Add the pumpkin cubes and vines. Boil all together until the pumpkin is soft but not mushy. Serve in individual soup bowls.

Smoked Pork and Bitter Eggplant

Nqaij Npuas Sawb Kib Xyaw Txiv Pos Lws Iab

Makes 4 servings

Bitter eggplants are small and green and shaped like a very small pumpkin.

INGREDIENTS

½ pound Hmong bitter eggplants, quartered
1 tablespoon vegetable oil
½ pound smoked pork, sliced thinly
½ stalk lemongrass, cleaned and cut in 2 pieces
½ teaspoon salt
1 teaspoon MSG (optional)
1 teaspoon black pepper

PREPARATION

Wash the eggplants and remove stems and leaves. Heat the oil in a skillet or wok to medium-hot. Add the eggplants, pork, lemongrass, salt, and MSG (if desired). Quickly stir-fry the mixture for a few minutes, until the eggplants are soft. Sprinkle with the black pepper.

Pork Meatballs

Qe Nqaij Npuas

These fun little meatballs can be deep-fried or steamed to be eaten as a snack, or gently boil them and add cubed squash or any other vegetable to the broth to make a tasty soup.

INGREDIENTS

1½ pounds ground lean pork
¼ cup minced lemongrass, tough outer leaves, top, and root
 removed first
3 green onions, white and green parts, chopped
3 cloves garlic, minced
1 teaspoon salt
1 teaspoon black pepper
1 teaspoon sugar
Vegetable oil (if deep-fried)

PREPARATION

You can use a mini-chopper to prepare the green onions and garlic, but the lemongrass should be chopped by hand because it is so fibrous. With gloved hands, mix the pork with all of the other ingredients. Form the mixture into 2-inch balls.

Pour 4 inches of vegetable oil in a wok. Heat to medium and then slip one layer of the meatballs into the hot oil. Fry until they are done and slightly crispy, about 10 minutes. Remove with a wire strainer and drain on paper towels. Continue until all the meatballs are fried. Or, instead of frying, steam on wax paper in the top of a steamer, or gently boil in water or broth until no longer pink inside. Serve as a snack accompanied by Hot Chili Garlic Sauce.

Hot Chili Garlic Sauce

Kua Txob Qej

Makes about 1 cup sauce

INGREDIENTS

    3 or 4 small hot chilies, minced (more or less,
      depending upon desired heat)
    ¼ cup chopped cilantro
    4 green onions, green and white parts, chopped
    1 clove garlic, minced
    3 tablespoons squid sauce
    Juice of 1 large lime
    1 tablespoon sugar
    ¼ cup chopped tomatoes (for an Americanized flavor)

PREPARATION

Chop up all ingredients and mix well.

Pig Brain Pâté

Hlwb Npua Tuav

Makes appetizers for 10

Finding pig brains is not always easy, even in Asian grocery stores. They sell very quickly because they are so popular. If you have never eaten pig brains, you may be surprised by their delicate flavor.

INGREDIENTS

    4 pig brains (very fresh)
    ½ cup chopped green onion, white and green parts
    ½ cup chopped cilantro
    2 hot Thai chili peppers (more or less, according to desired heat),
      minced
    ½ teaspoon salt
    Dash coarse-ground black pepper

Rinse the brains gently in cool water. Bring a medium-sized pot of water to boil and slip the brains into the water. Simmer for 15 minutes. While the brains cook, wash and chop the herbs and chili peppers. Remove the brains with a slotted spoon to a large mortar and pestle. Add the green onion, cilantro, chili peppers, salt, and black pepper. Pound the ingredients together until the brains are mushy and completely mixed with the herbs and seasonings.

Pig brain pâté is eaten in small spoonfuls along with a meal, or it is set out as an appetizer. Although it is not a Hmong custom, this pâté can be eaten spread on crackers, garnished with a thin slice of hot chili to give it an extra kick and a sprig of cilantro for color.

Pork and Chicken Salad with Peanuts

Nqaij Npuas thiab Nqaij Qaib Xav Lav

Makes 8 servings

Serve this salad along with sliced ripe mangos and sweet sticky rice for a warm summer evening's light meal.

INGREDIENTS

1 stalk lemongrass, tough outer leaves, root, and top of leaves
  removed
3 sprigs Thai basil
½ pound lean pork
1 whole boneless, skinless chicken breast
3 cloves garlic
2 cups raw, shelled peanuts
2 tablespoons fish sauce
2 tablespoons vinegar
1 teaspoon salt
1 teaspoon MSG (optional)
1 teaspoon sugar
1 large white onion, shredded
½ head cabbage, shredded
4 large carrots, thinly sliced

Cut the lemongrass into 3-inch lengths. Put the lemongrass and Thai basil sprigs in a saucepan of boiling water. Add the pork and chicken and simmer until the meat is cooked through, 15 to 20 minutes (no pink inside). Transfer the meat to a bowl to cool. Discard the herbs, and reserve 1½ cups of the cooking water. When the meat is cool, shred it with your fingers. Add the reserved water to the shredded meat.

Pound the garlic with a mortar and pestle. Add the peanuts, and continue to pound until they are mixed and the nuts are in tiny chunks. Transfer this mixture to a small bowl. Add the fish sauce, vinegar, salt, MSG (if desired), and sugar. Mix well with a wire whisk.

Wash the vegetables. Shred the cabbage and onion. Using a vegetable peeler, slice the carrots into thin strips. Mix everything together in a large serving bowl. Serve immediately.

Beef and Water Buffalo ~
Nqaij Nyuj thiab Nqaij Twm

Traditional Beef Soup 155
Quav Iab Nyuj

Hmong Dried Beef 158
Nqaij Nyuj Qhuav

Stir-Fried Dried Beef with Bamboo 160
Nqaij Nyuj Qhuav Kib Xyaw Ntsuag

Grilled Beef *Larb* 160
Laj Nqaij Nyuj Xaj los yog Suam

Beef Stew with Banana Blossoms and Eggplants 162
Kua Las ("Oh-La")

Beef and Luffa Squash with Basil 165
Nqaij Nyuj Xyaw Xwb Kuab

Chili and Thai Eggplant Condiment 166
Kua Txob Lws Tuav

Beef Soup with Sour Bamboo 167
Nqaij Nyuj Hau Xyaw Ntsuag Qaub

Beef Stir-Fried with Bitter Melon 168
Nqaij Nyuj Kib Xyaw Dib Iab

Beef Noodle Soup 168
Fawm (Phở)

Beef and String Bean Stir-Fry 170
Taum Ntev Kib Xyaw Nqaij Nyuj

Beef and Tomato Stir-Fry 171
Nqaij Nyuj Kib Xyaw Txiv Lws Suav

Beef and Water Buffalo ~
Nqaij Nyuj thiab Nqaij Twm

Portland community leader Ge Ly grinds very lean beef that will be mixed with rice powder, hot chilies, and herbs to make the traditional Lao meat salad called larb.

FEW HMONG PEOPLE TASTED Western-style beef before coming to the United States, because the only red meat readily available or affordable in Laos besides wild game was water buffalo. Therefore, few traditional recipes call for beef. Water buffalo or beef was reserved for funerals and special occasions, when the sacrifice of a cow was desired. At these big events the animal would be killed, butchered, cooked, and consumed all in one day, usually providing food for a large group of guests.

Such a crowd required that preparation be kept to a minimum. Often the meat was simply boiled.

In the United States, beef is less expensive and more widely available than water buffalo, so it is more often the meat of choice. But, when possible, Hmong people still like to eat water buffalo. Water buffalo are not the same as American buffalo, which are actually bison. Water buffalo are true buffalo, the same species that pulled plows in Laos. The meat is a very healthy option, since it is 44 percent lower in fat and 40 percent lower in cholesterol than traditional beef; it also has 55 percent fewer calories.

Because beef is scarce in Laos, many Hmong recipes using beef—simple stir-fries and soups—are of recent origin. However, recipes for traditional beef soup, "oh-la," *larb*, and dried beef originated in Laos. This chapter begins with those old-fashioned recipes and ends with the more modern ones.

Finding water buffalo meat is not easy for non-Hmong cooks. Hmong communities generally know which ranchers raise and sell water buffalo, but they seldom advertise in print or on the Internet. Inquire within a Hmong community to find out where it is sold.

Each recipe notes whether to use beef or water buffalo.

Traditional Beef Soup

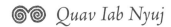 *Quav Iab Nyuj*

Makes 1 pot of soup

Anne Fadiman's popular book *The Spirit Catches You and You Fall Down: A Hmong Child, Her American Doctors, and the Collision of Two Cultures* contains a description of "cow-poo soup" that has left a lasting impression on many readers. The writer describes a soup made as part of a traditional Hmong healing ritual conducted by a shaman attempting to restore a little girl to health. The typically Hmong-style earthy name refers to the fact that the soup includes beef stomach and intestines, as well as organ meat. This soup is prepared when a cow or water buffalo is butchered, usually for a funeral or as part of a traditional ceremony. Contradicting its name, the soup is made of healthy ingredients and is very nutritious. However, this dish may not be for people who are one or more generations away from having to eat whatever is available in order to live. Tino Yang and his wife, Ia Vang, who contributed this recipe, both grew up in Thai refugee camps and still have vivid memories of the many days when they had no more to eat than a bowl of rice and some green vegetables. To them and many other Hmongs, this hearty soup was a marvelous luxury, eaten only on special occasions when a cow or water buffalo was sacrificed. It continues to be relished by many Hmong Americans, and it is often served at Hmong funerals.

This recipe is impractical for non-Hmong cooks, because getting many of the ingredients would be difficult without having access to a freshly butchered cow or water buffalo. If you do cook this soup, try to maintain a ratio of twice the amount of broth as meat, and about equal amounts of kinds of meat (entrails and organs, flesh meat and skin). The eggplants and herbs serve only to season the soup, not as main ingredients. Including a few bitter-tasting ingredients, such as bitter eggplants or gallbladder juice, is traditional.

Following this recipe is a second version with more precise measurements, using ingredients that can be purchased in a mainstream grocery store.

Amounts and proportions of ingredients depend upon the number of people being fed.

Beef or water buffalo entrails, organs, and skin in about equal
  amounts
Flesh meat (chuck, shank, or rib meat) from beef or water buffalo
Kaffir lime leaves
Ginger or galanga root, sliced
Salt
MSG (if desired)
Beef or water buffalo bones, including knuckle bones with meat
  attached (for a hearty broth)
Small bitter eggplants, sliced
Hmong herbs such as whole basil leaves, culantro (called saw-leaf
  or duck-tongue herb, txuj lom muas loob), *and Vietnamese*
  coriander (luam laws)
Beef bouillon cubes

PREPARATION

Traditional Beef Soup contains a variety of beef (or water buffalo) meat, including skin, entrails, organs, and flesh meat, in about equal amounts. All of the beef is sliced thin; Ia slices the meat about ¼ inch thick. The toughest parts are cooked the longest, to make them chewable.

Carefully clean the thick skin and then boil it for a long time (5 hours or more), until it is soft and chewy. Cut it into ¼-inch-thick slices.

Carefully clean the entrails and organs. Turn the stomach and intestines inside out and wash them with running water, salt, and lime juice. Remove any dirty or damaged areas and discard. Boil a pot of water and add the kaffir lime leaves, sliced ginger or galanga root, salt, and MSG (if desired). Put knuckle bones with meat into the pot. After the broth simmers for a while, add the sliced cooked skin. Slice the stomach and intestines into thin pieces and add them to the soup. Continue to boil until these items are soft. Next, add the organ meat, also sliced thin. To give the soup a bitter flavor, add tiny bitter eggplants that have been cleaned and sliced. Finally, slice and add the flesh meat, and cook until it is tender and no longer pink. Add Hmong herbs if desired. To boost flavor, Ia adds beef bouillon cubes while the soup boils.

Soup made for funerals never includes hot peppers or spicy seasonings, only salt and the pungent bitterness of traditional vegetables or herbs.

Recipe shared by Tino Yang and Ia Vang of St. Paul, Minnesota

Traditional Beef Soup, Version Two

Makes about 8 servings

INGREDIENTS

2 pounds oxtails, or beef joint bones with some meat attached

3 to 4 teaspoons salt, or to taste

4 quarts water

2 inches fresh ginger root, peeled and sliced ¼ inch thick

1 inch fresh galanga root, peeled and sliced ¼ inch thick
  (if available)

3 to 4 kaffir lime leaves (if available)

1 beef bouillon cube (Asian-style or regular)

1 teaspoon MSG (optional)

½ pound beef tripe, sliced into 1-inch strips ¼ inch thick

1½ pounds chuck roast, cut into ½-inch cubes

1 cup quartered small bitter eggplant or 1 bitter melon,
  seeds removed, quartered and sliced ¼ inch thick

1 cup mixture coarsely chopped Thai basil leaves and
  Vietnamese coriander

PREPARATION

Rinse the oxtails or beef bones in cold water. Pat dry with paper towels and sprinkle with a little of the salt. In a large pot, bring the water to a full boil. Add the oxtails, ginger root, galanga root, lime leaves, 2 teaspoons of the salt, beef bouillon cube, and MSG (if desired). Add the beef tripe strips and lower the heat so the soup boils slowly. Cook for about 1 hour, skimming off any foamy residue as it accumulates. Taste the tripe to see if it is chewable. Continue to cook another hour or more, until the tripe is soft and chewy and the meat begins to fall off the bones. Add more water or canned beef broth as the liquid boils away, to maintain the level of broth. While the soup cooks, cut up the chuck roast and chop the herbs. Add the cubes of beef and cook the soup 20 more minutes. Skim off the fat that rises to the surface. Taste the soup and add more salt if necessary. Add the bitter eggplant or bitter melon and the herbs. Cook the soup for about 15 to 20 more minutes, until all of the beef is tender and the eggplant or melon is soft but not mushy.

Hmong Dried Beef
 *Nqaij Nyuj Qhuav*

In Laos, meat was often preserved by drying it in the hot open air. In America, to replicate that old-time flavor, most Hmong people dry beef in the oven, or they buy dried Asian beef jerky at Asian grocery stores. You must refrigerate and then use oven-dried or purchased Asian dried beef within a week, because it has not been treated with chemicals to allow for long-term storage. The drying method explained here works for beef or water buffalo.

INGREDIENTS

Several pounds lean, boneless beef or water buffalo
Salt
MSG (optional)

PREPARATION

Preheat the oven to 150 degrees. Cut the meat into strips about 1 inch thick by 10 inches long and remove any fat. Rub the meat all over with plenty of salt mixed with a little MSG (if desired). Put the boneless strips of beef on a wire rack in the oven with a pan below to catch drips. Keep the oven door ajar to allow the moisture to escape. Dry the meat for 6 to 8 hours. Cut a slit in the thickest part of the meat to make sure it is no longer pink in the middle before ending the drying process. When it is done, remove the meat from the oven and allow it to cool. Store in airtight containers in the refrigerator.

Hmong Funerals Hmoob Nteeg Tuag

THE MOST IMPORTANT RITUAL in Hmong culture is the funeral, known as *kev ploj tuag* (the way of death). The details vary slightly in different clans and sub-clans, and certain elements of traditional funerals are not present in Hmong Christian funerals. Hmong funeral practices have been passed down basically unchanged from generation to generation. The more senior and respected the deceased, the bigger the funeral. It is very important for all descendants and other family members of the deceased to participate in the many rituals associated with death. The funeral itself lasts for at least three days and nights, and additional activities happen before and after. Such a funeral can cost a family thousands of dollars, and much of the money goes to feed the multitude of guests.

To prepare their loved one for the journey to the afterlife, close family members bathe and dress the deceased in new clothes. Among other things, many pieces of traditional embroidery, *paj ntaub*, are placed with the body. Old customs dictate that the clothing and other items to be buried with the deceased be made only of natural fibers. At Christian funerals, candles burn, hymns are sung, and prayers are spoken. The haunting notes of a Hmong bamboo pipe, called a *qeej*, and the rhythmic *tum, tum, tum* of a special wooden drum constructed exclusively for the service pervade the atmosphere of a traditional funeral. Three times a day a gong signals meals for all attendees. The deceased is symbolically fed. Then everyone attending the funeral is also fed, with rice, beef or buffalo, chicken, beverages, fruits, and snacks. For both Christian and traditional funerals, it is common for a family to have one or more cows or buffalo butchered and cooked each day to feed the crowd. Cauldrons of boiling meat, simply flavored with salt and perhaps a few herbs, are prepared. Mountains of rice are steamed. Several people work full-time to cook and serve the meals. As with many rituals and events, food is an essential component contributing to the solidarity of the Hmong people.

Stir-Fried Dried Beef with Bamboo

Nqaij Nyuj Qhuav Kib Xyaw Ntsuag

Makes 4 servings

This dish takes only about 15 minutes to prepare. Use homemade dried meat as in the preceding recipe, or buy it from an Asian grocery store.

INGREDIENTS

    2 cups dried beef or water buffalo, sliced thin
    3 cups canned bamboo, sliced thin
    ½ stalk lemongrass, cut into 2-inch pieces
    2 green onions, white and green parts, cut into 2-inch pieces
    1 clove garlic, chopped
    1 tablespoon vegetable oil
    2 teaspoons salt
    2 teaspoons soy sauce
    ¼ teaspoon Mrs. Dash or MSG (optional)

PREPARATION

Slice the meat and bamboo, and chop the lemongrass, green onions, and garlic. Heat the oil in a medium-sized wok or skillet and then add the garlic. Stir-fry for a few seconds, until it is golden brown and fragrant. Add the beef, lemongrass, salt, soy sauce, and Mrs. Dash or MSG (if desired), and stir-fry for a few minutes. Next, add the bamboo and continue to stir-fry for a few more minutes. Finally, add the green onions. Stir to mix, and then serve hot.

Grilled Beef *Larb*

Laj Nqaij Nyuj Xaj los yog Suam

Makes 8 servings

All of the ingredients for this recipe can be purchased at a mainstream grocery store, except for the Toasted Sticky Rice Flour and the fresh galanga root. Fresh ginger root can be substituted for the galanga, but there is no substitution for toasted rice flour. See page 61 for a recipe, or buy it ready-made at an Asian grocery store. This recipe requires a very tender cut of Western-style beef, not water buffalo.

The beauty of *larb* is its freshness. To have everything ready at the same time, first grill the beef. While it cools, prepare the rest of the ingredients.

Larb, wrapped in a lettuce leaf, is eaten with accompanying herbs and vegetables. To serve the *larb*, pile lettuce leaves and the accompanying vegetables on a platter. Diners select the vegetables they like and assemble their own wrap; they can squeeze additional lime juice on their salad.

For a more traditional *larb* recipe that uses raw beef, see page 237.

INGREDIENTS

*2 pounds sirloin steak (any lean and tender boneless beef
  will work)*
Juice of 1 large or 2 small limes
2 teaspoons minced fresh galanga root (or ginger root)
1 teaspoon minced hot chili peppers or crushed hot chili flakes
½ teaspoon MSG (optional)
½ teaspoon salt
½ teaspoon sugar
1 tablespoon fish sauce
2 tablespoons Toasted Sticky Rice Flour (page 61)
*1 bunch green onions, white and green parts, thinly sliced
  on the diagonal*
1 bunch cilantro, coarsely chopped
2 heaping cups coarsely chopped mint
*Leaf lettuce, 2 or 3 leaves for each diner, washed and dried
  (for wraps)*

ACCOMPANIMENTS

Select several of these herbs and vegetables to accompany the *larb*. Wash, dry, and arrange on a serving tray.

*2 limes, cut on the sides and quartered (to add additional zing
  to wraps)*
Hot chili peppers, very thinly sliced on the diagonal
Thai basil sprigs
Arugula leaves
Watercress

Bean sprouts
Cucumbers, cut into sticks
Radishes, thinly sliced

PREPARATION

Broil or grill the steak to medium-rare. Allow the meat to cool to room temperature. Slice into strips about 2 inches long, ½ inch wide, and ¼ inch thick. Place the sliced meat in a glass bowl and squeeze the lime juice over it. Add the ginger or galanga, hot chili or chili flakes, MSG (if desired), salt, sugar, fish sauce, and toasted rice flour. Mix well. Add the green onion, cilantro, and mint. Toss the meat and herbs together gently.

This dish works well for a buffet. On a platter, arrange the lettuce leaves, each topped with a generous scoop of meat salad. Diners take a leaf or two, add additional herbs and vegetables, and squeeze lime juice and perhaps a sprinkle of fish sauce or thinly sliced hot chilies on top—delicious!

Beef Stew with Banana Blossoms and Eggplants

 *Kua Las ("Oh-La")*

Makes 12 servings

This old-fashioned dish would have been made with water buffalo in Laos, but in America, cooks use meat from a beef leg, including the tendon. Either fresh or dried meat works in this recipe. May Tong Yang, who shared this recipe, dries the meat as described in the Hmong Dried Beef recipe (page 158) before adding it to the stew. If possible, include fried pork or beef skin, to give the stew extra flavor. When neither is available, creative Hmong cooks sometimes add packaged pork rinds just before serving. This stew is thickened with rice that has been soaked in water and then pureed.

Non-Hmong people will find this recipe impractical, because it requires ingredients that are available only when a cow is butchered.

INGREDIENTS

2 cups sticky rice
4 pounds beef leg meat with tendons, or buffalo meat,
    fresh or oven-dried
4 teaspoons salt

4 quarts water

2 stalks lemongrass, tough outer leaves and roots removed,
cut into 3 inch sections

2 or 3 eggplants, each about 14 inches long (about 1½ pounds),
sliced

12 to 14 Thai eggplants, sliced

1 package (2½ ounces) dried black fungus, soaked and rinsed,
then chopped

2 pounds fresh green beans, washed and stem ends snipped off

2 banana blossoms

1 bunch green onions, white and green parts, washed and sliced
into 2-inch pieces on the diagonal

1 bunch fresh dill weed, chopped coarsely

1 cup Vietnamese coriander sprigs, chopped coarsely

1 cup culantro leaves, chopped coarsely

1 bunch Thai basil, chopped coarsely

½ package (1½ ounces) fried pork rinds (optional)

PREPARE THE MEAT AND BROTH

Put the uncooked sticky (sweet) rice in a bowl and cover it with warm water. Soak for at least 2 hours. After the rice and water combination is soft, put it in a blender and process until completely pureed. This mixture will be added to thicken the stew later.

Wash the meat. If you are using buffalo meat with skin, scrape the skin clean of hair. Put the meat in a pan and use 2 teaspoons of the salt to salt it well on all sides. Heat the oven broiler to 450 degrees and broil the meat about 10 inches from the elements for 15 to 20 minutes. Turn the meat over and continue to broil for 15 to 20 more minutes. The broiling process brings out the flavor of the meat. Remove from the oven and allow the meat to cool. When cool, cut it into long, 2-inch-thick strips. Then slice the strips into ¼-inch-thick pieces and set them aside. Bring the quarts of water to boil in a large pot and add the lemongrass. Allow it to simmer while preparing the vegetables.

PREPARE THE VEGETABLES

Wash the eggplants and remove the stems and blossom ends. Slice the eggplants and put them in a bowl of water with some salt, so they don't turn brown. Soak the dried black fungus in a bowl of warm water for

About "Oh-La"

WHAT HMONG PEOPLE refer to as "oh-la" (*kua las*) is a traditional Laotian stew, called *or lam* when it is made with dried buffalo and thickened with eggplants, or *or ho* when it is made with meat or fish and a variety of vegetables and herbs. The Lao word *ho* loosely translated means "to put in" (whatever you have), and that is just what Hmong people do when making "oh-la." Green beans, eggplants, okra, luffa squash, banana blossoms, and mushrooms are often used. The stew can be thickened with softened rice or eggplants, and meat choices include fresh or dried deer, beef, buffalo, or squirrel. Dried buffalo, beef, and pork skin are also common ingredients. Hmong herbs, including dill, cilantro, culantro, Vietnamese coriander, basil, and green onions, are added as well. There are as many ways to make "oh-la" as there are Hmong cooks.

May Chue Lawson, of Oregon City, opens a banana blossom and discards the immature bananas inside, which are too bitter to eat. The petals are used in Chicken Curry Noodle Soup (Khaub Poob) and "Oh-La" (Lao stew).

30 minutes. When it is soft, drain and rinse, and pinch the tough center out of each piece. Then chop the fungus coarsely. Wash the green beans, snip the ends off, and cut the beans into 2-inch lengths. Discard the tough outer petals of the banana blossoms and any finger-like immature bananas (they are far too bitter to eat). Tear the remaining softer petals into bite-sized pieces. Put the torn-up petals in a bowl of water with a little salt, to keep them from turning brown. Wash and chop the green onions, dill, Vietnamese coriander, culantro leaves, and Thai basil.

PREPARE THE STEW

Remove the lemongrass from the broth and discard. Add the meat (and skin, if used) to the simmering broth. Add the drained eggplants, black fungus, and banana blossom petals. Simmer for 30 to 40 minutes. Add the green beans, green onions, dill, Vietnamese coriander, culantro leaves, Thai basil, and the remaining 2 teaspoons of salt. Stir the stew to distribute the ingredients. Simmer until the beans are cooked through. Taste, and add more salt if needed. Add the pureed rice and stir well. If desired, add the fried pork rinds and stir them into the mixture. Although they become soggy, they add a nice robust flavor. Serve with lots of hot jasmine rice.

Recipe shared by May Tong Yang of Portland, Oregon

Beef and Luffa Squash with Basil

Nqaij Nyuj Xyaw Xwb Kuab

Makes 6 servings

This dish, like many Hmong recipes, is a cross between a stir-fry and a soup. Only Western-style beef is appropriate for this dish.

INGREDIENTS

1 pound very lean ground beef
1 teaspoon vegetable oil
1 bulb lemongrass (base of a stalk), cut into 3-inch pieces and smashed
1 luffa squash, skin removed, cut into ½-inch cubes to equal about 4 cups

2 hot Thai chili peppers (optional, depending upon
how much heat you want)
2 cups water
2 cups green basil leaves
1½ teaspoons salt
1 teaspoon coarse-ground black pepper

PREPARATION

Have all ingredients ready before beginning to cook. Heat the oil to
medium-hot in a deep wok. Add the ground beef and lemongrass and fry
2 minutes. Stir and break the meat apart as it cooks. Remove from heat and
spoon off the excess fat. Return to heat and add the squash cubes and hot
chilies. Add the water, basil leaves, salt, and black pepper. Bring the mixture
to a simmer and cover the pan with a lid. Simmer for a few minutes, until
the squash is soft but not mushy. Serve hot.

Sami's husband, Don, likes this soup with plenty of hot chili condiment
made with Thai eggplants.

Chili and Thai Eggplant Condiment
 *Kua Txob Lws Tuav*

Makes 1 cup sauce

INGREDIENTS

4 Thai eggplants, stems and blossoms removed,
thinly sliced and then chopped
1 teaspoon salt
4 small hot chilies, minced
¼ cup chopped cilantro
4 green onions, mostly green part, chopped
1½ tablespoons fish sauce
1 teaspoon sugar
Juice of 1 large lime

Slice the eggplants thinly after removing the stem and blossom ends. Toss with the salt in a colander; let stand 20 minutes. Rinse well; squeeze out the excess liquid. Finely chop the eggplants and put in a small bowl. Add the rest of the ingredients and mix well. Taste and adjust seasonings. Serve freshly made.

Beef Soup with Sour Bamboo

Nqaij Nyuj Hau Xyaw Ntsuag Qaub

Makes 8 to 10 servings

This quick and easy recipe can be made with fresh or dried beef.

INGREDIENTS

2 cups sour bamboo strips
2 pounds beef ribs, chopped into bite-sized pieces
15 cups water
1 stalk lemongrass, tough outer leaves and root removed,
    tied in a knot
1 tablespoon salt (use half if using dried or smoked beef)
1 teaspoon MSG (optional)

PREPARATION

In a colander, rinse the bamboo. Allow it to drain while you chop the beef. Rinse the chopped beef and put it into a medium pot with the 15 cups of water. Turn the heat to high. Add the lemongrass, salt, and MSG (if desired), and bring to a boil. Boil for about 15 to 20 minutes. Add the bamboo and continue to boil for about 10 more minutes. Taste, and add more salt if necessary. Discard the lemongrass and serve hot.

Beef Stir-Fried with Bitter Melon

Nqaij Nyuj Kib Xyaw Dib Iab

Makes 4 servings

INGREDIENTS

> 1 pound top round beef roast, cut into ½-inch pieces
>   (or substitute water buffalo)
> 3 cups bitter melon, seeds and pith removed, cut into
>   ½-inch pieces
> 2 tablespoons vegetable oil
> ½ tablespoon salt (use less if using dried beef)
> 1 teaspoon MSG (optional)
> 1 tablespoon oyster sauce

PREPARATION

Wash and cut up the beef (or water buffalo) and bitter melon. In a medium-sized wok, heat the oil to medium-hot. Add the meat and stir-fry for 2 to 3 minutes. Add the bitter melon, salt, MSG (if desired), and oyster sauce. Continue to stir for about 5 minutes, until the melon is soft but not mushy. Serve with Everyday Rice.

Beef Noodle Soup

Fawm (Phở)

Makes 8 servings

This recipe is a simple family version of the *Phở* found in "Cooking for a Crowd." Beef is the best meat choice.

INGREDIENTS FOR BROTH

> 4 pounds oxtails (available at most grocery stores)
> 6 quarts water
> 1 whole yellow onion
> 3 slices fresh or dried ginger root
> 4 star anise pods
> 1 tablespoon salt

2 tablespoons fish sauce

3 tablespoons canned beef paste for Phở soup (available at
   Asian grocery stores)

1 package Phở seasoning mix (available at Asian grocery stores)

1 package (7 ounces) frozen Vietnamese beef meatballs, thawed
   and cut in half

¼ pound tripe (sold precooked in Asian markets), rinsed, dried,
   and sliced very thinly

INGREDIENTS FOR THE SOUP BOWLS

2 pounds small, flat rice noodles, dried or fresh (usually labeled
   "Phở noodles")

1 pound beef tenderloin, sliced very thinly (ask the butcher to
   do this)

Cilantro sprigs, several for each bowl

4 green onions, white and green parts, sliced on the diagonal

Coarse-ground black pepper

ACCOMPANIMENTS

2 cups fresh bean sprouts

1 bunch basil sprigs

1 bunch culantro (duck-tongue or saw-leaf herb)

1 jalapeño pepper, sliced thinly on the diagonal

2 limes, cut into wedges

Coarse-ground black pepper

PREPARATION

Rinse the oxtails well. Put them and the water in a large pot and bring to a boil. Peel the papery layer off of the onion and add the onion to the pot. Add the ginger root, star anise, salt, fish sauce, beef paste, and seasoning mix. Lower the heat and simmer the broth for about 1 hour, skimming off any scum that rises to the surface.

While the broth cooks, clean and arrange the fresh vegetables and herbs on a serving platter.

Taste the broth and adjust the seasonings. With a slotted spoon, remove the solids from the broth, refrigerate the meat, and discard the rest of the solids. For a very clear broth, strain it through a fine sieve and return to the cooking pot. Continue to simmer the broth.

If using dried noodles, soak them in warm water for 20 to 30 minutes before cooking. Fresh noodles need only to be rinsed in cool water before cooking. Add the meatballs and tripe to the broth. Have everything ready to assemble the bowls of soup. Just before the soup is to be served, bring a large pot of water to a rolling boil. Using a sieve (a long-handled vertical sieve is best), lower a serving of noodles into the boiling water and cook for only 10 to 20 seconds; the noodles should still be a little chewy. Pull the sieve out of the water and allow the noodles to drain completely. Transfer a helping of the noodles to a large Asian soup bowl. (Asian soup bowls are very large and deep, to hold all of the ingredients and keep the soup hot. Many styles and patterns are available in Asian groceries.) Put 2 or 3 slices of the tenderloin on the noodles and top with a few cilantro sprigs, some of the sliced green onions, and a little black pepper. Ladle the broth into the bowl, completely covering the noodles; the hot broth cooks the tenderloin. Make sure a few meatballs and some of the tripe strips are in each serving. Continue to fill each bowl with the noodles, beef, cilantro, green onions, pepper, and hot broth. Serve immediately. Diners can add a squeeze of lime juice, herbs, and other condiments, including seasoning sauce, hoisin sauce, soy sauce, fish sauce, and Sriracha chili sauce. Eat *Phở* with chopsticks and a spoon. Sipping and slurping are definitely permissible.

Beef and String Bean Stir-Fry

Taum Ntev Kib Xyaw Nqaij Nyuj

Makes 8 servings

INGREDIENTS

2 teaspoons vegetable oil
4 cloves garlic, mashed with the side of a knife and then chopped
3 cups lean beef, sliced thinly
1 teaspoon salt
1 teaspoon coarse-ground black pepper
2 tablespoons oyster sauce
2 pounds string beans, stem ends removed, cut into 3-inch pieces
1 tomato, sliced thinly

Heat the oil to medium-hot. Add the garlic, beef, salt, black pepper, and oyster sauce. Stir-fry for about 1 minute. Add the green beans. Continue to stir-fry for a few more minutes, until the beans are bright green but still a little crunchy. Add the tomato slices. Stir-fry until the sauce uniformly coats the beef and beans. Serve hot with rice.

Beef and Tomato Stir-Fry

Nqaij Nyuj Kib Xyaw Txiv Lws Suav

Makes 3 to 4 servings

This dish will satisfy anyone who craves hot peppers. Adjust the level of heat by varying the number of chilies. Have all of the ingredients ready before beginning to cook.

INGREDIENTS

½ pound lean beef, cut into bite-sized pieces
¼ cup vegetable oil
2 hot Thai chili peppers, thinly sliced
½ tablespoon fish sauce
½ teaspoon salt
1 tablespoon seasoning powder (such as Mrs. Dash)
½ cabbage, cut into 1-inch cubes
4 green onions, white and green parts, cut into 3-inch pieces
½ bunch cilantro, cut into 3-inch pieces
½ teaspoon coarse-ground black pepper
2 medium-sized tomatoes, cut into bite-sized pieces

PREPARATION

Cut up the beef and vegetables. In a large wok, heat the vegetable oil to medium-hot. Add the beef cubes, hot peppers, fish sauce, salt, and seasoning powder. Stir-fry for 3 to 4 minutes. Add the cabbage, green onions, cilantro, and black pepper. Stir-fry for 2 to 3 more minutes. Add the tomatoes and continue to cook until the mixture is hot, the tomatoes have released their liquid, and the beef is just pink in the middle. Serve with jasmine rice and Hot Chili and Eggplant Sauce (page 88).

Ka's Journal

AS EVENING TURNED TO NIGHT in Hmong Laotian homes, parents and grandparents would wrap their sleepy children in blankets and tell them stories about brave Hmong kings and wild forest spirits, and talk about what it meant to be a good Hmong man or woman. In America, children are more apt to fall asleep watching television. Storytelling is a thing of the past, and written records are not a Hmong tradition. However, Mai Xee (pronounced "my see") Vang of Portland, Oregon, is lucky enough to have such a record, written in her mother's hand, to remind her of her Hmong heritage. Mai Xee's mother, Ka Kue, recorded the events of her life and lessons for her children in a little spiral-bound notebook that became the precious inheritance of Mai Xee and her siblings.

Ka was born in Khang Hong village, Laos, in 1946. Her childhood was typical. She learned to care for her younger siblings, to respect her elders, and to sew, cook, and clean. When Christian missionaries visited her village, she listened to them preach about Jesus and the Kingdom of God. Ka was a spiritual child, and she found that the quiet prayers of Christians made more sense to her than calling out to *Xob* (the God of Thunder), *Nyiaj Yig* (the original provider of shamanic instruments), and *Nraug Hli* (Lord Moon). Years later, Ka recorded these memories in her journal. She wrote about walks in the forest, wondering about the mystery of the wind, the earth, and the sky. She wrote about her dreams, sometimes frightening and sometimes prophetic. They were filled with wild animals, and trees with limbs that climbed to heaven and roots that spread forever; dreams so vivid that, as an adult, she drew pictures of them in her journal.

Ka fell in love with a handsome soldier. At age fifteen, she went with him to his home and became his bride. In six years, Ka and her husband were blessed with four children: Toua, Pang, Bee, and Mai Xee. Bee was a high-spirited little boy who loved to laugh and race around. One day, while running down a path, he stepped on a rusty nail. He grew ill and was carried to a hospital, but the deadly bacteria had taken control of his body. He died in his mother's arms.

Two more babies were born to Ka and her husband. Then more losses followed as Ka and her family, along with thousands of other Hmongs, fled their country and the life they knew. Eventually they immigrated to Oregon, where Ka continued to care for her family, surrounded now by unfamiliar sights and sounds.

Ka had no formal education, but she wanted to learn to read and write. Mai Xee, then fifteen years old, began to teach her. They struggled together over English lessons, but Ka discovered she loved her own language best, and she continued to learn to read and write Hmong even after Mai Xee married and left home. It was then that Ka began to keep her secret journal. She fell ill with acute kidney disease. Feeling her time was limited, Ka pressed on to record her sorrows and joys, and the important lessons she wanted her children never to forget. She died when she was only fifty-four. Her family gave her a Christian funeral, with many of the old Hmong customs woven in. Relatives came from across the United States and from France. Five cows were killed in her honor, and the meat was cooked to feed the mourners. For days Ka's family and friends burned candles and devoted themselves to sending her to the heavenly home she so strongly believed in.

After the funeral, Mai Xee and her siblings found Ka's journal, wrapped tightly in a Hmong skirt and concealed in a basket under her bed. Mai Xee cherishes the journal. Its words and pictures seem to say, "Although you are American, never forget that you are Hmong." Two pages are particularly sweet. On them, her mother carefully drew pictures of the food-preparation implements that Ka felt her children would need for a good Hmong life. Some of the words in her journal are misspelled. A few of the items pictured are not familiar to Mai Xee; they are artifacts from Hmong life in Laos.

Ka wrote (in Green Hmong [*Hmoob Leeg*]): *Peb ua neej nyob yuav tsum muaj tej nuav mas txhaj paub ua peb lub neej nyob. Nuav yog qov ob huv peb lub neej.* Roughly translated, her words mean, "In our lives, we must have these things in order to make a living."

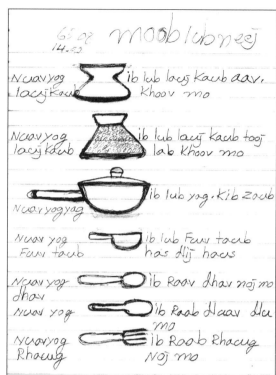

Pages from Ka Kue's journal.

Tug cug—a rice pounder

Lub zeb—a corn grinder (literally, a "round-shaped stone")

Lub ntoob (Lub thoob)—a bucket

Qov ntxhug (Qhov txos)—an oven (made of clay)

Xaab cub—a stove (made of clay)

Suav cib—a bamboo basket for draining rice

Vaab—a round bamboo winnowing tray

Chaus (Tshau)—a small strainer

Lauj kaub aav khoov mo(v)—a clay cooking pot for slow-cooking rice

Lauj kaub tooj lab khoov mo(v)—a copper/brass cooking pot for boiling rice

Yag kib zaub—a pot for stir-frying vegetables

Fuv taub has dlij haus (Fub taub has dlej haus)—a scoop (made of a dried pumpkin shell) to dip water for cooking or drinking

Dlav noj mo(v)—a spoon for eating

Dluav dlu mo(v)—a wooden paddle for stirring rice

Rhawg noj mo (Rawg noj mov)—a fork for eating

A Thai rice cooker with three kinds of rice commonly used in Hmong cooking: Regular or Jasmine Rice (*Txhuv Txua*), a component of Everyday Rice (*Noj Mov Txhua Hnub*), Purple Rice (*Txhuv Ntsav*), and Sticky Rice (*Txhuv Nplaum*) PAGES 51–53

ABOVE Rice Rolls (*Hmoov Ua Fawm Kauv*) (top) PAGE 63
and Party Egg Rolls (*Kab Yob*) PAGE 247

OPPOSITE Stuffed Bitter Melon (*Dib Iab Ntim Nqaij Hau Ua Kua*) PAGE 72

ABOVE Stir-Fried Baby Bok Choy with Pork Belly
(*Zaub Ntsuag Dawb Kib Xyaw Nqaij Npuas*) PAGE 79

OPPOSITE Fish *Larb* (*Laj Ntses*) (top) and Chicken *Larb* (*Laj Nqaij Qaib*)
PAGES 185 AND 107

OPPOSITE   Whole Fish Steamed in Banana Leaves (*Ntses Cub Xyaw Txuj Lom*)
PAGE 179

ABOVE   Chicken Curry Noodle Soup (*Khaub Poob*)   PAGE 255

ABOVE Green Papaya Salad (*Taub Ntoos Qaub*) PAGE 239

OPPOSITE Three-Color Dessert (*Nab Vam*) PAGES 224 AND 262

FOREGROUND Ripe Mango with Coconut Sticky Rice

(*Txiv Txhais Siav Xyaw Mov Plaum Nrog Kua Mav Phaub*) PAGE 217

BACKGROUND Tropical Fruit Cocktail with Almond Gelatin

(*Qab Zib Khov Xyaw Txiv Hmab Txiv Ntoo*) PAGE 220

Fish and Game ~
Ntses thiab Nqaij Nruab Nrag

Baked Striped Bass with Tomatoes and Herbs 178
Ntses Bass Ci

Whole Fish Steamed in Banana Leaves 179
Ntses Cub Xyaw Txuj Lom

Fried Whole Perch 181
Ntses Perch Kib

Fish Dip Sauce 182
Kua Txob Nab Pas

Grilled Stuffed Trout 183
Ntses Xwv

Steamed Fish Steaks with Ginger 184
Ntses Cub Xyaw Qhiav

Fish *Larb* 185
Laj Ntses

Trout Salad with Vermicelli Noodles 187
Trout Xav Lav Ntxuag Fawm

Deli-Style Fried Shrimp 188
Cw Muaj Taub Hau Kib

Stir-Fried Shrimp and Asparagus 190
Cw Kib Xyaw Asparagus

Chue's Famous Cracked Crab 193
Tswb Roob Ris Ncu

Sour and Spicy Seafood Soup 196
Khoom Nruab Deg Hau Ntsim thiab Qaub

Shrimp and Baby Octopus Hot and Sour Soup 197
Kua Ntsim Hau Xyaw Cw thiab Me Nyuam Octopus

Squab Soup with Asian Herbs 198
Nqaij Yij Hau Xyaw Txuj Lom

Sautéed or Broiled Quail/Frog Legs 199
Nqaij Ws/Nqaij Qav Ci los yog Kib

Fried Frog Legs with Coconut Cream 200
Ncej Paub Qav Nrog Kua Mav Phaub

Squirrel Stew with Eggplant ("Oh-La") 201
Nqaij Nas Hau Xyaw Txuj Lom

Venison Soup with Herbs 203
Nqaij Mos Lwj Hau Xyaw Txuj Lom

Cilantro Condiment for Game 204
Kua Txob Dos Zaub Txhwb

Fish and Game ⤳
Ntses thiab Nqaij Nruab Nrag

ELDER PHOUA HER, a shaman and medicine woman, from Suisun City, California, was born in a Laotian village located in the middle of a big jungle called *Naj Xaab*. She remembers:

> When I was a young girl, I walked with my parents to our plantations. Our mountains were very beautiful. I saw all kinds of birds, pheasants, squirrels, and monkeys that were calling and playing along the side of the road. There were many edible wild berries and plants. The streams were very fresh and the water tasted delicious. There were lots of fishes. The fishes that lived in the water stream tasted so good . . . My people's lives in the mountains depended on nature to help for hundreds of years.

The mountain forests of Laos, recalled with poignancy by Phoua, were populated by an amazing variety of wild animals. The Mekong River and its tributaries that flowed freely throughout the country were home to all kinds of aquatic life. Before the war disrupted their rural lifestyle, Hmong people trapped, hunted, and fished to help feed their families. The following recipes for fish and game reflect that bygone era.

The first four recipes are all variations on a theme: a whole fish is cooked with Hmong herbs and spices. These dishes reflect the individual tastes of different Hmong cooks.

Baked Striped Bass with Tomatoes and Herbs

◎◎ *Ntses Bass Ci*

Makes 4 servings

There are as many variations of this dish as there are Hmong cooks. The following recipe was shared by Chee Vang, of Denver, Colorado.

When Chee's son, Kong, was a young man, he liked to fish in the big reservoirs east of Denver and often brought home beautiful fresh striped bass for his mother to cook.

Chee likes to enhance the flavor of fish by first allowing it to sit, sprinkled with salt and pepper, for several hours in the refrigerator. To serve the fish for dinner, begin preparation in the morning. To serve the fish for breakfast, start the process the evening before.

INGREDIENTS

1 whole striped bass, about 1½ to 2 pounds

2 teaspoons salt

1 teaspoon coarse-ground black pepper

3 inches fresh ginger root, peeled and chopped fine

3 bulbs lemongrass, tough outer leaves and roots removed,
   sliced very fine

5 green onions, white and green parts, chopped fine

5 sprigs mint, chopped fine

1 to 2 fresh chili peppers, minced (depending upon desired heat)

1 large or 2 medium-sized tomatoes

1 tablespoon vegetable oil

2 cloves garlic, chopped

1 tablespoon oyster sauce

1 tablespoon Kwong Hung Seng Sauce (a sweet soybean sauce
   from Thailand)

PREPARATION

Gut, clean, and rinse the fish in cold water. With a fish scaler or a small, sharp knife, scrape off the scales by holding the fish firmly with one hand and scraping from tail to head. Pat the fish dry with paper towels. Cut 3 or 4 slits about halfway into the flesh and put the fish in a glass dish. Sprinkle the inside and outside of the fish with the salt and pepper. Cover the pan with aluminum foil and let sit in the refrigerator about 9 to 10 hours.

Preheat the oven to 400 degrees. Just before the fish is to be cooked, prepare the ginger, lemongrass, green onions, mint, and hot chilies. Put in a small bowl and set aside. Chop the tomatoes. Heat the vegetable oil to medium-high in a large, flat-bottomed skillet. Toss in the garlic and stir-fry until fragrant. Then add the chopped tomatoes and stir-fry just until limp. Add the fish and cook for about 5 minutes on each side or until the meat is opaque and white, but the fish has not browned. Add the ginger, lemongrass, green onions, mint, and chilies. Add the oyster sauce and the Kwong Hung Seng Sauce. Stir the herbs with a wooden spoon, being careful not to disturb the fish. Turn the fish over once to coat both sides with the mixture. Transfer the fish to a baking pan (the sauce is messy, so you may want to use a disposable pan). With a rubber scraper, scrape all of the sauce and herbs onto the fish. Cover the dish with a lid or aluminum foil and bake until the fish is hot throughout and all of the flavors are combined, about 20 minutes.

Recipe shared by Chee Vang of Denver, Colorado

Whole Fish Steamed in Banana Leaves
 Ntses Cub Xyaw Txuj Lom

Makes 4 servings

Co-author Sheng provided this recipe. It calls for many fresh Hmong herbs, such as culantro and Vietnamese coriander, but if you cannot find them all, use whatever you have available. The more you include, the more traditional the dish will taste. If you wish to double or triple the recipe, steam several packets of fish at a time.

INGREDIENTS

> *1 medium-sized catfish, perch, or striped bass*
> *1 tablespoon salt*
> *2 teaspoons black pepper*
> *1 teaspoon MSG (optional)*
> *¼ cup dried or fresh sliced galanga root (ginger root can be substituted)*
> *½ stalk lemongrass (the tender part), minced*

3 chili peppers, sliced very thinly on the diagonal

1 cup chopped cilantro

1 cup green onions, white and green parts, sliced on the diagonal

½ cup coarsely chopped mint

½ cup coarsely chopped Vietnamese coriander (luam laws)

½ cup coarsely chopped culantro

¼ cup whole kaffir lime leaves

6 cherry tomatoes

2 tablespoons Toasted Sticky Rice Flour (page 61)

2 or 3 medium-sized banana leaves

PREPARATION

Gut, clean, and rinse the fish, or, if purchased, have the butcher clean the fish for you. Pat the fish dry inside and out with paper towels and put it in a glass dish. Sprinkle with the salt, pepper, and MSG (if desired). Chop and slice all of the herbs and vegetables. Wash the banana leaves carefully. With a pair of scissors, trim off any tough, yellow edges. Dry the banana leaves gently with a paper towel, stroking along the grain to avoid tearing. Tear off a 3-foot-long section of heavy-duty wide aluminum foil and lay it on a flat work surface. Put 1 banana leaf on the foil and another leaf on top of the first, with the grains crossing each other. If the leaves are torn or if they are small, use an additional leaf, so the fish can be completely wrapped. Put the fish on the banana leaves. Pile the herbs and vegetables on top of and inside the fish. Sprinkle with the toasted rice flour. Wrap the banana leaves around the fish. Enclose the fish–banana leaf packet in the foil by bringing the long sides up and crimping them together and then folding them over to fit snug. Then bring the two short sides of the foil up and crimp them together on top of the packet. This seal will keep the liquid from dripping out while the fish cooks.

In the bottom part of a large, flat-bottomed steamer, bring several inches of water to boil. Lay the fish packet with the crimped side facing up in the steamer. Cover the pot and steam for 40 minutes.

When the fish is done, remove the packet and place on a serving platter. Carefully open the foil and discard. Open the banana leaves to expose the steamed fish, being careful to keep the sauce on the fish.

Fried Whole Perch

Ntses Perch Kib

Makes 4 servings

This combination of freshly caught fish, cilantro, and lime is typically Hmong. The fish are simply fried, complete with their heads and tails, until they are nice and crisp. They are then served topped with fresh herbs, surrounded with wedges of lime, and accompanied by Fish Dip Sauce. Diners can use their fingers or their forks to pull the tasty fish away from the bones.

Song, who contributed this recipe, says that walleye (a member of the perch family) is her family's favorite fish. When he has time, Song's husband fishes with their sons. Fish caught in the fall months have the best flavor.

INGREDIENTS

2 fresh fish (yellow perch or walleye), 1 pound each

1 tablespoon salt

1 cup vegetable oil

2 cloves garlic, minced

1 teaspoon coarse-ground black pepper

8 sprigs cilantro, cut into 2-inch pieces

4 green onions, white and green parts, shredded (use a hand-held
    green onion shredding tool available at Asian groceries)
    and then cut into 2-inch pieces

4 lemons, cut into wedges

PREPARATION

Clean the fish inside and out. Scrape the scales by holding the fish firmly with one hand and scraping from tail to head with a small, sharp knife or fish scaler. Cut 2 or 3 slits in the sides of the fish. Small fish require no slits. Sprinkle the salt on the fish and in the body cavity. In a frying pan large enough to hold both fish in a single layer, heat the oil to medium-hot. Add the garlic and sauté just until it is fragrant and golden. Add the fish and cook for 10 minutes on one side. Carefully turn them over and fry on the other side for 10 minutes. Remove the fish from the pan and arrange on a serving platter. Sprinkle with the black pepper. Squeeze a little lemon juice over the fish and top with cilantro and onion. Surround the fish with lemon wedges. Serve hot with plenty of jasmine rice and accompanied by Fish Dip Sauce (below).

Recipe shared by Song Moua of Eau Claire, Wisconsin

Fish Dip Sauce
Kua Txob Nab Pas

Makes 1 cup

This sauce is very hot.

INGREDIENTS

5 hot chili peppers, including seeds, minced
1 heaping tablespoon minced fresh lemongrass, tough outer leaves, base, and top few inches of leaves removed first
3 tablespoons chopped cilantro
3 tablespoons chopped green onions, white and green parts
Juice of 1 lemon
¼ teaspoon salt
½ teaspoon sugar
2 tablespoons fish sauce (Three Crabs brand is best)

PREPARATION

Mince the chilies and lemongrass. Chop the cilantro and green onions and put them all in a bowl. Add the lemon juice, salt, sugar, and fish sauce. Stir well until the salt and sugar are dissolved.

Grilled Stuffed Trout

Ntses Xwv

Makes 8 servings

INGREDIENTS FOR FISH

> *4 medium-sized whole trout, about 2 pounds each*
> *2 teaspoons salt*
> *1 teaspoon MSG (optional)*
> *Vegetable oil*

INGREDIENTS FOR STUFFING

> *1 tomato, sliced into wedges*
> *1 cup chopped cilantro*
> *4 green onions, white and green parts, chopped*
> *1 teaspoon chili flakes*

INGREDIENTS FOR BASTING SAUCE

> *2 cloves garlic, chopped*
> *2 tablespoons sugar, heated until liquid and mixed with*
> * 1 tablespoon water*
> *2 tablespoons oyster sauce*

PREPARATION

Buy cleaned trout or clean your own. Using a small, sharp knife, scrape off all of the scales from tail to head. Wash the fish under cold running water and pat dry with paper towels. Sprinkle the fish with the salt and MSG (if desired). Allow the salt to soak into the fish while you prepare the stuffing and make the basting sauce.

In a small saucepan, heat the sugar over low heat until it is liquid and golden. Remove from heat and carefully add the water, stirring constantly. Add the oyster sauce and set aside until ready to use.

Stuff the fish with the tomatoes, herbs, and chili flakes. If any herbs are left over, chop fine and add to the basting sauce. Using thick cotton string, tie the fish closed so the stuffing doesn't fall out. Put the fish side by side in a large, square grilling screen that holds them securely when closed and locked. Brush the fish with the vegetable oil on both sides. Grill over hot coals for about 15 minutes. Turn the fish over and continue to cook for about 10 more minutes. Brush the fish on both sides with the basting sauce and cook until the meat is solid. The sweet sauce burns easily, so apply it only at the very end of the cooking time. When the fish are cooked, open the grilling screen and carefully transfer them to a serving dish. Cut the strings, remove, and discard. Serve the fish hot, accompanied by a fresh green salad, grilled corn on the cob, and steamed rice.

Recipe shared by Lee Moua of Denver, Colorado

Steamed Fish Steaks with Ginger
Ntses Cub Xyaw Qhiav

Makes 4 servings

This dish demonstrates how young Hmong cooks mix Asian and Western influences. Serve it at a small dinner party; each serving looks like a gift. When the packets are unwrapped, the fragrant steam rises, giving diners a treat for the nose and taste buds as well as the eyes. Banana leaves, which can be purchased in Asian grocery stores, add a wonderful wild flavor. However, you can substitute parchment paper for the banana leaves. Almost any firm white fish can be substituted for the cod.

INGREDIENTS

1½ pounds fresh cod steaks, cut into 4 pieces
3-inch piece fresh ginger root, finely slivered
Juice of 1 lemon
6 large cloves garlic, finely slivered
2 tablespoons peanut oil
1 tablespoon sesame oil
3 tablespoons soy sauce
4 banana leaves or parchment paper (to wrap the fish in)
1 stalk lemongrass, 8 leaves removed and washed
   (to tie the fish packets)
¼ cup sesame seeds, for garnish

Wash and dry the fish fillets and set aside. Peel the ginger root, slice very thinly, and then cut into fine slivers. In a small bowl, marinate the ginger in the strained lemon juice. Slice the garlic and sliver it the same as the ginger. Heat the peanut and sesame oils in a small sauté pan over medium-low heat. Add the garlic. Cook 2 to 3 minutes, until the garlic is aromatic and light golden. Pour the garlic and oils into the bowl with the lemon juice and ginger. Add the soy sauce and mix well. Wipe out the sauté pan with a paper towel. Fry the sesame seeds in the dry pan over medium heat, until golden brown. Remove from the heat and set aside.

Lay a 10-by-12-inch piece of banana leaf on a flat surface. You may need to overlap smaller pieces to make the square. Put 1 piece of the fish in the center of the leaf. Top with ¼ of the lemon juice and ginger mixture and ¼ of the sesame seeds. Wrap the fish the way you would wrap a sandwich in waxed paper. Repeat for the remaining pieces of fish. Tie each fish package securely with the lemongrass or with string. Steam the packages for 20 minutes. Remove from the steamer with tongs and untie the lemongrass. Place each serving on a plate and carefully open each packet.

Fish *Larb*

Laj Ntses

Makes 10 servings

This dish is great to make with fresh-caught fish. When you add the lime juice to the raw fish, the acid from the limes changes the structure of the fish's proteins, essentially "cooking" the fish without using heat. During the process, the chopped fish becomes opaque and white.

As an entrée, *larb* is customarily offered to diners in a serving bowl accompanied by a plate filled with lettuce leaves and fresh herbs, such as cilantro and mint. Each person scoops a portion onto a lettuce leaf, adds herbs according to taste, and then rolls up the lettuce leaf to eat. For a beautiful appetizer, roll individual servings into lettuce or wild betel leaves and serve them on a platter.

Before you prepare the fish, carefully wash, dry, and chop the herbs. If you can't get all of the herbs listed, use what you can find. However, you must include mint, cilantro, green onions, and Vietnamese coriander.

Measure herbs loosely packed into the measuring cup, and use only fresh, blemish-free herbs. Chop them by hand, because using a food processor will bruise them.

This recipe is easy to halve or double.

INGREDIENTS

3 pounds fresh salmon, striped bass, or trout fillets
Juice of 4 limes (more if the limes are small)
½ cup minced galanga
1 stalk lemongrass, tough outer leaves, root, and top several inches
  removed before mincing
2 hot chili peppers, minced (or more, if you want more heat)
⅓ to ½ cup chopped fresh spearmint (sometimes called
  Asian mint)
⅓ to ½ cup chopped cilantro, stems and leaves
1 bunch green onions, green and white parts, chopped
⅓ to ½ cup chopped Vietnamese coriander
⅓ to ½ cup chopped culantro (duck-tongue or saw-leaf herb)
⅓ to ½ cup finely chopped rice paddy herb (often labeled with its
  Vietnamese name, Rau Om, in Asian grocery stores)
⅓ to ½ cup chopped Thai basil
¼ cup chopped Chinese boxthorn leaves
2 tablespoons fish sauce
1 teaspoon salt (or 1½ teaspoons if you do not use MSG)
1 teaspoon MSG (optional)
½ teaspoon ground Sichuan pepper
½ cup Toasted Sticky Rice Flour (page 61)

PREPARATION

Clean and fillet the fish, or buy already-filleted fish. Remove the skin. On a large, clean chopping board, chop the fish with a heavy knife or cleaver. As you chop, fold the fish over on itself. Continue to fold and chop until the fish is very finely chopped. Put the fish in a glass or ceramic bowl and squeeze the lime juice over it. Using your hands, mix the lime juice into the fish. After it is thoroughly mixed and the fish has turned opaque, squeeze the lime juice out of the fish one handful at a time and transfer the fish to another glass or ceramic bowl. Discard the squeezed-out juice. Add the galanga, lemongrass, chilies, mint, cilantro, green onions, Vietnamese coriander, culantro, rice paddy herb, Thai basil, and Chinese boxthorn. Sprinkle the fish sauce, salt, MSG (if desired), Sichuan pepper, and rice flour over the mixture. With gloved hands, toss and mix everything together. Serve immediately with additional fresh herbs and lettuce leaves.

Trout Salad with Vermicelli Noodles
Trout Xav Lav Ntxuag Fawm

Makes 6 servings

This recipe is almost fat-free. Use a fresh trout, or for a tasty variation, try smoked trout purchased from a grocery store.

INGREDIENTS

> *1 fresh trout, about 2½ to 3 pounds (or smoked trout)*
> *1 bag (3½ ounces) vermicelli noodles*
> *1 bunch fresh cilantro, coarsely chopped*
> *1 bunch fresh mint, coarsely chopped*
> *4 green onions, white and green parts, coarsely chopped*
> *Small bunch Vietnamese coriander (optional), coarsely chopped*
> *2 to 3 small cucumbers, cut lengthwise and then sliced*
> *Small head red leaf lettuce*

PREPARATION

Buy a whole cleaned trout, or use a freshly caught fish that has been cleaned and gutted. Remove the head and tail and scrape off the scales by holding the fish firmly with one hand and scraping from tail to head with a small, sharp knife or fish scaler. Rinse the fish under cold running water and pat dry with paper towels. Wrap the fish in aluminum foil and bake in an oven preheated to 350 degrees. Bake the fish for about 30 minutes, or until the meat is solid and flaky. While the fish is cooking, prepare the noodles and vegetables. Soak the noodles in hot water for about 20 minutes, until they are soft and pliable. Drain them and cut into 1-inch lengths with a pair of kitchen shears. Put the prepared vermicelli in a large bowl. Wash the cilantro, mint, green onions, and Vietnamese coriander (if available), chop the herbs coarsely, and add them to the bowl. Cut the cucumbers in half lengthwise and then slice. Wash the lettuce and separate the leaves.

When the fish is done, allow it to cool and then remove the meat from the bones. Break the fish into flakes with your fingers and add the meat to the bowl of noodles and herbs. Add the cucumbers to the mix and toss lightly. Serve with lettuce leaves and a side dish of Hot Chili Condiment (page 87).

Deli-Style Fried Shrimp
Cw Muaj Taub Hau Kib

Makes 6 servings

This shrimp dish is closely associated with the Hmong because you can find it at Hmong-operated delicatessens. However, the Hmong borrowed it from other Asian cultures and made it their own. And no wonder—these salty, peppery shrimp are impossible to resist.

INGREDIENTS

> 2 pounds medium-sized head-on shrimp
> 1½ tablespoons salt
> 1 teaspoon seasoning salt
> ½ tablespoon MSG (optional)
> 2 teaspoons Sriracha chili sauce
> ½ tablespoon coarse-ground black pepper
> 4 cups corn oil
> 1 cup tempura batter mix (dry, not mixed with water)
> 1 medium-sized white onion, cut in half and sliced into
>   ½-inch wedges
> 2 jalapeño peppers, thinly sliced

PREPARATION

Put the shrimp in a colander. Rinse them well under cold running water and pick off the long feelers. Allow the shrimp to drain and then put them in a bowl. Add the salts, MSG (if desired), chili sauce, and black pepper. Toss until the shrimp are evenly coated with the seasonings. Heat the oil over high heat in a deep wok or skillet. Sprinkle the tempura batter mix on the shrimp, tossing them as you do to lightly coat them. Fry the shrimp, a few at a time, for about 3 minutes in the hot oil. Do not crowd the shrimp, or they will stick together. With a mesh scoop, lift the shrimp out of the oil and put on a serving platter. After all of the shrimp are cooked, fry the onion and jalapeños briefly in the same oil. Do not overcook the onions, to keep them from becoming limp. Garnish the shrimp with the onions and jalapeños. Serve hot on a platter.

Sheng's daughter Angie prepares Deli-Style Fried Shrimp.

Stir-Fried Shrimp and Asparagus

Cw Kib Xyaw Asparagus

Makes 6 servings

This recipe blends Eastern and Western ingredients and techniques. In landlocked Laos, freshwater shrimp were caught in the many free-flowing rivers. In America, saltwater shrimp are the norm. Asparagus was not grown in Laos, but since Hmong cooks revel in green vegetables of all kinds, asparagus has been happily incorporated into their menus. Sometimes fresh asparagus shoots are simply steamed. However, this recipe pairs asparagus with shrimp and gives them an Asian treatment.

INGREDIENTS

2 pounds large fresh shrimp, shells and veins removed

3 pounds fresh asparagus, tough ends removed, cut into
   2-inch lengths

1 tablespoon vegetable oil

¼ cup chopped fresh garlic

¼ pound ground pork

¼ cup oyster sauce

4 green onions, white and green parts, shredded and cut into
   3-inch lengths (green onion shredding tools are available at
   Asian groceries)

PREPARATION

Clean the shrimp and asparagus. Cut the asparagus into 2-inch lengths. Set both aside. In a large wok, heat the oil to medium and sauté the garlic until it is soft and aromatic. Add the ground pork and sauté, stirring constantly, to break the pork apart. Toss in the shrimp and asparagus and continue to stir-fry for about 5 minutes. Cover the pan and allow the mixture to steam in its own juices for about 5 minutes. Remove the cover, add the oyster sauce, and stir to mix everything together. Transfer to a serving dish, garnish with the green onion, and serve immediately.

Catching Crabs in Laos

WHEN CHUE YANG lived in Eureka, California, her family would go crabbing in the ocean. She created the cracked crab recipe included in this book. Everyone says that they are "finger-lickin' good!"

Chue explains how she learned about crabs.

When I was a girl in Laos, almost a teenager, one morning my sister and I were going to our farm. We were walking down by a creek that ran through the forest away from my village. The sky turned very dark and I heard the rurrrrrr, rurrrrrr, rurrrrrrr *of thunder. It was the day of the first big rain after the dry season. The rain poured down and made everything very wet. That made all of the crabs that lived in the bank by the creek want to come out of the ground. My sister and I decided to catch the crabs, and we did. We picked them up with our hands and put them into two big bags. We carried them home on our backs, and*

*Chue Yang, of Sacramento, California, has a reputation
for making "finger-lickin' good" cracked crab.*

they tried to bite us on our shoulders and necks. These crabs were small and very red. My mother made the fire hot in our charcoal stove. We scrubbed the crabs and put them on the coals. That is how we cooked them in Laos.

Sometimes when I wanted to catch crabs I would go to a big rock that stuck out over the river. I sat down on the rock and looked down into the water. A line of big bubbles was coming up. Plip, plip, plip; that would be from a crab. There was a rainbow in the bubbles. My uncles said that rainbows meant there was a mermaid in the water. I believed them. I was only a little afraid of the water, but I liked to catch crabs and eat them.

Another story we heard in Laos explains why all crabs taste salty. On the back of a crab's shell is a design that looks just like a horse's hoofprint. Long ago crab shells were plain, but one time the northern Chinese people came down on their horses to do business with the people in the south. The crabs came to meet them, but the horses stepped on the crabs' shells and broke them. The crabs complained because they were hurt, so the Chinese people said that they would put medicine on them. Instead, the Chinese poured salt on their wounds and the salt went into the crabs' bodies.

Chue's Famous Cracked Crab

Tswb Roob Ris Ncu

Makes 16 servings (½ crab per person)

In Laos, good cooks made a tasty sauce to thickly coat cracked crab by combining "crab butter" (the viscera found inside the crab's top shell) and the crab's eggs, when present, with rice liquor, coconut milk, herbs, and spices. In most regions of America, harvesting female crabs is illegal, so egg whites can substitute for the crab eggs. Before using crab butter, check with the U.S. Department of Agriculture online or by phone to find out the current status of toxins in shellfish in your region. If levels of domoic acid are too high, clams and oysters as well as crab butter are not safe to eat. However, even under those circumstances crabmeat is not affected and is safe to eat.

Serve this crab warm, or for a special treat on a hot evening, chill the crab after it is cooked and then serve it with cold sticky rice. Set the table with lots of paper napkins and plenty of ice water and cold beer. Dinner guests can't worry about being neat, because the only way to truly enjoy this dish is to lick the sauce from your fingers and the shells, and to dig out every bit of the juicy, salty meat.

This recipe is not for the fainthearted, as it requires you to dismember live crabs. The dish tastes best this way, but if you want to enjoy the flavor without the trouble of live crabs, a simplified version of Chue's recipe using crabs that have already been cleaned and cooked follows this recipe.

INGREDIENTS

8 large fresh, live Dungeness crabs

2 tablespoons vegetable oil

3 cloves garlic, smashed and chopped

2 teaspoons salt

2 stalks lemongrass, tough outer leaves and ends removed,
each tied in a knot

5 large slices fresh or dried galanga

2 inches fresh ginger, peeled and sliced

¼ cup rice liquor (to reduce the "fishy" smell)

"Crab butter" from inside the crab shell

3 egg whites

1 bundle (about 10) fresh green onions, chopped

1 bunch cilantro, chopped to equal 1 cup

1 can (13½ ounces) coconut milk
1 jar (8 ounces) crab paste with bean oil
1 tablespoon hot and sour paste
1 Asian-style fish bouillon cube (optional)
3 sprigs Vietnamese coriander, chopped coarsely

PREPARATION

Scrub the crabs carefully with a stiff brush under cold running water. Re-move the upper shell from each crab, retaining the shell with the visceral material that adheres to the inside of it (the crab butter). Set the top shells aside. Break away, remove, and discard the gills, mouth, apron, and any dirty areas of the crabs' bodies. Using a sharp knife, cut each crab in half down the middle, and then cut in half again between the legs. Remove the smallest end leg segment from each of the four back legs, as these parts contain no meat. With the dull side of your knife, smack the large claws and leg sections once to crack the shell. This break makes it easier to remove the meat when eating the crab, and it also allows the seasonings to coat some of the meat inside.

In a very large pot, over medium-high heat, stir-fry the smashed garlic in the oil for 1 or 2 minutes, until it is golden and fragrant. Add the salt, lemongrass, galanga, and ginger. Add the crab quarters and rice liquor and stir-fry for about 10 minutes. Reduce the heat to medium-low and cover the pot with a well-fitting lid. Allow the crab to steam while you prepare the sauce.

If you are using the crab butter, remove it from inside the top shells. Discard the shells. Put the crab butter in a colander and rinse very well under cold running water. Drain, and then place the crab butter and egg whites in a bowl. Next, add the green onions, cilantro, and coconut milk. Finally, add the crab paste, hot and sour paste, and Asian fish bouillon (if desired). Stir the mixture very well and then pour it over the crab in the pot. Turn the heat up to medium. Stir the crab quarters until every part is coated with the sauce. Taste the sauce, and add more salt and rice liquor if needed. Stir once more and then cover the pot again. Steam until the crabmeat is thoroughly cooked, about 15 minutes. Remove and discard the lemongrass, ginger, and galanga.

Serve the crab, covered with the sauce, on a large platter.

Recipe shared by Chue Yang of Sacramento, California

Cracked Crab, Version Two

Makes 4 servings

Although our non-Asian friends love to eat Chue's luscious cracked crab, they suggested that we develop a Hmong-style recipe using crabs that are bought cooked and cleaned.

INGREDIENTS

2 large cooked and cleaned Dungeness crabs (available at mainstream grocery stores or fish markets)
2 tablespoons vegetable oil
2 cloves garlic, smashed and chopped
1 bulb lemongrass (base of a stalk), cut into ¼-inch slices
2 inches fresh ginger, peeled and cut into ¼-inch slices
2 teaspoons salt
¼ cup rice liquor
½ cup coconut milk
¼ cup Sriracha chili sauce
3 green onions, white and green parts, chopped
¼ cup chopped cilantro
Juice of 1 lime

PREPARATION

Measure and prepare all of the ingredients before beginning to cook. The already cleaned and cooked crabs will be cold and will only need to be heated up. Cut each crab into 4 pieces and crack the shells as in the preceding recipe. Set the crab aside. In a large wok, over medium-high heat, stir-fry the smashed garlic in the oil for a minute, until it is golden and fragrant. Add the lemongrass, ginger, and salt and stir-fry for another minute. Add the rice liquor, coconut milk, and chili sauce and stir until all of the ingredients are combined. Toss the crab with the sauce. Then cover with a lid. After the crab is heated through (about 10 minutes), remove the lid, stir again, and add the green onions, cilantro, and lime juice. Stir and cook a few more minutes until all of the flavors are combined. Discard the lemongrass and ginger. Serve hot.

Sour and Spicy Seafood Soup

Khoom Nruab Deg Hau Ntsim thiab Qaub

Makes 6 servings

This soup can be made with any firm-fleshed fish steaks, such as catfish or striped bass, or substitute a variety of seafood, including prawns, squid pieces, and clams. Most Asian markets stock sour soup base mix. It comes in either 1.4-ounce packets of powder or 16-ounce cans of thick liquid. Use about 1 tablespoon of the liquid for each serving. Watercress gives the soup a special bitter bite. However, non-Asians may prefer the dish without it.

INGREDIENTS

    2 pounds prepared seafood (see preparation instructions below)
    10 cups water
    ¼ cup dried or fresh sliced galanga
    1 stalk lemongrass, tough outer leaves and root removed, bulb smashed with the flat edge of a knife, and cut into 3-inch pieces
    4 to 6 kaffir lime leaves
    1½ teaspoons salt
    ½ teaspoon black pepper
    ½ teaspoon MSG (optional)
    2 to 3 hot Thai chili peppers, white and green parts, sliced thinly on the diagonal (optional)
    1 package (40 grams or 1.4 ounces) sour soup base mix
    ¼ cup green onion, white and green parts, sliced on the diagonal
    2 medium-sized tomatoes, cut into 1-inch cubes
    1 pound clean watercress
    Juice of 1 lime

PREPARATION

Clean and cut the fish steaks into 2-inch squares. If using prawns, wash, and remove their shells and intestinal veins. If using squid, cut into 1-inch pieces. If using clams, scrub well and rinse several times in cold running water. Set the seafood aside and bring the water to boil in a medium-sized stockpot. Add the galanga, lemongrass, lime leaves, salt, black pepper, MSG, and chilies (if desired). Add the soup base mix. Simmer the broth for about 10 minutes. Add the seafood and green onion, and then simmer just until the fish is solid and the prawns are pink, about 5 to 7 minutes. Discard clams with shells that do not open when cooked. Add the tomatoes and watercress, and then squeeze the lime juice into the broth. Simmer for a few more minutes. Serve hot.

Shrimp and Baby Octopus Hot and Sour Soup

Kua Ntsim Hau Xyaw Cw thiab Me Nyuam Octopus

Makes 4 servings

Jars of hot and sour paste can be purchased in Asian grocery stores. Garland chrysanthemum greens are popular in Japanese cuisine. When young, they have a delicate, almost perfumed taste. They become bitter as they mature.

INGREDIENTS

*10 to 12 small baby octopi, about ½ pound (available in most
    Asian and some mainstream grocery stores)*
8 medium-sized shrimp, heads and tails left on but shells peeled
6 cups water
1 teaspoon salt
⅛ teaspoon MSG (optional)
2 slices fresh or dried galanga or ginger
3-inch stalk lemongrass (the tender part)
1 tablespoon hot and sour paste
1 shallot, sliced thinly on the diagonal
4 to 5 small okra pods
½ cup pineapple cubes
2 cups young garland chrysanthemum greens

PREPARATION

Clean and prepare the octopi and shrimp, then set aside. Bring the water to a boil in a pot. Add the salt, MSG (if desired), galanga or ginger, lemongrass, hot and sour paste, and shallot. Reduce the heat slightly, so the water is gently boiling. Add the okra and cook for a few minutes, until the pods are soft but not mushy. Add the octopi, shrimp, pineapple, and garland chrysanthemum. Simmer until the shrimp is pink and the octopi are solid and white, about 6 to 8 minutes.

Squab Soup with Asian Herbs
Nqaij Yij Hau Xyaw Txuj Lom

Makes 4 servings

Squabs are young, commercially raised pigeons available at some gourmet grocery stores and Asian markets and online from game meat sellers. Hmong cooks favor squab because its dark, rich meat remains moist and tender when cooked, and its flavor has an accent of the wild. Squab reminds older Hmong people of the small game birds that were hunted in Laos. This dish brings together many typically Hmong flavors.

Be careful not to overcook squab. The meat is quite red, even when fully cooked.

INGREDIENTS

2 medium-sized squabs

¼ cup vegetable oil

2 cloves garlic, peeled and chopped

½ cup peeled, sliced ginger

1 stalk lemongrass, tough outer leaves and root removed,
   chopped into 3-inch pieces

1 chicken bouillon cube (Asian-style [contains MSG] or regular)

2 teaspoons salt

1 teaspoon coarse-ground black pepper

5 cups water

1 cup chopped tomato

1 cup basil, cut into 3-inch lengths

1 cup baby dill, cut into 3-inch lengths

1 cup cilantro, cut into 3-inch lengths

1 cup green onion, white and green parts, cut into 3-inch lengths

1 cup spearmint sprigs (found in Asian markets),
   cut into 2-to-3-inch lengths

1 cup Vietnamese coriander, cut into 2-to-3-inch lengths

1 jalapeño pepper, sliced into 4 pieces (if you like it hot)

PREPARATION

Wash the squabs and pat dry with paper towels. Using a cleaver, cut the squabs into bite-sized pieces, chopping right through the bones. Heat the oil over medium heat in a large wok. Add the garlic, ginger, and lemongrass.

Stir-fry for 1 or 2 minutes, just until the garlic begins to brown. Add the squab meat, chicken bouillon, salt, and black pepper. Stir-fry for about 5 minutes. Add the water and bring to a simmer. Cover and cook for 10 minutes. Add the chopped tomato. Cover the soup again and return it to a boil. Then add the basil, dill, cilantro, green onion, mint, Vietnamese coriander, and sliced jalapeño pepper (if desired). Cook for 5 more minutes uncovered. Ladle into soup bowls and serve hot.

Sautéed or Broiled Quail/Frog Legs
Nqaij Ws/Nqaij Qav Ci los yog Kib

Makes 6 servings

In Laos, boys practiced their hunting skills using slingshots. Any small bird they shot became part of the dinner menu. In America, some men enjoy hunting quail, but most of the time quail are purchased frozen at an Asian or gourmet market, six to a package.

Be careful not to overcook these little birds.

INGREDIENTS

6 quail or 3 pounds frog legs
1 tablespoon salt (or less, to taste)
½ teaspoon Accent or MSG (optional)
1 teaspoon coarse-ground black pepper
1 teaspoon Sriracha chili sauce
1 cup vegetable oil
2 cloves garlic, finely chopped

PREPARATION

If the quail are frozen, thaw them completely. Cut the birds down the middle, through the breastbone, and rinse well in cold running water. Pat dry with paper towels and flatten each bird, so that the halves are butterflied. Put the quail in a bowl. Add the salt, Accent or MSG (if desired), black pepper, and chili sauce. With your hands, mix and rub the seasonings all over the birds. To sauté the quail, heat the oil in a large frying pan until it is medium-hot. Sauté the garlic for 1 or 2 minutes, until it is golden brown. Add as many quail to the pan as will fit. Fry the quail for about

14 to 18 minutes, turning them occasionally so that all surfaces become brown and crispy. Drain on paper towels, and sauté the remaining birds. Arrange the birds on a platter and serve with rice and hot chili condiment. To broil the quail, add the garlic to the seasonings and then place the quail on an oiled broiling pan. Broil at 400 degrees, 8 inches from the heat, for about 15 minutes, turning the birds over once so they brown on both sides.

Frog legs can be prepared in the same way as quail. Use 3 pounds of frog legs. To keep them from becoming dry when cooking, add 2 tablespoons of oil or melted butter to the seasonings, chili sauce, and garlic, and marinate them in the mixture for 30 minutes prior to cooking. Cook as for quail.

Fried Frog Legs with Coconut Cream
Ncej Paub Qav Nrog Kua Mav Phaub

Makes 4 servings

In Laos, frogs were plentiful. On warm evenings, young men visited streams and ponds to catch as many frogs as they could. The frogs were then gutted, cleaned, put on a spit, and grilled whole over a wood fire. Sometimes they were chopped up and made into soup. In the West, whole frogs and frog legs can be found in the frozen section of large Asian grocery stores. Some markets sell live frogs. The butcher will dress them according to order.

The following recipe has a Vietnamese flair, thanks to contributor True Ly's mother, who was Hmong Vietnamese.

INGREDIENTS

> 2 pounds jumbo skinned frog legs
> ½ stalk lemongrass (the tender part), minced (to equal ¼ cup)
> 2 fresh red chili peppers, chopped
> 2 green onions, white and green parts, chopped
> 3 cloves garlic, crushed
> 1½ teaspoons sugar
> 1 teaspoon salt
> 2 tablespoons fish sauce
> 2 ounces bean thread noodles
> 2 tablespoons vegetable oil
> 1 small yellow onion, chopped

½ cup water

1 chicken bouillon cube (Asian-style [contains MSG] or regular)

½ cup coconut cream

Fresh-ground black pepper

Cilantro sprigs, for garnish

PREPARATION

Rinse the frog legs and put them in a glass container. Using a mortar and pestle, pound the lemongrass, chilies, green onions, garlic, sugar, salt, and 1 tablespoon of the fish sauce until the ingredients are well mixed and mashed. Mix the paste with the frog legs, cover, and marinate in the refrigerator for 30 minutes. Soak the bean thread noodles in warm water for 20 minutes, then drain and cut into 2-inch lengths. Heat the oil in a wok over high heat. Add the onion and sauté until soft but not brown. Add the frog legs and sauté for 10 to 12 minutes, turning to brown all sides. Add the water and bouillon cube, and bring to a boil. Reduce the heat, cover, and simmer for 15 minutes. Uncover the wok and add the coconut cream and remaining fish sauce. Cook gently for 10 more minutes. Add the bean thread noodles and bring to a boil. Remove from the heat. Sprinkle with black pepper and garnish with cilantro sprigs. Serve hot with rice.

Recipe shared by True Ly on a visit from Paris to Portland, Oregon

Squirrel Stew with Eggplant ("Oh-La")
 *Nqaij Nas Hau Xyaw Txuj Lom*

Makes 6 servings

This recipe is unusual for a modern cookbook, but it is included because many Hmong men enjoy hunting wild squirrels. In a Hmong home, no meat is ever wasted, so Hmong women still make this old-fashioned stew. Squirrel is not available in any store, and hunting squirrel requires a license.

INGREDIENTS

1 large squirrel, fur removed, cleaned and chopped into
  bite-sized pieces

1 bottle dark beer

1 tablespoon vegetable oil

2 cloves garlic, finely chopped

1 stalk lemongrass, tough outer leaves and root removed,
  then smashed and cut into 3-inch pieces

3 to 4 small red chili peppers

6 kaffir lime leaves

1 tablespoon chopped fresh galanga

1 tablespoon chopped fresh ginger

5 cups water

½ tablespoon salt

½ tablespoon fish sauce

¼ teaspoon MSG (optional)

6 to 7 whole okra pods

8 small Thai eggplants

1 cup loosely packed basil leaves

¼ teaspoon ground Sichuan pepper

HERBS

Use as many of these herbs, chopped into 1-inch pieces,
as are available. Other Hmong herbs can be added as well.

1 bunch culantro

6 Chinese boxthorn leaves

6 green onions

½ bunch cilantro

1 bunch mint

1 bunch Vietnamese coriander

PREPARATION

To remove some of the squirrel's wild flavor, soak the squirrel meat in the beer for several hours, and then drain. Clean and cut the herbs into 1-inch pieces and set them aside. In a large soup pan, heat the oil to medium-high. Add the garlic, lemongrass, chilies, lime leaves, galanga, and ginger. Stir for about a minute until the mixture is fragrant, and then add the meat. Continue to cook and stir for several minutes. Add the water, salt, fish sauce, and MSG (if desired). Cover and let simmer for about 10 minutes. Add the okra, eggplants, basil, and Sichuan pepper. Cover again and continue to cook for about another 10 minutes, stirring occasionally. Add the herbs and let the stew simmer about 5 or 10 more minutes. Serve accompanied by warm rice—a wonderful winter meal.

Venison Soup with Herbs

◎◎ *Nqaij Mos Lwj Hau Xyaw Txuj Lom*

Makes 8 servings

Venison gets a typical Hmong treatment in this recipe.

INGREDIENTS

8 cups water
1 stalk lemongrass, tough outer leaves and root removed
¼ cup thinly sliced fresh galanga
¼ cup thinly sliced fresh ginger
4 cups venison, cut in 2-inch cubes (rib meat is good,
* with some bones)*
1½ tablespoons salt
¼ teaspoon MSG (optional)
5 whole kaffir lime leaves
4 to 5 Chinese boxthorn leaves (optional)
¼ cup culantro
¼ cup mint
¼ cup Vietnamese coriander
¼ cup cilantro sprigs
¼ cup coarsely chopped green onion, white and green parts
1 cup whole basil leaves
¼ teaspoon black pepper

PREPARATION

Put the water in a medium-sized pot. Add the lemongrass, galanga, and ginger. Bring to a boil, then add the venison, salt, and MSG (if desired). Simmer for 10 minutes. Add the kaffir lime and Chinese boxthorn leaves (if desired). Cook for another 5 to 10 minutes. Then add the rest of the herbs and the black pepper. Ladle into individual bowls and serve hot with Cilantro Condiment for Game (below).

Cilantro Condiment for Game

Kua Txob Dos Zaub Txhwb

Makes 5 cups, enough for a large crowd

When served with game, chili condiments do not include fish sauce.

INGREDIENTS

> ¼ cup hot Thai chili peppers, chopped
> 1 to 1½ tablespoons salt
> ½ tablespoon MSG (optional)
> 3 cups coarsely chopped cilantro
> 2 cups coarsely chopped green onion, white and green parts
> 2 tablespoons lime or lemon juice

PREPARATION

Put the chilies, salt, and MSG (if desired) into a medium-sized mortar and pound with the pestle. Add the cilantro, green onion, and lime or lemon juice, and continue to pound until all the ingredients are mixed. Serve in a small bowl with game meat dishes.

Beverages and Desserts ↽
Dej Qab Zib thiab Khoom Txom Ncauj

Rice Juice 209
Kua Ntxhai

Cucumber Juice 209
Kua Dib

Pumpkin Juice 209
Kua Taub

Green Vegetable Juice 210
Kua Zaub Tsuag

Tamarind Bark Tea 210
Kua Ntoo Txiv Quav Miv

Mommy Nyaj's Rice Wine Dessert 211
Mommy Nyaj Mov Cawv Qab Zib

Fruit—Sour, Salty, Hot, and Sweet 216
Txiv Hmab Txiv Ntoo—Qaub, Qab Ntsev, Kub, thiab Qab Zib

Young Coconuts 217
Kua Mav Phaub Mos

Sweet Tamarind 217
Txiv Quav Miv Qab Zib

Ripe Mango with Coconut Sticky Rice 217
Txiv Txhais Siav Xyaw Mov Plaum Nrog Kua Mav Phaub

Homemade Coconut Milk 218
Kua Mav Phaub Ua Tom Tsev

Coconut Gelatin 219
Qab Zib Khov Xyaw Kua Mav Phaub

Tropical Fruit Cocktail with Almond Gelatin 220
Qab Zib Khov Xyaw Txiv Hmab Txiv Ntoo

Cassava Root and Plantain Tapioca Dessert 221
Nab Vam thiab Qos Ntoo Ntug Qab Zib

Sweet Pumpkin with Coconut 222
Taub Cub Xyaw Mav Phaub thiab Qab Zib

Corn Tapioca Pudding 222
Nab Vam Qab Zib Hau Xyaw Pob Kws

Three-Color Dessert 224
Nab Vam

"Frog Eggs" 225
"Qe Qav" Noob Zaub Txwg Theem

Tapioca Pearl Drinks (Crystal Delights) 226
Qe Qav Hlaws Xyaw Dej Qab Zib

Beverages and Desserts ～
Dej Qab Zib thiab Khoom Txom Ncauj

Hmong celebrations always include the icy-cold, coconut-rich Three-Color Dessert (Nab Vam).

GUESTS TO A HMONG AMERICAN HOME are always offered something to eat and drink. Nowadays the beverage is likely to be an American or Asian soft drink, a sweet coffee beverage, or a bottle of water. In Laotian villages, purchased beverages were not always an option. To quench thirst, everyone drank water carried from a nearby stream. At meals, people drank the liquids in which meat and vegetables were cooked. Teas brewed from a variety of health-giving plant material were common beverages for adults. Men drank homemade beer and wine, and occasionally hard liquor. When the war in Southeast Asia disrupted village life, and Hmong people moved into urban areas, they added store-bought beverages and fancy dessert-beverages, such as "bubble tea" and Three-Color Dessert (*Nab Vam*), to their menus.

Eating a sweet dish at the end of a meal is not a Hmong custom. People enjoy sweet beverages and other treats, but never at the end of a meal, because then everyone is too full. Fresh fruit and sweet dishes are usually eaten as snacks, or to stave off hunger while a meal is being prepared.

This chapter opens with five old-fashioned beverages.

Distilled and Brewed Alcohol Cawv Cub

LEE XIONG of Monroe, North Carolina, remembers making alcohol in Laos:

When we lived in Laos, it was not easy to get liquor. We didn't have a liquor store just down the street. We had to make our own, and it was a difficult job, but we have to have good wine for our ancestors—we give the ancestors our very best food and drink. One thing was important to remember when we made liquor: don't talk about it. If you did, the alcohol would not be any good.

Many older men and women remember how hard it was to distill alcohol by hand. Sweet (sticky) rice was the preferred grain, although corn also was used. First, the grain was ground and then cooked. An alternative was to accumulate and use leftover sticky rice. Then the grain was mixed with distiller's yeast and allowed to ferment undisturbed for several weeks. Homemade distilling equipment included a low earthenware stove, a large wooden barrel, two large woks (one to hold boiling water and one for cold water), a steaming tray (to hold the mash above the boiling water), a ladle to collect the distilled spirits, and a tube to siphon off the finished alcohol. Making liquor was a hot, labor-intensive endeavor. The fire underneath the apparatus needed constant stoking. Cold water—needed to make the steam condense—usually came from a nearby stream and had to be carried in buckets to the still.

Beer and wine were made from natural ingredients as well.

Traditional marriage, funeral, and New Year's rites all require sips of alcohol. In America, Hmong people like to use vodka or brandy for these formal occasions. Hmong men sometimes end a festive evening by toasting one another.

Rice Juice

 *Kua Ntxhai*

The water that is used to soak rice a second time is called rice juice (*kua ntxhai*). It is warm, nutritious, and never wasted. People drink it and make pickles with it.

Cucumber Juice

 *Kua Dib*

Cool and refreshing, this dish is made and eaten by women as they prepare dinner. Any cucumbers will work, but best are the large, ripe, yellow Hmong cucumbers (*dib laus*). To make cucumber juice, cut a cucumber in half lengthwise. Scrape the flesh from the cucumber into a bowl using the handle end of a metal Asian soup spoon. Add sugar to taste and combine with ice, if desired. Sip the pulpy mixture from a spoon.

Pumpkin Juice

 *Kua Taub*

Part sweet treat and part beverage, a glass of pumpkin juice is set at each place by many old-fashioned cooks. To make pumpkin juice, select a mature Hmong pumpkin. This medium-sized, round pumpkin has a splotchy green and gray-orange shell with super-sweet, bright yellow-orange flesh inside. A regular pumpkin can also be used.

First, use a sharp knife to slice away the peel. Then cut the pumpkin into quarters and discard the seeds and stringy pulp. Cut the solid flesh into 1-inch cubes. Cook the cubes in boiling water until they are soft but still hold their shape. Turn off the heat and add sugar to taste, and stir until the sugar is completely dissolved. The drink should be sweet, but the sugar shouldn't overpower the wonderful pumpkin flavor. To serve, ladle several cubes of pumpkin and the cooking water into a glass for each guest. Serve warm or at room temperature.

Green Vegetable Juice

◎◎ *Kua Zaub Tsuag*

To American southerners, this beverage is "pot liquor." Hmong people call it "green vegetable juice." It is served like pumpkin juice, but it is not sweetened. In the summer, when fresh garden greens are bountiful, Hmong Americans cook and freeze them for winter. To prepare Green Vegetable Juice, put 4 cups of frozen, cooked greens, such as bamboo mustard cabbage or oilseed rape, in 2 quarts of water and bring to a boil. Ladle the water and some greens into each glass. Serve warm or at room temperature.

Tamarind Bark Tea

◎◎ *Kua Ntoo Txiv Quav Miv*

The leaves, bark, and roots of many plants have health-maintaining and healing qualities. Tamarind bark tea aids digestion and reduces a woman's nausea in the first months of pregnancy.

Hmong herbalists often sell tamarind bark at farmers' markets. Buy 2 or 3 pieces.

Boil 4 cups of water in a saucepan. Add the bark pieces and simmer for about 15 minutes. Turn the heat off, and when the tea is cool enough to drink, pour some of the liquid into a cup. Never add sugar to medicinal teas.

Most medicinal teas and tonics (*tshuaj yej*) are made from a mixture of several natural ingredients. Many elderly Hmong people know what to use for various common ailments. Herbalists package combinations to treat specific problems such as aching joints, hay fever symptoms, listlessness, constipation, and skin rashes. At farmers' markets and New Year's fairs, herbalists offer a variety of items, some imported from Southeast Asia and others locally grown, and they help customers find the proper treatments.

A Hmong woman sells a wide array of traditional medicinal plant products at the Sacramento New Year's celebration.

Mommy Nyaj's Rice Wine Dessert

Mommy Nyaj Mov Cawv Qab Zib

Makes 5 to 7 servings

Fhoua Chee Yang is the head pastry chef and Kao Yee Xiong is the business manager of Cakes by Fhoua, the Hmong bakery they own in St. Paul, Minnesota. They created this dessert specifically for this cookbook. It combines Fhoua's modern Cordon Bleu patisserie training with Kao Yee's mother's age-old recipe for fermented sticky rice. Fhoua and Kao Yee use a sponge cake for this dish because it is light and absorbs the rice wine and caramelized syrup without losing its fine texture; however, ladyfingers are an acceptable substitution. The rice topping takes four days to prepare, so plan in advance when you want to serve this slightly alcoholic, delicious cake.

Cakes by Fhoua

BOTH FHOUA CHEE YANG and her cousin and business partner, Kao Yee Xiong, have made a conscious decision to focus on their bakery, Cakes by Fhoua, instead of beginning their own families. After high school, they attended college, and Fhoua went on to training at the Minneapolis/St. Paul Cordon Bleu Patisserie and Baking School. Often, when they were teased and urged by their elders to get married and have children, their choice was not comfortable or easy. Yet Kao Yee's mother, Chia Yang, contributed the start-up money to buy the commercial ovens, mixers, and other equipment they needed. Many other friends and family members withheld approval until the business was up and running. Fhoua says:

> *The naysayers made us that much more determined to follow our dream and to succeed. They helped us achieve our goal almost as much as those people who gave us encouragement. That is the way Hmong society works. It challenges young people to prove themselves.*
>
> *Being successful is all part of understanding who you are. Being Hmong is unique, because we are a people without a country. That fact has made us adaptable. We must become leaders wherever we are. Each of the people in my generation is finding for themselves a successful place within our own society and also in the greater society. We are responsible for our own success and that of our society. That often means we need to be good examples for our elders as well as good role models for the younger kids.*

Early each morning Fhoua spends two or three hours in the rented commercial kitchen baking cakes, croissants, muffins, and cookies and decorating made-to-order cakes. Cakes by Fhoua caters to a diverse clientele that includes Somalians, African Americans, Vietnamese, Hmong, and Caucasians. One goal has been to make their products appealing to Hmong elders. Fhoua uses a commercial nondairy cream in some of her icings and fillings because of Asians' lactose intolerance. She also has developed recipes with low sugar content for Hmong elders who desire less-sweet products. Fhoua decorates cakes according to her customers' whims, drawing pictures freehand with icing. In addition, she

Fhoua Yang (left) and Kao Yee Xiong, of St. Paul, Minnesota, are business partners. Together they operate the city's first Hmong bakery. This cake, called Mommy Nyaj's Rice Wine Dessert, is one of their many Hmong-themed creations.

uses images generated on a special printer that uses edible ink on edible paper. That way, any image, including photographs, can be applied to a cake. Fhoua also caters to Hmong aesthetic preferences. She offers a traditionally dressed Hmong couple wedding cake topper and often pipes designs inspired by colorful Hmong embroidery (*paj ntaub*) onto her cakes.

Kao Yee explains:

We are constantly promoting our products and often have to explain why our products are better than the ones from Safeway or Sam's Club. After we explain that our cakes are always fresh, never frozen, and that the customer can have any decoration they choose, we gain repeat customers.

Fhoua and Kao Yee still don't have time to devote to husbands, in-laws, and children. They both have second full-time jobs, because all proceeds from the bakery get funneled back into their business. For now, their goal is growing the bakery; soon they hope to open a storefront and mail-order business. They realize that the path they have chosen is very different from the ones their parents chose. Fhoua states, "We do things differently than our elders, but we have the same values."

The Rice Wine Dessert that Fhoua and Kao Yee created for this cookbook reflects a mixture of old and new. The fermented rice recipe has been passed down in Hmong households from generation to generation, and it is combined with contemporary ingredients using recently acquired skills. Thus the dessert represents the balance of modern and traditional elements of Fhoua and Kao Yee's world. For more information about Cakes by Fhoua, go to their Web site: http://www.cakesbyfhoua.com.

> *2 cups uncooked sticky rice (short- or long-grain)*
> *1 cup water*
> *½ ball Chinese distiller's yeast (available in Asian groceries)*

OTHER INGREDIENTS

> *½ cup sugar*
> *¼ cup water*
> *1 pint heavy whipping cream*
> *3 tablespoons powdered sugar*
> *1 cup sweetened coconut flakes*
> *1 sponge cake, 7-inch diameter (Chinese bakeries usually sell*
> *undecorated sponge cakes)*

PREPARATION

DAY 1: PREPARE THE FERMENTED RICE

Soak the rice in warm water for at least 3 hours. Cook the rice using a Thai rice steamer. Spread the cooked rice on a large piece of freezer paper on a flat surface and allow to cool completely. Put the cooled rice in an airtight container and sprinkle with the cup of water. Crush the yeast ball until it is a fine powder and sprinkle about half of it over the rice. Mix gently, secure the lid, and let sit in a warm place for four days. When the fermentation process is done, a slightly alcoholic liquid will have accumulated in the rice. The mixture should smell mellow and taste sweet. If it becomes pungent, it is overfermented.

DAY 4: ASSEMBLE THE DESSERT

Refrigerate the fermented sticky rice.

Make caramelized syrup: Put the ½ cup granulated sugar into a small, heavy saucepan and heat on low, stirring constantly, until the sugar melts and becomes light brown. Remove the pan from the stove. Slowly and carefully add the ¼ cup water, again stirring constantly, until the sugar is completely dissolved. Be very careful because the hot melted sugar will bubble and pop. Allow the syrup to cool completely.

Prepare the whipped cream: In a mixing bowl, whip the cream at high speed, adding the powdered sugar a little at a time. Whip the cream and sugar until soft peaks form. With a rubber spatula, gently fold in ¾ cup of the coconut flakes.

Assemble the dessert: Buy or bake a sponge cake. Slice it into two layers and brush away any crumbs. Make a decorative pattern on a flat cake plate by drizzling zigzags of the caramelized sugar back and forth across it. Place the bottom cake layer in the center of the plate. Using a basting brush, brush some of the rice liquid on the bottom layer, allowing it to soak into the cake. Spread whipped cream on the bottom layer, about ½ inch thick. Position the second cake layer on top. Brush more of the rice liquid on the top layer. Spread the rest of the whipped cream on top. Using a small ice cream scoop, scoop little balls of the fermented rice onto the top of the cake. Drizzle with more caramelized sugar and then sprinkle with the remaining coconut. (Eliminate the coconut if you don't like it.)

If you substitute ladyfingers, make individual servings on small plates instead, placing two ladyfingers over the drizzled caramelized sugar. Brush with the rice liquid, and top with whipped cream and a small scoop of fermented rice. Sprinkle with coconut. Do the same for the other servings.

Recipe shared by Fhoua Chee Yang and Kao Yee Xiong of St. Paul, Minnesota

Fruit—Sour, Salty, Hot, and Sweet

Txiv Hmab Txiv Ntoo—Qaub, Qab Ntsev, Kub, thiab Qab Zib

American cooks almost always pair fruit with sugar, but Hmong people like to eat fruits that are naturally sour, such as unripe plums and mangos, and fruits that have been enhanced with salt, lime juice, and hot chilies. Somxai and Souzana Vue, of Denver, offer this quick recipe for a snack that combines these flavors.

Peel and slice a green (unripe) mango (*ntsuab txiv txhais*). Then sprinkle the slices with fresh lime juice and a mixture of salt, minced hot chilies, and a touch of sugar. For a shortcut, look in the seasonings section of an Asian grocery store for a spice jar labeled "Chili and Salt Seasoning for Fruits" (*Bột Muối Ớt*). Sprinkle any tart, crunchy fruit, such as Gravenstein apples or Asian pears, with lime juice and some of the seasoning. Or try the mixture with persimmons (*txiv qhaib nplaig*), another Hmong favorite fruit.

Young Coconuts

Kua Mav Phaub Mos

Tables piled high with rough, white coconuts appear at every Hmong New Year's celebration. These are young coconuts. Although their interior is filled with juice and meat, they are not completely mature. Select one, and the vendor will chop off the top in one stroke with a heavy knife and hand the coconut back to you, complete with a straw for sipping the delicate juice. After all the juice is gone, peel the coconut meat from inside the shell and eat it. The flesh of a new coconut is soft and slightly sweet.

Sweet Tamarind

Txiv Quav Miv Qab Zib

Sweet tamarind is another favorite snack for Hmong people, especially for the elderly. These fat, long, bumpy brown seedpods can be purchased in a box or by the pound in Asian grocery stores. The soft, slightly gooey edible part is inside the brittle shell that surrounds the seeds. Sweet tamarind has a mild flavor, not unlike a ripe fig. It is considered good for digestion.

Ripe Mango with Coconut Sticky Rice

Txiv Txhais Siav Xyaw Mov Plaum Nrog Kua Mav Phaub

Makes 8 servings

When Hmong people eat something sweet, they like it very sweet. Nothing is sweeter and richer than sticky rice infused with coconut milk and sugar, and no fruit packs more tart-sweet flavor than a bright orange, ripe mango. This dessert appears on the menu in most Hmong, Thai, and Lao restaurants.

You can make coconut milk by hand (see below), and it tastes better than canned or powdered coconut milk, but all three options produce a flavorful result. If you use canned coconut milk, shake the can well before you open it, because the thick cream rises to the top. Be sure the consistency is uniform before adding the milk to the other ingredients.

3 cups uncooked sticky rice

1 can (14 ounces) coconut milk, or substitute either
homemade coconut milk or powdered coconut milk
reconstituted with water

½ cup powdered sugar

½ cup grated sweetened coconut

4 ripe mangos, peeled and sliced

Mint sprigs, for garnish

PREPARATION

Soak the sticky rice overnight in cool water. Drain, and then steam in a Thai basket steamer. While the rice is cooking, heat the coconut milk in a saucepan. Stir in the powdered sugar. Bring the mixture just to a boil. Stir the hot mixture until the sugar is completely dissolved, and then remove the pan from the heat. When the rice is soft, turn it out into a large bowl. Pour the coconut mixture over the rice and fold it into the rice. Stir in the grated coconut. Slice the mangos. For each serving, arrange a scoop of coconut sticky rice on a dessert plate with the slices of half a mango fanned out around the rice. Garnish with the sprigs of mint. Serve at room temperature.

Homemade Coconut Milk

Kua Mav Phaub Ua Tom Tsev

1 large coconut makes 2 cups of coconut milk

Coconut milk is not the clear, watery liquid in the middle of a fresh coconut; that liquid is called coconut juice. Coconut milk is the thick, creamy extraction from finely grated coconut meat. In one way coconut milk is like whole cow's milk: it separates after sitting for a while. The thickest part, called coconut cream, rises to the top. Making coconut milk isn't hard. Simply follow these steps.

First, pierce two of the three soft "eyes" at the top of the coconut with a sharp instrument and drain the juice. Then place the coconut on a cement or stone surface and crack it open with a hammer. Taste the meat to make sure it is sweet. If it smells or tastes bad, discard that coconut and try another one. With a paring knife, pry the white meat from inside the shell and chop it into small, uniform pieces. Put half of the coconut meat into a blender and add about 1 cup of boiling water. Secure the lid and blend on high for about 30 seconds. Line a large sieve with two layers of fine cheesecloth and set the sieve over a deep bowl. Pour the blended coconut mixture into the cheesecloth so the liquid drips into the bowl. Blend the other half of the chopped coconut the same way and add it to the sieve. When the mixture is cool enough to handle, gather the edges of the cheesecloth and wring hard to extract as much liquid as possible. One coconut makes about 2 cups of coconut milk. Transfer the coconut milk to a glass container. Coconut milk does not keep well, so it must be used right away or refrigerated. If a recipe calls for coconut cream, allow the coconut milk to sit until it separates, and then use the thickest third of the liquid. If a recipe calls for coconut milk, mix well and use the needed amount.

Coconut Gelatin
Qab Zib Khov Xyaw Kua Mav Phaub

Makes one 8-by-8-inch pan of gelatin (16 big cubes)

INGREDIENTS

2¼ cups water
1 cup sugar
1 tablespoon agar-agar powder
1 cup coconut milk (homemade, canned, or reconstituted
    powdered)

PREPARATION

Mix the water and sugar together in a medium-sized saucepan. Sprinkle in the agar-agar powder and stir with a wire whisk. Bring the water to a simmer, and then cook and stir for about 5 minutes. Add the coconut milk and stir briskly with the whisk until the mixture returns to a low boil.

Pour the liquid into an 8-by-8-inch pan, and allow to cool and gel (you don't need to refrigerate). Cut into 16 cubes and stack on a serving plate. Diners pick up the cubes with their fingers.

Tropical Fruit Cocktail with Almond Gelatin

Qab Zib Khov Xyaw Txiv Hmab Txiv Ntoo

Makes about 14 servings, 1 cup each

INGREDIENTS

> 2 ¼ cups water
> ½ cup sugar
> ¼ teaspoon salt
> 1 tablespoon agar-agar powder
> 1 can (14 ounces) sweetened condensed milk
> 1 tablespoon almond extract
> 6 cups bite-sized pieces tropical fruit, canned or fresh
> Mint sprigs, for garnish

PREPARATION

Make the gelatin as in the previous recipe, but reduce the sugar to ½ cup, add the salt, and substitute sweetened condensed milk for the coconut milk. Add the almond extract after the mixture has returned to a boil. Pour the gelatin into two 8-by-8-inch pans and allow to gel. Select 3 or 4 kinds of tropical fruit, either canned or fresh. Lychee nuts, ripe mangos, ripe papayas, pineapple, Asian pears, jackfruit, and strawberries are good choices. You will need about 6 cups of bite-sized fruit pieces. Peel the fruits that have skins, and cut all into bite-sized pieces. Put the pieces in a large bowl along with the syrup from the canned fruit (if you use canned). Just before serving, cut the gelatin into bite-sized diamond shapes and add it to the fruit. Serve in individual parfait glasses or bowls. Add some of the syrup to each serving. Garnish with a sprig of mint (and half a strawberry, if available).

Cassava Root and Plantain Tapioca Dessert

◎◎ *Nab Vam thiab Qos Ntoo Ntug Qab Zib*

Makes 6 servings

Plantains look like large bananas, but they have a much firmer texture. Both plantains and cassava roots should be peeled and steamed before eating.

INGREDIENTS

1 large ripe plantain, peeled, cut into ½-inch cubes
1 cassava root (about same size as plantain), peeled,
 cut into ½-inch cubes
1 lemon, for juice
½ cup small tapioca pearls
6 cups water (to cook tapioca)
1 can (14 ounces) coconut cream
1 cup sugar
½ teaspoon salt

PREPARATION

Peel the plantain and cut it into ½-inch cubes. Put the cubes in a bowl and cover with water. Squeeze the lemon juice into the water. With a sharp knife or vegetable peeler, peel the cassava root and cut away any damaged areas. Cut the cassava into ½-inch cubes and add them to the bowl of water. Soak for 10 minutes. Drain the plantain and cassava cubes. Steam them about 15 minutes over boiling water, until they are soft but still retain their shape. In a saucepan, bring the water to a boil and slowly add the tapioca pearls. When the tapioca rises to the surface, turn the heat down to maintain a low boil and cover the pan. Cook the tapioca for 10 minutes, stirring occasionally. Turn off the heat and allow to sit for 5 minutes. Using a sieve, rinse the tapioca pearls gently in tap water until the water runs clear. While the tapioca is cooking, mix the coconut cream, sugar, and salt together in another saucepan. Bring the mixture to a boil and then turn the heat down to keep it hot but not boiling. After the plantain and cassava root have finished steaming, add them to the coconut mixture. Add the drained tapioca. Stir well and allow the dessert to sit for 20 minutes. Serve warm or at room temperature in individual custard cups.

Sweet Pumpkin with Coconut

Taub Cub Xyaw Mav Phaub thiab Qab Zib

Makes about 20 pieces

INGREDIENTS

1 Hmong pumpkin (winter pumpkin with gray-green skin
  and bright orange flesh)
2 cups powdered sugar
1½ cups grated coconut, packaged or fresh

PREPARATION

Wash the pumpkin with soap and water and rinse well. With a sharp knife,
cut the pumpkin in half, and then scrape out the seeds and stringy pulp and
discard along with the stem. Do not cut away the shell. Cut the pumpkin
into pieces about 3 inches square. Pile the pumpkin squares into a steamer
and steam until the pumpkin flesh is soft but not mushy. Allow to cool
enough to handle. Carefully lift the pumpkin pieces out of the steamer and
onto a work surface, flesh side up. Sprinkle each square first with powdered
sugar and then with grated coconut. Serve warm.

Corn Tapioca Pudding

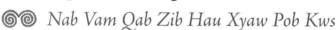 *Nab Vam Qab Zib Hau Xyaw Pob Kws*

Makes 8 servings

Sweet corn is often an ingredient in Hmong desserts. You can use fresh or
canned corn for this dish, or substitute mung beans (see the variation at
the end of this recipe).

INGREDIENTS

1 cup small tapioca pearls
16 cups water, divided (to cook tapioca)
2 cups corn kernels, canned or fresh
1½ cups water (to cook corn)
1 can (13½ or 14 ounces) coconut milk

⅔ cup sugar
½ teaspoon salt
Mint leaves, for garnish (optional)

If you use fresh corn, remove all of the silk and cut the kernels off the cobs. If you use canned corn, drain the kernels before measuring.

To reduce the gooeyness of the tapioca pearls, boil them in two steps. Bring 8 cups of the water to boil in a medium-sized saucepan. Add the tapioca pearls, stirring as you do so. When the tapioca rises to the top, reduce the heat so the water just simmers. Cook the tapioca for 7 minutes, stirring occasionally. Drain the tapioca and rinse twice in cold water. At the same time, discard the original water and bring 8 more cups of water to a boil. Pour the partly cooked tapioca pearls into the water and return it to a boil. Cook for 5 to 7 minutes. Turn off the heat and allow the tapioca to sit in the water for 10 minutes more. Drain the tapioca and rinse as before. Now, bring 1½ cups water to a boil. Add the corn and cook for 2 minutes. Add the coconut milk, sugar, and salt and return to a low boil. Cook for about 5 minutes. Add the tapioca pearls. Stir, and return the pudding to a boil. Remove from the heat and allow to cool at least 30 minutes before serving. Serve cool or cold in individual pudding cups. If desired, garnish with mint leaves.

Mung Bean Variation

Soak 1½ cups dried mung beans in warm water overnight. Drain, rinse well, and drain again. Then steam the mung beans over boiling water for 15 minutes. Substitute the steamed mung beans for the corn in the above recipe.

Three-Color Dessert

Nab Vam

Makes 10 servings

The following recipe is adapted from the more complex recipe that serves 30 to 40 people found in "Cooking for a Crowd." This version is good for everyday use, because it begins with what is best described as a *"nab vam kit"* that you can buy at some Asian grocery stores. These plastic bags usually include premade starch strings and sometimes sweet corn or soybeans and sweetened coconut milk. Strips and small cubes of agar-agar gelatin (prepared as in the Coconut Gelatin recipe above) can be used instead of the starch strings.

INGREDIENTS

1½ cups sugar

1 cup water

1 package medium-sized tapioca pearls, bright or pastel colors

2 packages ready-made starch strings in coconut milk

3 or 4 kinds fresh or canned fruit (jackfruit, palm nuts, coconut
   jelly, young coconut, attap fruit, or fresh fruit or melons),
   cut into bite-sized pieces, to equal about 6 cups

5 cups small ice cubes

PREPARATION

Make sugar syrup by cooking the sugar over medium-low heat until it melts and becomes a caramel color. Slowly add the water and mix until the sugar is completely dissolved. Remove from the heat and allow to cool. Cook the tapioca pearls according to package instructions. Then drain them and rinse gently in a sieve under tap water until the water runs clear. Transfer to a bowl. Cover the tapioca with the syrup. Open the canned fruit, and drain and discard the liquid. Cut large chunks into bite-sized pieces. With a melon baller, scoop the melon into little balls. Pour the starch strings and coconut milk into a large bowl. Add the tapioca pearls and the fruit. Then add the ice cubes. Ladle into individual bowls to serve.

"Frog Eggs"
"Qe Qav" Noob Zaub Txwg Theem

Makes about 3 cups

Non-Hmongs might be startled by what look like tiny eggs in their dessert, but the Hmong consider a dish more fun to eat if it contains these small balls that are soft on the outside and crunchy in the middle. Some people call them "frog eggs." They are added to Three-Color Dessert, Tapioca Pearl Drinks, and fruit shakes.

There are two ways to add this interesting visual and textural element to a dessert. The old-fashioned way is to soak dried basil seeds in warm water. They swell up and have a dark, hard spot in the middle, surrounded by a soft outer covering. We make a more modern version of frog eggs using water chestnuts.

INGREDIENTS

1 large can (1 pound 4 ounces) whole water chestnuts,
*   drained and cubed*
2 tablespoons cold water
1 teaspoon red food coloring
12-ounce package tapioca flour

PREPARATION

First, slice the water chestnuts into ¼-inch slices, and then use an onion dicer to cut each slice into uniform ¼-inch cubes. (The dicer has a cutting grid, a lid that is closed to push the food through the grid, and a reservoir to hold the diced product. Asian grocery stores often stock dicers.) Next, soak the cubes for about 5 minutes in a mix of the cold water and red food coloring. This process turns the water chestnuts red. Drain, then cover with cool water, and gently rinse the water chestnuts. Now completely drain the water chestnuts. In a large bowl, toss the water chestnuts with the tapioca flour, being careful to coat each cube. Meanwhile, bring a large pot of water to boil. After the cubes are well coated with the tapioca flour, slowly shake them one by one into the boiling water, stirring the pot to keep the cubes from clumping together. Simmer, but do not boil, for 4 to 5 minutes. The cubes will rise to the surface. Fill a large pan with cold water. Drain the cubes and gently add them to the cold water. Pour off this water and add new cold water, to solidify the starch. The cubes should be bright red, soft on the outside and crunchy on the inside. They can be stored in cool water in the refrigerator for up to 8 hours. Or the cubes can be mixed gently with a can of coconut milk and stored.

Tapioca Pearl Drinks (Crystal Delights)
Qe Qav Hlaws Xyaw Dej Qab Zib

Westerners are used to solid and liquid food being separate. That is not so for the Hmong (and Asians in general), who delight in a variety of slippery, crunchy, chewy, and watery sensations all happening in the same dish. Tapioca pearl drinks, sometimes called bubble tea, exemplify this phenomenon. Invented by a creative Taiwanese café owner in the 1980s, they are combinations of tea, coffee, or fruit and fruit juices, often blended with sweetened milk and ice. Chewy tapioca pearls nestle in the bottom of the glass, to be drunk, along with the beverage, through a fat straw. Tapioca pearl drinks are a take-out café food. In cities with Asian populations, bubble tea shops have become almost as popular as Starbucks. In these cafés, the drinks are usually made from packaged mixes, but Sami found a wonderful Hmong-owned restaurant that serves handmade tapioca pearl drinks brim-full of fresh fruits, sweetened milk, and brewed tea or coffee—the Rice Palace Restaurant in Milwaukee, Wisconsin. The owners, Chuedang and Gao Youa Vue, call their healthy creations Crystal Delights. The basic recipes that follow are at-home variations of the drinks they serve to their customers.

Making tapioca pearl drinks is a several-step process. First, prepare the sugar syrup; next, cook the tapioca pearls; and then chill all of the ingredients. The final step is to blend with ice and serve.

PREPARE THE SUGAR SYRUP

Makes enough for about 8 servings

4 cups sugar
1¾ cups water

Mix the sugar and water in a medium-sized saucepan. Bring the mixture to a boil and cook just until the sugar is entirely dissolved. Remove from heat and let cool, and then refrigerate.

PREPARE THE TAPIOCA PEARLS

Makes enough for about 8 servings

12 cups water
1 bag large-sized, dry tapioca pearls (8.8 ounces/250 grams)

Many colors of dry tapioca pearls are available in Asian markets. Black ones are often used for pearl drinks because their dark color contrasts with the pastel beverage.

In a medium-sized saucepan, bring the water to a full boil. Slowly stir the tapioca pearls into the boiling water. Stir until the tapioca pearls rise to the top. Reduce the heat enough so that when the pan is covered, the water will remain boiling but not boil over. Cover and allow the pearls to cook for about 25 minutes, stirring occasionally. Turn off the heat and soak the tapioca pearls for another 10 minutes, again stirring occasionally. Drain the pearls and rinse in cold tap water until the water runs clear. Drain all of the water from the tapioca pearls, and cover them with the cooled syrup, stirring once. Refrigerate in a covered, airtight container. Use the pearls the same day, because they will expand and lose their texture if left to soak in the syrup.

Thai Iced Tea and Thai Iced Coffee Bubble Drink

Makes 4 servings

1 cup fresh-ground Thai coffee or Thai tea leaves
4 cups water (for brewing coffee or tea)
1 can (14 ounces) sweetened condensed milk
Sugar syrup, to taste
¼ cup cooked tapioca pearls
Ice cubes

Brew strong coffee or tea in a standard drip coffeemaker. Pour the beverage into an 8-cup glass measuring cup and allow it to cool. Add the can of condensed milk and sugar syrup to taste. Pour into tall glasses filled with ice, or blend with ice. Add tapioca pearls, and stir. Sip through a fat straw.

Fresh Fruit Bubble Drink

Makes 1 serving

1 cup fresh fruit (mango, strawberries, pineapple, honeydew,
*   or combination)*
⅔ to ¾ cup cold sugar syrup
1 cup ice cubes (always use more ice than sugar syrup)
¼ cup tapioca pearls
Fresh fruit chunks and whipped cream, for garnish (optional)

For the ultimate frozen beverage, put the fresh fruit in the freezer for 15 to 20 minutes before making this drink, but do not use previously frozen fruit. In a blender, blend all of the ingredients except the tapioca pearls. Check to see if the mixture is well blended. If not, turn off the blender, push the mixture down to the bottom of the blender with a rubber spatula, cover, and blend again. Put tapioca pearls in the bottom of a tall glass and pour the fruit shake on top. If desired, garnish with whipped cream and fresh fruit chunks. Nothing tastes better on a warm summer afternoon.

Recipes shared by Chuedang Vue of Milwaukee, Wisconsin

Chasing a Hmong American Dream

SOME PEOPLE CALLED Chuedang Vue and his wife, Gao Youa, crazy when they gave up their professional jobs to open a restaurant. But each time Chuedang took business associates to lunch, he wished he could take them to a restaurant that was representative of his own culture—a place that served real Hmong food. As time went by, this thought became a vision, and with a tremendous amount of work and expense it became the Rice Palace Restaurant in Milwaukee, Wisconsin.

Chuedang and Gao Youa were both born in Laos. The war's end forced their families to flee to the Ban Viani refugee camp in Thailand. In that tumultuous setting, the two teenagers met and fell in love. They married in the camp and then immigrated to the United States. All five of their children were born in America. Farming, parenting, and housework were the skills they brought with them, but over time they learned English and completed their educations. Chuedang landed a good job in a design engineering firm, and Gao Youa became an accountant. They seemed to have found the American Dream. They had cars, a lovely home, full-time jobs, and enough money to put their children through college. Yet Chuedang could not stop thinking about owning a Hmong restaurant. He explains:

> Our culture demands that each person strives to find their unique calling and works hard to become a success at whatever that is. I wanted to do more than earn a living. I wanted to introduce the greater community to the healthy nature of Hmong cooking. I wanted our restaurant to represent where we have come from and who we are today. Some Hmong people are ashamed of who they are, but I wanted to stand up tall and demonstrate something about our people.

Convincing his wife took a long time. Then together they developed recipes and wrote a business plan, detailing their vision. They submitted it to the bank and secured a half-million-dollar loan. In 2003 they opened their restaurant in a building that had been a bowling alley. Later they added a take-out bakery and delicatessen. Finally, Chuedang remodeled the bowling alley lanes, doing most

Chuedang Vue makes each Crystal Delight dessert from scratch at his restaurant, the Rice Palace, in Milwaukee, Wisconsin.

of the work himself, turning the space into a banquet hall. To attract customers, they decided to offer, in addition to Hmong food, Laotian, Thai, Japanese, and Vietnamese dishes. For a traditional Hmong eating experience, they serve fresh-made Hmong Herbal Chicken (*Nqaij Qaib Hau*) and Dilled Mustard (*Zaub Pos*). Gao Youa states:

> It is very challenging to make everything fresh, the way Hmong people do. It is very challenging to bring our cooking into the mainstream. When we make qaub poob (*chicken curry noodle soup*), we start out with the whole chicken and make the broth by hand in small batches. We make the egg rolls by hand when they are ordered. We always use fresh fruit, herbs, and vegetables for everything we serve. That takes a lot of work. Sometimes, when we work twelve-hour days, I think that we might be crazy!

Everything about the restaurant speaks to the Hmongs' reverence for their staple food—rice. An interior wall is devoted to a huge mural of Hmong mountain farms, one side depicting dry-land rice cultivation and the other, wet-field rice cultivation. Framed photographs show Hmong people in Laos planting, tending, harvesting, and pounding rice. Other frames hold colorful embroidered cloth story-pictures (*paj ntaub*) that illustrate the many labors of village and farm life. These objects remind Chuedang and Gao Youa of their Hmong culture, and they are always enveloped with aromas of traditional cooking. However, moving up the socioeconomic ladder in America has meant that they no longer have time for some of their traditions, such as caring for grandchildren and the elderly. They hang on to what they can but find themselves constantly adjusting and adapting.

One hand-crafted specialty of the house is a variety of drinks they call Crystal Delights. These made-to-order beverages/desserts are composed of fresh fruit, brewed Thai coffee or tea, sugar, cream, and tapioca pearls. They are reminiscent of the festive drinks sold by street vendors in Laos and Thailand. Chuedang adapted two variations for this cookbook. He invites everyone to visit the Rice Palace Restaurant at 3730 W. National Ave., Milwaukee, Wisconsin 53215; phone: (414) 383-3156; fax: (414) 383-0325.

Cooking for a Crowd ~ Npaj Ib Pluag Loj

Green Salad with Ground Pork 236
Xav Lav Hmoob Xyaw Nqaij

Steak Tartare *Larb* 237
Laj Nqaij Nyuj

Green Papaya Salad 239
Taub Ntoos Qaub

Garlicky Green Bean Stir-Fry 243
Taum Kib Xyaw Qej

Sweet Pork 244
Nqaij Qabzib

Party Egg Rolls 247
Kab Yob

Zesty Dipping Sauce 249
Kua Txob Ntsw Kab Yob

Hot Chili Condiment for a Crowd 250
Kua Txob Ntsw

Sticky Rice with Salty Pork and Mung Beans
   Wrapped in Banana Leaves 250
Ncuav Qhwv Plooj Tsawb Xyaw Nqaij

Stir-Fried Cellophane Noodles with Ground Pork 252
Fawm Do Xyaw Nqaij

Chicken and Tofu Meatballs 253
Qe Nqaij Qaib Xyaw Taum Paj

Sheng's Broiled Chicken Wings 254
See Kooj Tis Qaib Ci

Chicken Curry Noodle Soup 255
Khaub Poob

Beef Noodle Soup for a Crowd 260
Fawm (Phở)

Three-Color Dessert 262
Nab Vam

Ka's Sweet Potato Vermicelli Salad 265
Kha Qos Liab Fawm Xav Lav

Cooking for a Crowd ➳ Npaj Ib Pluag Loj

Mao Xiong (Mrs. Lue Vang) prepares enough curry noodle soup to feed the entire congregation of the Hmong Missionary Alliance Church in Portland, Oregon.

TO SOME DEGREE, EVERY HMONG American faces an identity crisis. The elderly worry that their children and grandchildren will not learn or employ the traditional practices necessary for the health of the collective "Hmong soul" (*ntsuj plig Hmoob*). Younger Hmong people struggle to understand who they are and how they fit in to both Hmong culture and American culture. While some Hmong people cling adamantly to the traditional ways, others embrace Christianity, Western health care, and new family structures and speak English almost exclusively. Some people still "cook Hmong" at home every day, while others opt for mainstream American dishes. Regardless of the many different paths Hmong Americans walk, some things remain integral to their society: gathering together, and sharing fellowship and meals with extended family and friends.

This chapter includes the dishes most often served at such gatherings. Some are Hmong, and some are borrowed from other Asian cultures. All of them are favorites at big Hmong American parties.

Green Salad with Ground Pork

Xav Lav Hmoob Xyaw Nqaij

Makes 25 servings

Sheng's family loves this salad. They eat it at least twice a week. Cut this recipe in half for family meals, or double it for a big party.

INGREDIENTS

4 heads romaine lettuce
2 heads iceberg lettuce
2 bunches green onions, white and green parts, shredded
3 bunches cilantro, both stems and leaves, cut into 2-inch pieces
5 cucumbers, peeled and sliced
8 tomatoes, quartered and sliced
3 large carrots, shredded
2 dozen hard-boiled eggs, shells removed, sliced
1 pound ground pork
4 tablespoons fish sauce
8 teaspoons lemon juice
1 cup extra-virgin olive oil
1½ tablespoons salt
1 tablespoon black pepper

PREPARATION

Carefully wash the lettuces, drain off the excess moisture, and break the leaves into bite-sized pieces. Put the lettuces, green onions, cilantro, cucumbers, tomatoes, carrots, and sliced eggs into a very large bowl. Stir-fry the ground pork over medium heat for about 8 minutes, breaking the meat apart as it cooks. Remove from heat. When the meat has cooled a little, add the fish sauce, lemon juice, olive oil, salt, and black pepper. Mix well with a wooden spoon. Pour the meat mixture over the salad. Toss together well. Serve immediately.

Steak Tartare *Larb*

 *Laj Nqaij Nyuj*

Makes 30 servings

The Hmong use a Lao term for eating raw meat—*lav nyoos suam* (eating rough). For this recipe, we prefer to use the French term *tartare*. The elderly love this old-fashioned recipe. It contains ingredients that are not popular with young Hmong, including raw beef, bitter gallbladder (*kua tsib*) juice (the cooking liquid from boiling a beef gallbladder), beef tripe, and dried beef skin. If eating raw beef makes you uncomfortable, substitute very lean minced beef that has been sautéed just until it loses its pink color. Steak Tartare *Larb* is prepared only when the beef is extremely fresh, after a cow has been butchered for a special occasion, such as for a baby-naming ceremony (*hu me nyuam plig*). For a more Americanized beef *larb* recipe that uses grilled beef, see page 160.

This recipe requires many kitchen helpers. While the men mince the meat, the women prepare the herbs and vegetables and cook the tripe and gallbladder. Only the most experienced cooks mix the ingredients, tasting now and then to make sure the flavor is just right.

When Sheng's uncle prepares this dish, everyone agrees that it tastes great because he puts his heart and soul into the cooking. His happiness makes the food better.

INGREDIENTS

> 8 pounds very tender fat-free beef, minced
>
> Juice of 5 or 6 lemons
>
> 2 pounds cleaned beef tripe, boiled until done (it will be chewy, almost rubbery) and very thinly sliced (if purchased, it will be precooked)
>
> 1 pound chopped, cooked beef skin with no fat (or substitute Asian beef jerky from an Asian deli)
>
> 1½ cups minced lemongrass, tough outer leaves, tops, and root removed
>
> ½ cup finely chopped kaffir lime leaves
>
> ½ cup minced fresh galanga
>
> Small hot chilies, minced or very thinly sliced on the diagonal, to equal ½ cup

2 bunches green onions, white and green parts, thinly sliced on
  the diagonal
1½ bunches cilantro, coarsely chopped
3 cups chopped fresh mint
3 cups chopped Vietnamese coriander
2 to 3 cups Toasted Sticky Rice Flour (page 61, or purchase
  ready-made from an Asian grocery)
3 to 4 tablespoons salt
2 tablespoons MSG (optional)
1 to 1½ tablespoons ground Asian peppercorns, sometimes called
  Sichuan pepper
¼ to ½ cup fish sauce
2 to 3 tablespoons gallbladder juice (optional)

ACCOMPANIMENTS

Leaf lettuce, washed and dried
10 limes, cut on the sides and quartered (for additional zing)
Hot chili peppers, very thinly sliced on the diagonal
  (for those who like it very hot!)
Thai basil sprigs
Mint sprigs
Celery
Daikon radish, thinly sliced

PREPARATION

To protect your hands, wear disposable gloves when cutting the hot chilies.
Prepare all of the herbs and vegetables. Arrange the lettuce and accompanying limes, vegetables, and herbs on one or two large trays.

   Put the minced steak in a large bowl and squeeze the lemon juice over
it. Mix in the tripe and beef skin or jerky. Add the lemongrass, kaffir lime
leaves, galanga, hot chilies, green onions, cilantro, mint, and Vietnamese
coriander. Add the toasted rice flour, salt, MSG (if desired), and Sichuan
pepper. Stir in ¼ cup of the fish sauce and 2 tablespoons of the gallbladder
juice (if bitter taste is desired). Toss everything together. Taste, and add
more of the fish sauce and gallbladder juice, depending upon the degree of
salt and bitterness you want.

Serve the *larb* in a bowl alongside the trays of accompanying herbs and vegetables. Diners can wrap the lettuce leaves around the meat salad and accompaniments.

Green Papaya Salad
Taub Ntoos Qaub

Order papaya salad in a Thai or Vietnamese restaurant and you will get a plate of julienned cabbage, green papaya, and carrots, seasoned with a delicate sweet and sour dressing, and sprinkled with a few boiled shrimp halves and several peanuts. Occasionally restaurants add a little fire by including a few chili flakes or some cayenne pepper in the dressing.

In contrast, Hmong-style green papaya salad is jam-packed with intense flavors. And if you are after *real* Hmong-style green papaya salad, go to a Hmong New Year's celebration. There, vendors spend hours mixing the dish "to order" for customer after customer. Some want it so hot that their eyes water; some people like it extra-sour. Some people add ground peanuts. But in general, Hmong people like papaya salad made with lots of crushed garlic cloves, fresh hot chili peppers, sour tamarind paste, pungent fish sauce or crab or shrimp paste, juicy limes, sugar, MSG, bright cherry tomato halves, and mounds of freshly shredded green papaya, all pounded together with a large mortar and pestle.

Large Asian grocery stores sometimes sell already-julienned papaya, but it is usually limp. A better option is to buy large green papayas and the special tool for shredding them. When preparing papaya salad for a lot of people, first make a paste of sour tamarind, crab or shrimp paste, and fish sauce. Then, for

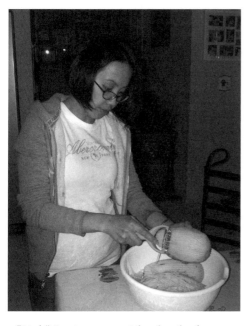

"Little" Sami uses a special tool to shred green papaya.

each serving, add a spoon or two of the mixture, depending on how sour and salty a person likes it.

A simpler, family-sized version of papaya salad appears on page 81.

INGREDIENTS FOR 3 CUPS SOUR/SALTY PASTE (ABOUT 25 SERVINGS)

> 1 brick (16 ounces) sour tamarind
> 1 jar (8 ounces) crab or shrimp paste (or a mixture of both)
> ¼ cup fish sauce
> ½ tablespoon MSG (optional)

OTHER INGREDIENTS (PER SERVING)

> 1 or 2 small hot chili peppers, minced (more or less,
>   depending upon desired heat)
> 2 cloves garlic, chopped
> 1 tablespoon sugar
> 3 cups long shreds of green papaya
> 6 cherry tomatoes, cut in half
> Juice of 1 lime

PREPARATION

To make the sour/salty paste, break apart the brick of tamarind and mix it together with the crab or shrimp paste, fish sauce, and MSG (if desired) in a saucepan. Turn the heat to medium-low and cook until they are combined. Store the mixture in a covered container in the refrigerator until ready to use.

For each serving of papaya salad, place the hot chilies and garlic in a large stone mortar. Pound them with a heavy wooden or stone pestle; this mashing and grinding heightens the aromas and flavors. Continue until the chilies and garlic are well combined and mashed. Add the sugar and a heaping tablespoon (or more, depending upon desired taste) of the sour/salty paste. Pound for a few more minutes. Toss in the shredded papaya and continue to mix well. Add the tomatoes and squeeze the lime juice over the salad. Some people like to add a bit of the lime pulp. Discard any lime seeds that end up in the salad. Mix, and let the diner taste. Make desired adjustments.

Hmong New Year Xyoo Tshiab

NEW YEAR IS the only major holiday the Hmong observe. In Laos, New Year's celebrations were held after the rice was harvested, during the full moon at the end of the twelfth lunar calendar month, and also at the beginning of the first lunar calendar month. Today, Hmong people all over the world celebrate in November, December, or January. In each city and town, community leaders plan festivals to take place at different times so that people can invite one another to visit and celebrate with them. Music performances, both traditional and modern, beauty pageants, and sports events are staged in big public venues. They last from three to seven days and attract hundreds or thousands of people, depending upon the size of the community.

Romance and the spicy-sour taste of papaya salad pervade Hmong New Year. During New Year's festivities, young men and women are given the go-ahead to

Sweethearts Julie Lor and John Hang, of Seattle, share a spicy serving of green papaya salad during Hmong New Year.

select and woo their mates. Courtships often begin with a couple strolling up and down the rows of food vendors, sharing bites of Hmong sausage, purple sticky rice, barbequed chicken, and everyone's favorite—green papaya salad. It is a time to wear one's finest embroidered clothing and silver jewelry. As the day progresses, young men and women face each other in two lines, tossing back and forth soft balls made of cloth (*pov pob*). The boys maneuver to stand across from girls who have caught their eyes. Anyone who drops a ball will forfeit a small token or sing a folk song (*hais kwv txhiaj*). Later on, if the couple wants to pursue the relationship, the tokens are returned in a more private setting. Traditionally, this was the only time that old-fashioned Hmong parents openly condoned romance.

Individual clans and family groups hold smaller formal banquets, where catered food is the norm, and men, women, and young people dance in a rhythmic circle, a borrowed Laotian custom. During New Year, Hmong families who follow the traditional ways hold various rituals to ensure the welfare of their family, to honor their ancestors, and to revere deities. The details of these rituals vary according to clan or descent group ("those who share the same household spirits": *ib tus dab qhuas*).

Food plays a major part of all celebrations and rituals associated with Hmong New Year. Sticky rice is cooked, pounded, shaped into little cakes, and eaten with sweet palm syrup. A pig is butchered, and mounds of *larb* and sweet meat are prepared. Each family prepares their favorite foods to share with visitors. In traditional homes, the best food is set at an altar for the ancestors. Hard-cooked eggs are shared with family members. The celebration of New Year is just as important in Christian homes as in traditional homes, and all non-spiritual customs are observed. In short, Hmong New Year is the time that all Hmong people celebrate their heritage and their "Hmong-ness."

Garlicky Green Bean Stir-Fry

Taum Kib Xyaw Qej

Makes 25 servings

Fresh green beans get a flavorful coating and a healthy treatment in this crowd-pleasing dish. This recipe can be doubled, but remember: the bigger the batch, the more muscle required to stir-fry it. A large wok can accommodate a single batch, but when doubling the recipe it is best to set up an outside propane burner and stand to do the cooking.

INGREDIENTS

5 pounds fresh green beans, washed and stem ends snipped off
⅔ cup vegetable oil
½ cup chopped garlic
½ large yellow onion, sliced
1 tablespoon salt
¼ cup water
½ cup oyster sauce

PREPARATION

Clean the green beans and snip off the stem ends. Heat the oil to medium-hot in a large, lidded, round-bottomed pan. Toss in the garlic and onion and stir-fry just until their flavors are released, about 20 seconds. Add the green beans and the salt. Stir-fry for a few minutes. Then add the water and cover the pan. Let the beans steam for 5 minutes. Uncover the pan, add the oyster sauce, and stir 2 to 3 minutes, until the beans are uniformly covered with the shiny sauce. They should retain some of their crunch.

Sweet Pork
Nqaij Qabzib

Makes 40 servings

Although this dish is always made with pork (*nqaij*), Hmongs usually call it "sweet meat." Whenever there is a freshly butchered pig to cook, Sweet Pork is on the menu. It is a simple dish, composed mainly of pork, sugar, and hard-cooked eggs. As the eggs simmer in the liquid, they become deep brown and infused with sweet ginger. The eggs are everyone's favorite part of the dish.

Start preparing this soupy stew early in the day, because it needs to cook slowly for a long time. This dish is a good choice for cooking outdoors in a very large pot over a propane burner. The following recipe is for a large crowd. A smaller, more Americanized version appears on page 133.

INGREDIENTS

8 cups sugar
10 pounds pork meat, including pig's feet, lower legs,
    and ribs with meat, cleaned and cut into 2-inch cubes
2 to 3 cups sliced fresh ginger or galanga root, peeled before slicing
3 lemongrass bulbs, cleaned and cut into several pieces
20 cups water
5 tablespoons salt
1 tablespoon MSG (optional)
½ cup dark soy sauce
4 dozen hard-cooked eggs, shells removed

PREPARATION

In a large pot, heat the sugar at a medium-low temperature, stirring constantly until it becomes liquid and turns dark brown. Reduce the heat and add the meat, ginger root, and lemongrass, stirring the mixture as you do. Add the water slowly, again stirring constantly. Be careful, because the hot liquid sugar may bubble up and spatter. Add the salt, MSG (if desired), and soy sauce. Bring the soup back up to a simmer. Stir well to dissolve the sugar syrup in the water. Put a lid on the pot and cook slowly for 2 hours. Add the eggs and gently stir them into the pork mixture. Cover the pot again and cook another hour, until the meat is tender but not falling apart and the eggs are a deep, rich, dark brown.

The Year My Family Decided Not to Have Papaya Salad and Egg Rolls for Thanksgiving

By May Lee-Yang

The year my family decided not to have papaya salad and egg rolls for Thanksgiving was the same year I made the four-hour trek from Madison back to St. Paul. That stretch of highway had allowed me to run away from home for four years.

The year my family decided not to have papaya salad and egg rolls for Thanksgiving was the same year my father tried to commit suicide and my brothers spent thousands of dollars trying to ward off evil spirits through the *ua neeb* and *hu plig* ceremonies, promising to obey and respect him even as they started treating him like a little child.

The year my family decided not to have papaya salad and egg rolls for Thanksgiving was the same year my heart was broken by my white boyfriend. The one I'd been waiting for all of my life. The one who told me two weeks before Thanksgiving, "I'm not a trophy."

The year my family decided not to have papaya salad and egg rolls for Thanksgiving was the same year I returned to my mom's house on Sherburne Avenue, a faded blue house that had not been part of childhood memories, but only came to be when I was seventeen, a house that was part of her attempt to create stability for my family.

The year my family decided not to have papaya salad and egg rolls for Thanksgiving was the same year that my eight-year-old nephew, Aaron, asked me simply, "How come you don't like us anymore?"

The year my family decided not to have papaya salad and egg rolls for Thanksgiving was the same year that I lay in the dark and held back tears of nostalgia for a time I always remembered and dreamed about, a time that preceded being a grown-up.

The year my family decided not to have papaya salad and egg rolls for Thanksgiving was the same year I woke up to find our house empty. I remembered countless Thanksgivings in which relatives streamed in and out while all the women in our family hurriedly made sure everyone else got enough turkey, rice, egg rolls, and papaya salad to eat, even while we never quite got anything afterward except dirty dishes, dirty kids, and dirty floors to clean up.

The year my family decided not to have papaya salad and egg rolls for Thanksgiving was the same year my family sat at our dining room table without relatives. The same year our turkey sat before my brother, Kai, *un*-carved and with no traces of the usual oyster sauce and lemongrass marinade. The year *Nyab*'s giblet and apple raisin stuffing took the place of a Stove Top concoction mixed with *peev choj*. The same year that there were mashed potatoes and gravy made from scratch. The same year that the salad did not contain slices of lime, shrimp paste, or pungent fish sauce. The same year that there was a green bean casserole smothered in cream of mushroom soup, shredded cheese, and dried onion bits instead of *zaub ntsuab*. And the same year that our Thanksgiving table, for once, looked normal, and American, like something I'd always dreamed of when I was a kid.

And yet the year my family decided not to have papaya salad and egg rolls for Thanksgiving, I found myself longing. I longed for papaya salad so hot and so tasty, I was willing to have bad breath and watery nostrils just to eat it. I longed for mid-mornings spent with my sisters and aunts rolling out hundreds of egg rolls while we talked about good men, bad men, and when I was going to marry one of these same men. I longed for the loudness of family gatherings that brought together cousins I hadn't seen since my teenage years, cousins with whom I'd reminisce about childhood experiences and contemplate adult dreams. I longed for moments lost with my nieces and nephews—birthdays, volleyball games, lazy afternoons at the local parks—moments I'd forfeited when I left for college and didn't return. I longed to see my parents as I remembered them—young, happy, and active—and not as they were now: growing old before my very eyes. Most of all, the year we didn't have papaya salad and egg rolls for Thanksgiving, I longed for connections, not to a place or a feeling, but to people. And so that same year, I returned home.

Hu plig—calling-in-the-soul ritual
Nyab—sister-in-law or daughter-in-law
Peev choj—small rice noodles
Ua neeb—healing ritual
Zaub ntsuab—mustard greens/leafy cabbage

Party Egg Rolls

Kab Yob

Makes 150 egg rolls

Everyone loves Hmong egg rolls (*kab yob*, pronounced "ka-yo"). They are crispy-brown on the outside and filled with tidbits of ground pork, shrimp, vermicelli noodles, vegetables, and herbs. Many parties start a day in advance with a group of friends assembling dozens of egg rolls, which get refrigerated until the next day. Then they are deep-fried and served piping hot with a dipping sauce (see the recipe below). Don't count on any leftovers!

Markets sell many kinds of spring roll and egg roll wrappers. Use the cream-colored ones, made of wheat flour, that are labeled "spring roll pastry."

INGREDIENTS

3 packages (50 wrappers per package) 5-inch-square
   spring roll pastry
5 pounds fresh shrimp (25 to 30 per pound)
2 packages (3½ ounces each) rice vermicelli noodles
1½ pounds ground pork
1 pound fresh bean sprouts (or substitute finely shredded cabbage)
2 large carrots, peeled and grated
1 bunch cilantro, chopped
1 bunch green onions, white and green parts, chopped
3 teaspoons salt
1 teaspoon black pepper
1 teaspoon MSG (optional)
4 eggs, beaten (for filling)
3 egg yolks, beaten (for assembling egg rolls)
Large bottle corn oil (for frying egg rolls)

PREPARATION

If the wrappers are frozen, allow them to come to room temperature before assembling the egg rolls. Do not thaw them in a microwave.

Remove shells from the shrimp, and clean and devein. Set aside. Soak the vermicelli and drain according to package directions, which typically means soaking in warm water about 20 minutes before draining. With kitchen shears, cut the vermicelli into 1-inch lengths. In a large mixing bowl, combine the vermicelli with the ground pork, bean sprouts (or cabbage), carrots, cilantro, green onions, salt, black pepper, and MSG (if desired). Add the beaten eggs and mix thoroughly with your hands.

ASSEMBLE THE EGG ROLLS

In a small dish, beat the egg yolks. The beaten yolks serve as the "glue" that seals the wrappers so the filling doesn't leak out when the egg rolls are fried.

Use a dinner plate as a work surface. Peel a wrapper from the stack of spring roll wrappers and lay it flat with one corner of the square pointing toward you. Place a heaping tablespoon of the pork mixture on the wrapper halfway between the middle and the corner closest to you. Pat the filling into a 3-by-½-inch log. Experience will help you judge how much filling to use. Put one shrimp on top of the pork mixture. Bring the corner closest to you up and over the filling. Fold the left and right corners of the wrapper into the middle. With the back of a small spoon, smear a little beaten egg yolk on the unfolded corner. Continue to roll the wrapper up into a neat log. The finished egg roll will be plump and about 3 inches long. Lay the egg rolls next to each other on a baking sheet covered in plastic wrap. Put a sheet of plastic wrap between each layer of egg rolls. Refrigerate until ready to cook.

COOK THE EGG ROLLS

Egg rolls taste best when freshly made. Fill a large wok or pan three-fourths full of corn oil. Turn the heat to medium. After the oil is hot (about 365 degrees), slip the egg rolls, one at a time, into the hot oil. They should begin to boil but not turn brown right away. If the egg roll just sits in the oil, the oil is not hot enough. You can fry several egg rolls at a time, but do not crowd them, because they may stick together. Deep-fry the egg rolls about 5 minutes, or until the outside is a crisp golden brown. Drain the egg rolls on paper towels. Serve right away. Sprinkle with ground roasted peanuts and dip in Zesty Dipping Sauce.

Roasted Peanuts

Txiv Laum Huab Xeeb Kib

Shell raw peanuts or buy shelled raw peanuts. Put a single layer of peanuts in a dry sauté pan. Over medium heat, roast the nuts, shaking the pan to keep them turned. Sauté the peanuts until they are brown and fragrant, but be careful not to burn them. With a mortar and pestle, pound the peanuts until they are medium-sized bits (or use either a nut grinder or a food processor).

Zesty Dipping Sauce

Kua Txob Ntsw Kab Yob

Many people like to dip egg rolls in a prepared sweet and sour sauce, like Mama Sita's brand Sweet and Sour Sauce, or a prepared sweet chili sauce. Below is a homemade zesty sweet and sour sauce.

INGREDIENTS

3 tablespoons cornstarch
¼ cup brown sugar
1 cup pineapple juice
2 tablespoons dark soy sauce
Juice of 1 large lime
3 tablespoons ground chili paste

PREPARATION

Mix the cornstarch and brown sugar in a small saucepan. Add the pineapple juice and soy sauce. Stir and bring to a boil over medium-high heat. Reduce heat and cook until thick. Remove from heat. Add the lime juice and chili paste. Stir with a wire whisk.

Hot Chili Condiment for a Crowd

Kua Txob Ntsw

Makes 3 cups

Hmong people seldom serve dinner without a little dish of hot chili dipping sauce on the table. Use this recipe when cooking for a crowd.

INGREDIENTS

½ cup minced hot chili peppers (small red and green Thai chilies are good choices)

½ cup chopped cilantro

½ cup chopped green onions, white and green parts

¼ cup minced fresh lemongrass, tough outer leaves, root, and top few inches of leaves removed

1 cup fish sauce (3 Crabs brand is best)

¼ cup lime juice

1 teaspoon salt or MSG

2 teaspoons sugar

PREPARATION

Wear rubber gloves when mincing the chilies, since they are very hot and can burn your skin. Mix the chilies, cilantro, green onion, and lemongrass together in a bowl. Add the fish sauce, lime juice, salt or MSG, and sugar. Stir until everything is blended.

Sticky Rice with Salty Pork and Mung Beans Wrapped in Banana Leaves

Ncuav Qhwv Plooj Tsawb Xyaw Nqaij

Makes 30 large packets of rice

These rice packets are full of savory, salty surprises, and the banana-leaf wrapper adds a sweet, earthy taste. This recipe calls for mung beans, sausage, and fatty pork, but you can be creative with the filling. Some people like to add coconut cream to the rice, as in the Sticky Rice in Banana Leaves recipe on page 54. That addition makes the rice packets both salty and sweet. This dish takes a long time to prepare, so begin it a day or two before a party. First, the rice and mung beans must be soaked for several hours, or overnight. Then the banana-leaf packets are assembled and boiled; having a lot of kitchen helpers makes the assembly easier and more fun. The cooked banana-leaf packets can be refrigerated for a day before being served.

These packets are not meant to be part of a meal. A good hostess will offer them to guests while a meal is being prepared or as a "to-go" snack.

INGREDIENTS

1 bag (5 pounds) sticky rice
1 bag (14 ounces) dried, split mung beans
1 tablespoon salt
1 package (16 ounces) preserved Chinese sausage
1 piece pork belly, or other pork meat, about 1½ pounds
3 packages (20 to 25 leaves each) frozen banana leaves
1 ball plastic raffia string, to tie packets

PREPARATION

Pour the sticky rice grains into a very large bowl or tub. Cover with warm water to about 2 inches above the level of the rice. Empty the mung beans into a medium-sized bowl and cover with warm water 2 inches above the level of the beans. Soak the rice and mung beans for at least 4 hours, or as long as overnight. Rinse the rice several times in clear water. Drain well. Leave the rice in the bowl or tub in which it was soaked.

Take the banana leaves out of the freezer and let them sit at room temperature for 1 hour, or more.

While the leaves thaw, drain the mung beans and then steam them over boiling water for 30 minutes, until they are very soft. Transfer the cooked mung beans to a bowl and let them cool. Once they have cooled, transfer them to a large mortar and pestle, add the salt, and pound the mung beans until they are completely mashed.

To prepare the banana leaves to be stuffed, lay each one flat and wash it gently following the grain of the leaf, so as not to tear it. With scissors, cut away any damaged areas and discard. Cut the leaves in half and set them aside. Each piece should be about 9 by 14 inches.

Cut the sausage and pork meat into large, bite-sized chunks and refrigerate until you are ready to assemble the rice packets.

To assemble the packets, lay half of a banana leaf over another, so the grain of the top leaf crosses the grain of the bottom leaf. Put a heaping ½ cup of the rice grains in the middle of the crossed leaves. On top of that, put a heaping tablespoon of the mashed mung beans and 2 pieces of the sausage on either side of a piece of pork. Top that with another tablespoon of mashed beans and another heaping ½ cup of rice grains. Try to keep the rice, beans, and meat in a compact unit, without stray grains escaping. Wrap up the package by folding opposite sides of the banana leaf over the top so they overlap, enfolding the rice and meat. Then fold the other two sides up, overlapping each other. Tuck in stray corners and turn the package over so that the overlapped sides are underneath. Use a long piece of the plastic raffia to tie the package tightly. Continue assembling packets until all of the rice, beans, and meat are used.

Put the rice packets in a very large pot. Cover them with hot water and bring to a boil. Cover the pot and reduce the heat so the water remains simmering. Cook for about 1½ hours, until the rice becomes very soft. Remove the packets from the water and let them cool. These snacks are usually served at room temperature, although they can be reheated for 30 minutes in a steamer. If you don't serve them right away, store them in a refrigerator.

Recipe shared by Mai Her (Sheng's mother) of Sacramento, California

Stir-Fried Cellophane Noodles with Ground Pork
Fawm Do Xyaw Nqaij

Makes 30 servings

This easy dish pleases everyone, old and young.

INGREDIENTS

> 5 packages (8 ounces each) cellophane noodles
> ½ cup vegetable oil
> ¼ cup chopped garlic
> 5 pounds lean ground pork
> ½ cup bottled hot chili sauce
> ½ cup oyster sauce
> 2 tablespoons fish sauce

1 tablespoon dark soy sauce

1½ tablespoons salt

1½ tablespoons black pepper

4 cups cherry tomatoes, cut in half

2 cans (12 ounces each) straw mushrooms, drained and sliced
  in half (or fresh straw mushrooms, washed and separated)

3 cans (12 ounces each) bamboo shoots, drained and sliced into
  thin strips

1 bunch green onions, white and green parts, cut into
  2-inch lengths

1 bunch cilantro, cut into 2-inch lengths

PREPARATION

Soak the cellophane noodles in warm water for 20 minutes, or until they are tender. Drain the noodles in a large mesh strainer in the sink until ready to use.

Heat ¼ cup of the oil in a large wok or skillet and sauté the garlic until it is fragrant but not brown. Add the pork and stir-fry until it is thoroughly cooked (no hint of pink remains) and broken into bits. Add the chili sauce, oyster sauce, fish sauce, soy sauce, salt, and black pepper. Stir well and then add the cherry tomatoes, straw mushrooms, and bamboo shoots. Stir and cook for a few minutes, until some of the liquid from the tomatoes has cooked away.

Pour the remaining oil into a large wok or pot with curved sides set over an outdoor propane burner. When the oil has heated, transfer the noodles and meat mixture into the pot and stir-fry until everything is mixed and hot. Add the green onions and cilantro and then toss until all the ingredients are combined. Taste, and add more seasonings if desired. Serve hot.

Chicken and Tofu Meatballs
Qe Nqaij Qaib Xyaw Taum Paj

Makes 50 servings

This recipe is a recent Hmong American creation. The easy-to-make dish is good to serve at a large gathering. Ground pork can be substituted for the ground chicken.

Set a large kettle of water (about 2 gallons) to boil over high heat on an outdoor propane burner. Add 8 slices of fresh or dried galanga and 3 stalks of lemongrass.

INGREDIENTS FOR MEATBALLS

2 to 3 cups chopped cilantro
1 to 2 cups chopped green onions, white and green parts
10 bricks tofu (12 ounces each)
6 pounds ground lean chicken
3 tablespoons salt
1 tablespoon MSG (optional)
1 tablespoon black pepper

PREPARATION

Chop the cilantro and green onions and put them in a very large bowl. Add the tofu, crumbling it with your hands. Add the ground chicken, salt, MSG (if desired), and black pepper. Using your hands, mix everything together. Form the mixture into golf ball–sized meatballs and then drop them one at a time into the gently boiling water.

To serve, ladle the meatballs and some of the broth into serving dishes. Guests sip the tasty broth from the serving dish with their spoons and dish the meatballs onto their plates.

Sheng's Broiled Chicken Wings

See Kooj Tis Qaib Ci

Makes about 65 pieces

Since kids prefer less traditional dishes than older people do, co-author Sheng often includes these slightly sweet, more Americanized crispy chicken wings in her menus. They are always a hit.

INGREDIENTS

6 pounds chicken wings (about 30 to 35 wings)
2 teaspoons salt

½ teaspoon MSG or Accent (optional)

1 teaspoon black pepper

2 tablespoons Sriracha chili sauce

4 cloves garlic, minced

½ cup finely minced lemongrass, tough outer leaves, base, and
   tops removed

¼ cup soy sauce

PREPARATION

Wash the chicken wings in cold water and dry on paper towels. Cut the tip off each wing and discard. Cut each wing into two pieces, at the joint. Combine the rest of the ingredients in a large bowl and then add the wing pieces. Stir so the wings are uniformly coated with the sauce. Arrange in a single layer on broiler pans. Turn the broiler to 400 degrees and broil about 15 minutes on one side. Turn the wings over and continue to cook about 15 more minutes, or until they are done and the meat inside is no longer pink.

Chicken Curry Noodle Soup

Khaub Poob

Makes 50 servings

No festive gathering is complete without *khaub poob* (pronounced "kah-poong"). A great bowl of this traditional dish can make a cook's reputation.

Khaub poob is vibrant with an almost startling variety of flavors and textures. However, Hmong people debate the merits of many of the ingredients. Some believe *khaub poob* is not *khaub poob* without plenty of garlic to flavor the curry and kaffir lime leaves to flavor the broth. Others declare these ingredients are heresy! Slivered banana blossoms are traditionally included along with the herbs and vegetables, but some young Hmong people do not care for the mildly bitter flavor and instead serve them on the side. Many people are disappointed if their soup is not made with whole dressed chickens that have been cut up. Such a soup comes complete with chicken feet, necks, and wings, and it gives diners the chance to nibble tasty meat from small bones—a favorite Asian eating experience. Other cooks prefer to use only shredded white chicken meat. To add an interesting taste and visual element, hard-boiled, shelled quail eggs are occasionally added. However, everyone agrees that *khaub poob* must include plenty of chewy rice noodles, thinly sliced bamboo shoots, and a rich broth full of meat and spicy coconut-curry seasoning, as well as a mound of fresh herbs and vegetables.

Making the soup requires several "sub-assemblies," and serving the soup requires several last-minute steps, so plan out each detail and do as much as possible in advance. Before preparing the soup, get ready by setting a buffet table with enough large Asian soup bowls (which are very large and deep, to hold all of the ingredients and keep the soup hot), soup spoons, chopsticks, and napkins for all the guests. Also set out the condiments, such as seasoning sauce, soy sauce, sliced hot chilies, and coarse-ground black pepper. Then make the broth, cut up the vegetables, cook the noodles, and prepare the curry mixture. Once the Thai chilies are sliced, the banana blossoms slivered, and the limes quartered, put them in bowls and add them to the buffet table.

Serving the savory soup is also an assembly process. After all of the preparation is complete, each eager diner receives a large Asian soup bowl. In the bottom of the bowl goes a handful of the fresh herbs and vegetables. Next, the cooked noodles are added. Then, just enough of the hot soup to cover the vegetables and noodles is poured on top. Finally, each diner chooses additional herbs and condiments to individually season the soup.

INGREDIENTS FOR BROTH

8 gallons water
2 stalks lemongrass, tough outer leaves and base removed,
  each stalk tied in a knot
20 whole kaffir lime leaves (about 1 cup)
1 cup dried or fresh sliced galanga
½ cup peeled, sliced fresh ginger root (optional)
4 chicken bouillon cubes (Asian-style, for most authentic-tasting
  broth, but they contain MSG)
4 whole, large, bone-in chicken breasts, or 2 whole chickens,
  cleaned and each cut into about 16 pieces
7 pounds (1 jumbo-sized can) bamboo shoots, shredded

2 banana blossoms

3 or 4 limes (for preparing banana blossoms)

1 large cabbage, very thinly shredded

2 bunches green onions, white and green parts, cut into
¼-inch pieces

2 bunches fresh mint, cut into ½-inch pieces

2 bunches cilantro, cut into ½-inch pieces

2 pounds fresh bean sprouts

15 packages (12 ounces each) medium-sized flat rice vermicelli
noodles (about 3 to 4 ounces per serving)

INGREDIENTS FOR CURRY MIXTURE

½ cup vegetable oil

1 cup fresh chopped garlic

1 can (14 ounces) namya curry paste

3 tablespoons shrimp paste

½ cup fish sauce

4 cans (14 ounces each) coconut milk (or 1 large box powdered
coconut milk mixed with water per package instructions)

½ cup sugar

1 tablespoon MSG (optional)

½ cup salt

1 to 2 tablespoons black pepper

CONDIMENTS

1 cup hot Thai chilies, very thinly sliced on the diagonal

15 limes, cut into wedges

Additional condiments: seasoning sauce, Sriracha chili sauce,
hoisin sauce, soy sauce, fish sauce, dried fried garlic,
coarse-ground black pepper

PREPARATION

To make the broth, bring the water to a boil in a 40-quart pot over an
outdoor propane burner. Add the lemongrass, lime leaves, galanga, peeled
ginger root (if desired), bouillon cubes, and chicken. Return to a boil and
then turn the heat down so the water continues to simmer. Cook the herbs

and chicken for about 30 minutes. Be sure not to let the broth boil hard, or it will become cloudy. Remove the chicken and put it in a bowl to cool. If using breasts, shred the meat with your fingers, pulling it apart into thin strips. Discard the bone and skin. If using whole cut-up chickens, leave the pieces intact. Let the broth continue to gently simmer while the vegetables, noodles, and curry mixture are prepared. Refrigerate the chicken in a covered container until you are ready to add it to the soup.

Next, drain the bamboo shoots. Using a sharp knife, pull strips off the length of each shoot until all bamboo shoots are reduced to long, thin strips. This task is good for a few people who want to chat, because it takes a long time. Set the shredded bamboo shoots aside in a bowl.

To prepare the ingredients for the bottom of the bowl, discard the tough outer petals of the banana blossoms and any finger-like immature bananas (they are too bitter to eat). Slice the softer banana flower petals into very fine slivers. Squeeze the juice and pulp of the limes into a bowl of water and add the banana blossom slivers. The lime juice keeps them from turning brown. These curly shreds add a bit of crunch and a mildly bitter taste. However, some people don't like the flavor, so the banana flower is often served separately from the other ingredients. Shred the cabbage and chop the green onions, mint, and cilantro. In a large bowl, mix them together with the bean sprouts to be used when the soup is assembled. Just before serving, drain the water from the banana blossoms and add to the mix, or serve separately.

To prepare the dry noodles, put them in a large bowl and cover them with warm tap water. Allow them to soak for 30 to 40 minutes, until they are pliable. Bring 10 quarts of water to boil in a very large pot and then add the noodles. Return the water to a rolling boil and cook for about 5 to 10 minutes, or until the noodles are soft but still a little chewy. Remove the noodles from the boiling water with a long-handled strainer, put them in a large container filled with cold water, and rinse. Pour off the water, refill with more cold water, and rinse a second time. With one hand, remove some of the noodles from the rinse water so that the strands hang down and are not tangled. With the other hand, gently squeeze excess water from the noodles. Coil each handful in a figure eight and place gently in a large bowl until you are ready to assemble the soup.

To prepare the curry mixture, heat the oil in a large pot and then add the garlic. Sauté until the garlic is soft and fragrant, then stir in the namya curry paste, shrimp paste, fish sauce, coconut milk, sugar, MSG (if desired), salt, and black pepper. Cook the curry mixture over medium heat for about 15 minutes, or until all of the flavors are combined and the sugar is dissolved. The curry mixture will be very salty; the salt becomes diluted when all of the soup ingredients are combined.

Remove the lemongrass, kaffir lime leaves, galanga, and ginger from the simmering broth. Add the shredded chicken meat or chicken pieces, shredded bamboo shoots, and curry mixture to the broth. Taste and add more seasonings if necessary.

Each diner's bowl should include a handful of the fresh vegetables and herbs (cabbage, green onions, mint, cilantro, and bean sprouts) as well as banana blossoms (if desired) and, over that, one or two coils of noodles. Ladle the hot soup into each bowl to just cover the vegetables and noodles. Finally, each diner adds other herbs, spices, and condiments. Then everyone settles in for a lot of satisfied soup-slurping!

Kathy (Ka) Vang, of Hillsboro, Oregon, coils rice noodles a few strands at a time. The smaller the coils, the longer the noodles will remain firm and ready to add to Chicken Curry Noodle Soup (Khaub Poob).

Beef Noodle Soup for a Crowd

Fawm (Phở)

Beef Noodle Soup is a Vietnamese dish and Hmong people call it by its Vietnamese name, *Phở* (rhymes with "duh"). This cookbook includes the soup because Hmong Americans make big, steaming pots of it for their parties. As with any dish Hmong people prepare, there is a lot of individualization of *Phở*. Cooks vary ingredients and quantities, and diners are invited to garnish their bowls with various condiments and many kinds of fresh herbs and vegetables. Below is a basic recipe for *Phở* for serving a crowd. A family-sized version appears on page 168.

INGREDIENTS FOR BROTH

2 large yellow onions, peeled and cut in half

3 pieces (each about 5 inches long) fresh galanga,
    or ginger root, peeled

4½ gallons water

8 to 10 meaty beef soup bones (knuckle bones and leg bones,
    or oxtails), cut into 3-inch lengths

2 pounds inexpensive cut of beef, cubed

20 star anise pods

4 tablespoons salt

1 tablespoon MSG (optional)

¼ cup sugar (for authentic Vietnamese taste, use yellow
    rock sugar)

2 packages Phở seasoning mix (optional)

1 bunch green onions, cleaned and shredded

5 packages (7 ounces each) Vietnamese beef meatballs
    (in the refrigerated or frozen food section of Asian
    groceries), thawed, each meatball cut in half

3 pounds tripe (bought precooked)

INGREDIENTS FOR BOWLS

5 pounds fresh or dried Phở rice noodles, about 3 to 4 ounces
    per serving

3½ pounds top sirloin steak (about 2 to 3 ounces per serving),
    very thinly sliced (have butcher slice it)

> *3 bunches cilantro, cut into 3-inch lengths*
> *2 bunches green onions, white and green parts, shredded*
> *2 pounds fresh bean sprouts*
> *4 bunches basil sprigs*
> *4 bunches or packages culantro*
> *3 heads red leaf lettuce, leaves separated*
> *4 jalapeño peppers, thinly sliced on the diagonal*
> *4 limes, cut into wedges*

CONDIMENTS

> *Seasoning sauce*
> *Hoisin sauce*
> *Soy sauce*
> *Fish sauce*
> *Dried fried garlic*
> *Dried fried onion*
> *Coarse-ground black pepper*

PREPARATION

To sear the onions and galanga or ginger, place a heavy pan over high heat and add the onion and galanga or ginger. Don't use any oil. As each side becomes charred, turn them over until all sides have some black areas. Cool, and then peel away the black areas.

Make the broth in a very large kettle outdoors over a propane burner. Bring the water to a rolling boil. Wash the bones carefully so that no gritty bits end up in the soup. Add the bones, cubed meat, onions, galanga (or ginger), star anise, salt, MSG (if desired), and sugar to the water. Simmer gently for 1½ hours, skimming off any foam and impurities that accumulate on the surface. Taste the broth and add some or all of the *Phở* seasoning powder for a stronger flavor, if desired. Hmong cooks do not parboil the bones as the Vietnamese do, so this soup has a distinctly earthy quality. While the broth simmers, prepare the vegetables, herbs, and condiments. Arrange the herbs and vegetables on serving trays.

Before serving, remove and discard the bones, meat, onions, and star anise from the broth. Skim off extra fat. Clean and shred the green onions. Add them plus the meatballs and tripe to the broth. Turn the heat to high and bring the broth to a full rolling boil.

If your noodles are fresh, untangle them and put them in a colander. Rinse them gently with cool tap water. If you are using dry noodles, soak them for 30 to 40 minutes in cool tap water before cooking. Each serving of noodles must be cooked individually. Over a second burner, bring a big pot of water to a rolling boil. Using a sieve (a long-handled vertical sieve is best), lower a serving of noodles into the boiling water and cook for only 10 to 20 seconds, until the noodles have lost their stiffness. Pull the sieve out of the water and drain the noodles completely. Transfer the hot noodles to a large Asian soup bowl. (Asian soup bowls are very large and deep, to hold all of the ingredients and keep the soup hot. Many styles and patterns are available in Asian groceries.) Place 2 or 3 slices of steak in the bowl and ladle the hot broth over the meat and noodles, making sure to include a few meatballs and some tripe in each serving. Diners pile on additional herbs, vegetables, and any or all of the other condiments to their soup.

Three-Color Dessert
Nab Vam

Makes 30 to 40 servings

This refreshing, bright dessert has a marvelous array of chewy, slippery, and smooth textures. Icy-cold *Nab Vam* (pronounced "na-va") is fun to eat!

Most Southeast Asian countries enjoy variations of Three-Color Dessert. Hmong people pride themselves on their wonderful variety of ingredients. The basic components are coconut milk, canned and fresh fruits, sugar, starch strings, and tapioca pearls. Some people like to add softened basil seeds and a drop of banana flavoring. This dessert is seldom made the same way twice. Creativity is definitely a key ingredient. When the starch strings are made from scratch, Three-Color Dessert is a time-consuming and tricky project. However, you can buy dry, ready-to-cook tapioca at Asian grocery stores in many shapes, sizes, and colors. For a big gathering, several cooks share the work by making the different components. Then, on the day of the party, they combine all of the ingredients. The finished dessert should be about one-third starch strings and tapioca pearls, one-third fruit, and one-third liquid (including ice).

A family-sized, quick version of Three-Color Dessert appears on page 224.

1 package (12 ounces) flour for steamed rice cakes
1 package (12 ounces) potato starch
20 cups cold water
1 tablespoon green food coloring
1 tablespoon red food coloring

INGREDIENTS FOR SUGAR SYRUP

8 cups sugar
4 cups water

OTHER INGREDIENTS

4 bags (8 ounces each) tapioca pearls or other tapioca shapes
in bright colors
2 cans (14 ounces each) coconut milk (or reconstituted
coconut milk powder)

FRUITS

12 to 15 cups of 2 or 3 different fruits, your choice:
Fresh or canned jackfruit, cubed
Canned coconut jelly
Canned palm seeds
Cantaloupe and honeydew melon, cubed

OPTIONAL INGREDIENTS

1 or 2 drops Amyle Essence Flavour (liquid banana flavoring
made in Thailand that is available in Asian grocery stores)
1 package (2 ounces) dry sweet basil seeds

MAKE THE STARCH STRINGS (CAN BE DONE A DAY IN ADVANCE)

Mix the 2 packages of dry starch together in a bowl and use half of the mixture for each color. The strings can be made with only steamed rice cake flour, but they will not keep their shape very long. Adding the potato starch allows the strings to be stored for a day.

Put 10 cups of cool water into a large saucepan and add enough of one food color to tint the water a deep green or red. Slowly add half of the starch mixture, stirring constantly with a large wooden spoon until it is completely dissolved. Put the pan on the stove and heat the mixture

Thick tapioca paste is pushed through the holes of a steamer to make the colorful strings in Three-Color Dessert. The strings drop into a tub of ice water and become firm.

slowly to a boil, stirring constantly. Cook for about 10 to 15 minutes. The mixture will become very thick.

Fill a large bucket with water and add some ice. Now transfer the starch mixture into the top part of a large metal steamer, the kind with medium-sized holes in the bottom. This operation requires two cooks. One person holds the pan steady above the water-and-ice-filled bucket. The second person pushes the starch mixture through the holes using a flat-bottomed pusher, creating "strings" that drop into the cold water (see the photograph).

An alternative to making starch strings by hand is to make thin sheets of agar-agar gelatin (page 22) dyed with food coloring. When the gelatin has set, cut it into long, thin strips.

After all of the starch has been pushed through the steamer, slowly pour off the water and then add more cold water to rinse the strings well. Rinse one or more times, until the water is no longer cloudy. Gently separate the strings with your fingers so they do not stick together.

Repeat the entire process, using the second color. Often, though, Hmong cooks make only green strings by hand. Other colors come from tapioca pearls, fruits, and jellies.

Store the starch strings, covered with water, in a closed container in the refrigerator.

MAKE THE SUGAR SYRUP (CAN BE DONE A DAY OR TWO IN ADVANCE)

In a heavy pan, warm the sugar over medium heat, stirring constantly until the sugar melts and turns caramel-colored. Remove the pan from the burner and allow the caramelized sugar to cool slightly. Stir in the water, but be careful, because the hot liquid sugar can bubble up and spatter. Turn the heat very low and continue to stir until the sugar is completely dissolved, making a thick syrup. Add more water when assembling the dish if the dessert is too sweet. Store the syrup in a closed container in the refrigerator.

Asian markets stock a variety of dried tapioca pearls and other shapes. Choose one or two and prepare according to the package directions. If you make them ahead of time, store in the sugar syrup in the refrigerator.

ASSEMBLE THE DESSERT (MUST BE DONE JUST BEFORE SERVING)

Now it is time to be creative! Use at least two or three kinds of canned and fresh fruit—the more colorful, the better. Drain the canned fruit and discard the liquid. Cut the canned fruit into bite-sized pieces, and use a melon baller to shape any melons.

If you like basil seeds, called "frog's eyes," prepare them now. Soaked in warm water, these tiny, hard, black seeds swell up and become gelatinous on the outside yet stay crunchy in the middle. Although basil seeds have little flavor, they add an interesting texture.

Pour the sugar syrup into a 3-gallon container. Drain the water from the starch strings and add them to the container. Pour in the tapioca pearls (if not already in the syrup). Add the canned coconut milk or reconstituted powdered coconut milk. Then add the fruit. If desired, add the Amyle Essence Flavour and the soaked basil seeds. Stir gently and taste. If the liquid is too sweet, add more water, a little at a time, continuing to check the sweetness. Just before serving, add a bag of small-sized ice cubes. Ladle into cups or bowls and eat with a spoon.

Ka's Sweet Potato Vermicelli Salad

Kha Qos Liab Fawm Xav Lav

Makes 10 servings

As the finishing touches were being added to this book, Sami spent a morning cooking with a group of Hmong people in Portland, Oregon. Preparing a luncheon for a large community group, they made a host of Hmong favorites, including tubs of rice, beef *larb*, green salad, chicken curry noodle soup, and stir-fried green beans. However, one dish was new to Sami. The salad featured sweet potato vermicelli, along with bacon, shrimp, and an array of herbs. Sami closely watched the cook, Ka Vang, and took lots of notes. She even saved the packaging from the vermicelli. Later, when she turned the package over, she discovered a recipe for "Korean *chop chae*" and a picture of the dish Ka had made. At least it was very similar. Ka had substituted several ingredients and altered the seasonings, but her salad was unmistakably a variation of the dish.

Excitedly, Sami called Sheng in Sacramento, California, to talk about the discovery. Ka's salad reflected American and Asian influences, but it remained Hmong at heart. Above all, the dish exemplified the creativity and individuality that are fundamental aspects of Hmong culture.

Make Ka's noodle salad. It is a fine example of Hmong cooking in America.

INGREDIENTS

1 dozen eggs

3 tablespoons vegetable oil, plus more for cooking eggs

1 tablespoon plus 1 teaspoon salt

¼ cup plus 1 tablespoon soy sauce

2 pounds thick-sliced fresh bacon (not cured) or
  Hmong smoked pork, cut into 1-inch pieces

1 large package (20 ounces) sweet potato vermicelli noodles

3 cloves fresh garlic, minced

5 cups carrots, cut into match stick–sized pieces
  (buy them already cut up)

4 hot Thai chili peppers, very thinly sliced on the diagonal

2 pounds shrimp, shells and intestinal veins removed

1 large bunch fresh garlic chives

4 tablespoons oyster sauce

2 teaspoons sesame oil

1 tablespoon sugar

1 bunch cilantro, cut into 4-inch pieces

PREPARATION

Before beginning to cook, clean and prepare the shrimp and all of the vegetables.

Crack the eggs into a bowl and whisk until the yolks and whites are completely blended. Stir in 1 teaspoon of the salt and 1 tablespoon of the soy sauce. Put 2 teaspoons of vegetable oil into a small, flat-bottomed skillet and heat to medium. Pour ⅔ cup of the egg mixture into the skillet and cook on one side until the egg patty is set, puffy, and a little browned, about 4 minutes. Carefully lift the edges with a spatula and turn the patty over in one piece. Cook on the second side until the egg is completely done and a little browned, another 3 to 4 minutes. Transfer the egg patty to a plate. Repeat the process until all of the egg mixture is cooked. Cut the egg patties into ½-inch strips.

Cut the bacon or smoked pork into 1-inch pieces and stir-fry in a skillet until they are a little crispy. Drain off the fat and discard it, and set the bacon aside.

Add a few drops of vegetable oil to a large saucepan two-thirds full of water, and bring to a boil over high heat. Add the vermicelli noodles and cook for 5 minutes. When the noodles are soft, drain and quickly immerse in cold water. Rinse for 1 or 2 minutes in cold running water. With kitchen shears, cut the noodles into 4-inch pieces.

In a large wok, heat 1 tablespoon of the oil to medium-hot. Add the garlic and stir-fry until fragrant but not brown. Add the carrots and chilies, and stir-fry for a minute. Add the shrimp and chives, then stir-fry for 6 minutes, just until the shrimp turn pink. Add the bacon, the ¼ cup of soy sauce, the remaining tablespoon of salt, and the oyster sauce, sesame oil, and sugar. Mix and cook together for another minute. Add 2 more tablespoons of the vegetable oil. Add the noodles, half the cilantro, and half the egg strips and stir-fry until the ingredients are mixed. Transfer to a serving dish and top with the rest of the cilantro and egg strips. Serve hot or cold.

Index ⤳ Kev Teeb Txheeb Ntaub Ntawv Raws ABC

NOTE *Italic page numbers indicate photographs.*

*It makes sense that the Hmong words for "index" are not commonly known,
since only recently have books been written in Hmong. The words mean,
"written document organized alphabetically to find a path to listings in a book."*

beef soup
    phở, 168–170, 260–262
    with sour bamboo, 167
    traditional, 155–158
beefsteak plant, 40
beer, 207, 208
betel, 40
beverages
    alcohol, 103, 207, 208
    broth as, 43
    coconut milk, 218–219
    cucumber juice, 209
    fresh fruit bubble drink, 228
    green vegetable juice, 210
    in Laos, 207
    pumpkin juice, 209
    rice juice, 209
    tamarind bark tea, 210
    tapioca pearl drinks, 226–228
    Thai iced tea and coffee bubble drink,
      227
bitter eggplant and smoked pork, 145
bitter liver, 138–139
bitter melon, 30
    and chicken soup, 98
    stir-fried with beef, 168
    stuffed, 72–73
black pepper, 22
black rice, 50
blood pudding, 143
blossoms
    banana, and eggplants with beef stew,
      162–163, 165
    squash, with pork, 142
bok choy, 27–28
    with pork belly, stir-fried, 79–80
Boston lettuce, 28
bottle gourd, 30
bouillon cubes, 22
boxthorn, Chinese, 40
brain, pig, pâté, 147–148
bread machines, pounding rice with,
    57
broccoli, Chinese, 28

bubble drinks, 227–228
bubble tea. *See* tapioca, pearl drinks

cabbage, 28
    leaves, stuffed, 73–74
    with pork sausage, 135–136
    and tomato stir-fry, 77–78
cake: Mommy Nyaj's rice wine dessert, 211,
    215–216
Cakes by Fhoua, 211, 212–214
Calrose rice, 49. *See also* rice
cardamom, 40
carrots, 32
    Sheng's green papaya salad, 81–82
cassava root, 32
    and plantain tapioca dessert, 221
celebrations
    jingle-bell parties, 131, 140–141
    New Year, 5, 57, 126, 131, 135, 211,
      241–242
    traditional gatherings, 4–5
    weddings, 4, 8, 70, 102–104
cellophane (bean thread) noodles, 26
    with ground pork, stir-fried, 252–253
    See also vermicelli noodles
Cha, Chong, 69
Cha, Dia, 93
cherry tomatoes, 31
chicken, 93
    and bean sprout salad, 110–111
    blood pudding, 143
    with cucumber and bitter melon, stir-fried,
      106–107
    drumsticks with Hmong-style barbeque
      sauce, 116
    in Hmong weddings, 103–104
    larb, 107–110
    with luffa squash, stir-fried, 101–105
    and pork salad with peanuts, 148–149
    rice porridge with, 62
    roasted with coconut, 114–115
    and tofu meatballs, 253–254
    with tomatoes, stir-fried, 105–106
    with wild bamboo, stir-fried, 80

fresh chicken with Hmong herbs (soup), 94–95, 97
herbed eggs, 127–128
medicinal, 37–42, 96, 97
squab soup with Asian herbs, 198–199
with venison soup, 203
See also specific herbs
Hmong
brief history of, 2–3, 6–7
culinary herbs, 35–37
culture of, in America, 7–9
eating habits of, 13–14, 17, 43
equipment for cooking, *16*, 18–20
medicinal herbs, 37–42
table settings, 43
traditional gatherings, 4–5
Hmong Missionary Alliance Church, 235
Hmong Recipe Cook Book, 76, 85, 115

jackfruit, 23
Japanese rush, 41
jasmine rice, 49. *See also* rice
jicama, 32
"jingle-bell party," 131, 140–141
juice
cucumber, 209
green vegetable, 210
pumpkin, 209
rice, 209

kaffir lime leaves, 36
knotweed, fragrant, 37
kohlrabi, 32
"ko-pia," 100
Kue, Bee, *172*
Kue, Ka, 172–174
Kue, Pang, *172*
Kue, Toua, *172*

laab. See larb
laap. See larb
Laos
animal sacrifices in, 141, 153
beverages and desserts in, 207

catching crabs in, 191
civil war in, 3
corn in, 60
game in, 177
hunting and fishing in, 54
making tofu in, 75
traditional beliefs in, 119
wedding traditions in, 102–104
wild foods eaten in, 33–34
larb, 11–12, 108
beef, 160–162
chicken, 107–109
fish, 185–187
pork, 137–138
steak tartare, 237–239
larp. See larb
Lawson, May Chue, *164*
Lee, Angie, *189*
Lee, Edward, *102*
Lee, Ia, *57*
Lee, MaiKia, *102*
Lee-Yang, May, 13–14, 245–246
lemongrass, 36–37
lettuce, 28
"live blood," 143
lob. See larb
Lor, Julie, *241*
Lor, Kou, 20–21
Lor, Nansee, *119*
luffa squash, 31
and beef with basil, 165–166
with chicken, stir-fried, 101, 105
vines, stir-fried, 76
Ly, Chou, *49*
Ly, Ge, *153*
Ly, True, *201*

mango
with coconut sticky rice, 217–218
fruit snack, 216
meatballs
chicken and tofu, 253–254
pork, 146
meat salad. See *larb*

medicinal chicken, 96–97

medicinal eggs, 128

medicinal herbs, 37–42, 96, 97, 211

mint, 37

mizuna, 29

moneywort, 41

monosodium glutamate (MSG), 11, 24

Moua, Lee, 56, 184

Moua, Song, 181, 182

MSG. *See* monosodium glutamate

mugwort, 41

mung beans, 34
  and sticky rice with salty pork, 250–252
  tapioca pudding, 223

mushrooms
  chicken and oyster mushroom soup,
    98
  dried, 23–24
  oyster, 34

mustard, Chinese, 29

mustard greens, 29
  and pork soup, 132

New Year celebrations, 5, 57, 126, 135, 211,
    241–242

noodles, 24–26, 259
  beef noodle soup, 168–170, 260–262
  cellophane noodles with ground pork,
    stir-fried, 252–253
  chicken curry noodle soup, 255–259
  chicken noodle soup, 100–101
  Ka's sweet potato vermicelli salad,
    265–267
  trout salad with vermicelli, 187–188

nuts. *See* peanuts

octopus and shrimp hot and sour soup, 197

"Oh-La," 164
  beef stew with banana blossoms and
    eggplants, 162–163, 165
  squirrel stew with eggplant, 201–202

oilseed rape, 29
  garlicky Chinese green flower, 78–79

okra, 31

omelets
  egg and ginger, 125
  Hmong-style, 124–125

onions, green, 36

oyster sauce, 26

packaged ingredients, 22–27

pancakes, Saly's rice and corn, 60–61

papaya
  green papaya salad, 239–240
  Sheng's green papaya salad, 81–82

pastes, 23. *See also* chili condiments and sauces

pâté, pig brain, 147–148

peanuts
  chili-peanut dipping sauce, 114
  ground toasted, 64
  pork and chicken salad with, 148–149
  roasted, 249

peas, sweet, 34
  vines, stir-fried, 76–77

pea vine tips, 34

pennywort, 41

pepper leaf, 40

peppers, 31

perch, fried, 181–182

perilla, 41

persimmons, 216

phở, 168–170, 260–262

pickles
  fried green-vegetable pickles, 86
  scrambled eggs with pickled greens, 123–124
  sour green-vegetable pickles, 84–85

plantain
  and cassava root tapioca dessert, 221
  filling with sticky rice in banana leaves, 56

pork, 131
  blood pudding, 143
  and chicken salad with peanuts, 148
  ground, with green salad, 236
  larb, 137–138
  liver, sour and bitter, 138–139
  meatballs, 146
  and mustard greens soup, 132
  pâté, pig brain, 147–148

rice porridge with, 62
sausage, Hmong, 134–136
skin, fried, 144
smoked, and bitter eggplant, 145
smoked, and young Asian pumpkins,
    144–145
with squash tendrils and blossoms, 142
sticky rice with salty pork and mung beans,
    250–252
stir-fried baby bok choy with pork belly,
    79–80
stir-fried, with cellophane noodles,
    252–253
sweet, 244
sweet pig's feet, 133
watercress salad with, 83
porridge, rice, 61–62
poultry. *See* chicken
pumpkin
    juice, 209
    smoked pork and young Asian pumpkins,
        144–145
    sweet pumpkin with coconut, 22
    vines, stir-fried, 76

quail legs, sautéed or broiled, 199–200

rattan, 34
    chicken soup, 99
rice, 6, 49, 49–50
    cakes, pounded, 58
    cakes, sweet steamed, 59
    with coconut cream, 54
    and corn pancakes, 60–61
    everyday, 51–52
    juice, 209
    mango with coconut sticky rice, 217–218
    porridge, plain, 61–62
    porridge with meat, 62
    pounded, 57–58
    purple, 53
    rolls, 63–64
    sticky, basic recipe, 53
    sticky rice in banana leaves, 54–56

sticky rice with salty pork and mung
    beans, 250–252
rice flour, 24, 25
    toasted sticky, 61
rice noodles, 25, 259
rice paddy herb, 37
Rice Palace Restaurant, 229–231
rice paper, 25–26
"Rice Rain" (poem, Song Yang), 65

salad
    bamboo, 82–83
    chicken and bean sprout, 110–111
    Der's egg and cucumber, 121–122
    green, with ground pork, 236
    green papaya, 239–240
    meat. *See* larb
    pork and chicken, with peanuts, 148–149
    Sheng's green papaya, 81–82
    sweet potato vermicelli, 265–267
    trout, with vermicelli noodles, 187–188
    watercress, with pork, 83
sauces
    barbeque, 116
    fish, 24
    fish dip, 182
    oyster, 26
    See also chili condiments and sauces
sausage
    filling with sticky rice in banana leaves,
        56
    Hmong sausage, 134–135
Sawyer, Sharon, 76, 85, 115
Scripter, Sami, 35, 96, 121
seafood. *See* fish; shellfish
sedum, 41
shaman rituals, 93, 126, 140–141
shellfish
    cracked crab, 193–195
    deli-style fried shrimp, 188–189, *189*
    shrimp and asparagus, stir-fried, 190
    shrimp and baby octopus hot and sour
        soup, 197
    sour and spicy seafood soup, 196–197

shrimp
  and asparagus, stir-fried, 190
  and baby octopus hot and sour soup, 197
  deli-style fried, 188–189
  paste, 81
Sichuan pepper, 26–27
"Slices with a Hmong Knife" (poem,
    Kou Lor), 20–21
slippery vegetable, 41
smelly-insect vegetable, 40
soup
  egg, 123
  pork and mustard greens, 132
  shrimp and baby octopus hot and sour, 197
  sour and spicy seafood, 196–197
  See also beef soup; chicken soup
soybean curd. See tofu
Spice House, 27
Spirit Catches You and You Fall Down, The
    (book, Fadiman), 155
squab soup with Asian herbs, 198–199
squash
  tendrils and blossoms with pork, 142
  See also luffa squash
squirrel stew with eggplant, 201–202
star anise, 27
stem lettuce, 29
stew
  beef stew with banana blossoms and
    eggplants, 162–163, 165
  squirrel stew with eggplant, 201–202
stir-fry
  baby bok choy with pork belly, 79–80
  beef with bitter melon, 168
  beef and string bean, 170–171
  cabbage and tomato, 77–78
  cellophane noodles with ground pork,
    252–253
  chicken with cucumber and bitter melon,
    106–107
  chicken with luffa squash, 101, 105
  chicken with tomatoes, 105–106
  dried beef with bamboo, 160
  green beans with garlic, 243

pumpkin vines, 76
shrimp and asparagus, 190
water spinach, 76–77
wild bamboo with chicken, 80
sweet fern, 41
sweet flag, 41
sweet potatoes, 32

tamarind, 27
  bark tea, 210
  sweet, 217
tapioca
  cassava root and plantain tapioca dessert,
    221
  and corn pudding, 222–223
  paste, 264
  pearl drinks (bubble tea, Crystal Delights),
    226–228
  starch-flour noodles, 25
taro roots, 32–33
tea, 207
  tamarind bark, 210
  Thai iced tea and coffee bubble drink, 227
tofu, 33
  basic recipe, 75–76
  and chicken meatballs, 253–254
  chicken soup with, 98
  pork-stuffed, 136–137
tomatoes, 31
  baked striped bass with herbs and, 178–179
  and beef stir-fry, 171
  and cabbage stir-fry, 77–78
  with chicken, stir-fried, 105–106
traditional recipes
  baked striped bass with tomatoes and
    herbs, 178–179
  beef soup, 155–158
  beef stew with banana blossoms and
    eggplants, 162, 165
  cassava root and plantain tapioca dessert,
    221
  chicken soup, 95, 98–99
  chili and Thai eggplant condiment,
    166–167